R406
T1
1869

PRECIOUS THOUGHTS:

Moral and Religious.

GATHERED FROM THE WORKS OF

JOHN RUSKIN, A.M.

BY

Mrs. L. C. TUTHILL.

"A very Sea of Thought; neither calm nor clear, if you will, yet wherein the toughest pearl-diver may dive to his utmost depth, and return not only with sea-wreck but with true orients."

Sartor Resartus.

NEW YORK:
JOHN WILEY & SON, PUBLISHERS,
2 Clinton Hall, Astor Place.
1869.

Entered, according to Act of Congress, in the year 1865, by
JOHN WILEY & SON,
In the Clerk's Office of the District Court of the United States for the
Southern District of New York.

PREFATORY.

MUCH time is wasted by human beings, in general, on establishment of systems; and it often takes more labour to master the intricacies of an artificial connexion, than to remember the separate facts which are so carefully connected. I suspect that system-makers, in general, are not of much more use, each in his own domain, than, in that of Pomona, the old women who tie cherries upon sticks, for the more convenient portableness of the same. To cultivate well, and choose well, your cherries, is of some importance; but if they can be had in their own wild way of clustering about their crabbed stalk, it is a better connexion for them than any other; and, if they cannot, then, so that they be not bruised, it makes to a boy of a practical disposition, not much difference whether he gets them by *handfuls*,* or in beaded symmetry on the exalting stick. I purpose, therefore, henceforward to trouble myself little with sticks or twine, but to arrange my chapters with a view to convenient reference, rather than to any careful division of subjects, and to follow out, in any by-ways that may open, on right hand or left, whatever question it seems useful at any moment to settle.

* Or *basketfuls*?

DEDICATORY AND EXPLANATORY.

TO

S. S. B.

The volume of Selections from the numerous works of John Ruskin, which was published some years since, I devoted mainly to "Nature" and to "Art," Ruskin's specialty, leaving only a small portion of the book to "Morals" and "Religion." Consequently, manifold thoughts, on these latter topics, remained in those voluminous works as hidden treasure, inaccessible to the many—thoughts valuable to the Christian philosopher, the statesman, and, indeed, to readers in general.

Without repeating any of the former selections, I have culled from that great treasure-house of thought the gems for this volume, which I take special pleasure in dedicating to you, my dear S., as an appreciative admirer of the writings of John Ruskin.

Affectionately and fervently yours,

LOUISA C. TUTHILL.

Princeton, N. J.

CONTENTS.

T.

U

V.

W.

PRECIOUS THOUGHTS.

DOWNRIGHT FACTS PLAINLY TOLD.

I HAVE been much impressed lately by one of the results of the quantity of our books; namely, the stern impossibility of getting anything understood, that required patience to understand. I observe always, in the case of my own writings, that if ever I state anything which has cost me any trouble to ascertain, and which, therefore, will probably require a minute or two of reflection from the reader before it can be accepted,—that statement will not only be misunderstood, but in all probability taken to mean something very nearly the reverse of what it does mean. Now, whatever faults there may be in my modes of expression, I know that the words I use will always be found, by Johnson's dictionary, to bear, first of all, the sense I use them in; and that the sentences, whether awkwardly turned or not, will, by the ordinary rules of grammar, bear no other interpretation than that I mean them to bear; so that the misunderstanding of them must result, ultimately, from the mere fact that their matter sometimes requires a little patience. And I see the same kind of misinterpretation put on the words of other writers, whenever they require the same kind of thought.

I was at first a little despondent about this; but, on the whole, I believe it will have a good effect upon our literature for some time to come; and then, perhaps, the public may recover its patience again. For certainly it is excellent discipline for an author to feel that he must say all he has to say in the fewest possible words, or his reader is sure to skip them; and in the plainest possible words, or his reader will certainly misunderstand them. Generally, also, a downright fact may be told in a plain way; and we want downright facts at present more than anything else.

———o———

FAITH, TRUTH, AND OBEDIENCE.

In the pressing or recommending of any act or manner of acting, we have choice of two separate lines of argument: one based on representation of the expediency or inherent value of the work, which is often small, and always disputable; the other based on proofs of its relations to the higher orders of human virtue, and of its acceptableness, so far as it goes, to Him who is the origin of virtue. The former is commonly the more persuasive method, the latter assuredly the more conclusive; only it is liable to give offence, as if there were irreverence in adducing considerations so weighty in treating subjects of small temporal importance. I believe, however, that no error is more thoughtless than this. What is true of the Deity is equally true of His Revelation. I have been blamed for the familiar introduction of its sacred words. I am grieved to have given pain by so doing; but my excuse must be my wish that those words were made the ground of every argument and the test of every action. We have them not often enough on our lips, nor deeply enough in our memories, nor loyally enough in our lives. The snow, the vapor, and the stormy wind fulfil His word. Are our acts and thoughts lighter and wilder than these—that we should forget it?

I have therefore ventured, at the risk of giving to some passages the appearance of irreverence, to take the higher line of argument wherever it appeared clearly traceable; and this, I would ask the reader especially to observe, not merely because I think it the best mode of reaching ultimate truth, still less because I think the subject of more importance than many others; but because every subject should surely, at a period like the present, be taken up in this spirit, or not at all. The aspect of the years that approach us is as solemn as it is full of mystery; and the weight of evil against which we have to contend, is increasing like the letting out of water. It is no time for the idleness of metaphysics, or the entertainment of the arts. The blasphemies of the earth are sounding louder, and its miseries heaped heavier every day; and if, in the midst of the exertion which every good man is called upon to put forth for their repression or relief, it is lawful to ask for a thought, for a moment, for a lifting of the finger, in any direction but that of the immediate and overwhelming need, it is at least incumbent upon us to approach the questions in which we would engage him, in the spirit which has become the habit of his mind, and in the hope that neither his zeal nor his usefulness may be checked by the withdrawal of an hour which has shown him how even those things which seemed mechanical, indifferent, or contemptible, depend for their perfection upon the acknowledgment of the sacred principles of faith, truth, and obedience, for which it has been the occupation of his life to contend.

———o———

ADVANCEMENT.

Between youth and age there will be found differences of seeking, which are not wrong, nor of false choice in either, but of different temperament, the youth sympathizing more with the gladness, fulness, and magnificence of things, and the gray hairs with their completion, sufficiency, and repose And so, neither condemning the delights of others, nor altogether distrustful of our own, we must advance, as we live on, from what is brilliant to what is pure, and from what is promised to what is fulfilled, and from what is our strength to what is our crown, only observing in all things how that which is indeed wrong, and to be cut up from the root, is dislike, and not affection.

———o———

GREAT RESULTS.

Men often look to bring about great results by violent and unprepared effort. But it is only in fair and forecast order, "as the earth bringeth forth her bud," that righteousness and praise may spring forth before the nations.

———o———

TRUE CONTENTMENT.

The things to be desired for man in a healthy state, are that he should not see dreams, but realities; that he should not destroy life, but save it; and that he should be not rich, but content.

Towards which last state of contentment I do not see that the world is at present approximating. There are, indeed, two forms of discontent; one laborious, the other indolent and complaining. We respect the man of laborious desire, but let us not suppose that his restlessness is peace, or his ambition meekness. It is because of the special connexion of meekness with contentment that it is promised that the meek shall "inherit the earth." Neither covetous men nor the Grave, can inherit anything;* they can but consume. Only contentment can possess.

The most helpful and sacred work, therefore, which can at present be done for humanity, is to teach people (chiefly by example, as all best teaching must be done) not how "to better themselves," but how to "satisfy themselves." It is the curse of every evil nation and evil creature to eat, and *not* be satisfied. The words of blessing are, that they shall eat and be satisfied. And as there is only one kind of water which quenches all thirst, so there is only one kind of bread which satisfies all hunger, the bread of justice or righteousness; which hungering after, men shall always be filled, that being the bread of Heaven; but hungering after the bread, or wages, of unrighteousness, shall not be filled, that being the bread of Sodom.

And, in order to teach men how to be satisfied, it is necessary fully to understand the art and joy of humble life,—this, at present, of all arts or sciences being the one most needing study. Humble life—that is to say, proposing to itself no future exaltation, but only a sweet continuance; not excluding the idea of foresight, but wholly of fore-sorrow, and taking no troublous thought for coming days: so, also, not excluding the idea of providence, or provision,† but wholly of accumulation;—the life of domestic affection and domestic peace, full of sensitiveness to all elements of costless and

* "There are three things that are never satisfied, yea, four things say not, It is enough: the grave; and the barren womb; the earth that is not filled with water; and the fire, that saith not, It is enough!"

† A bad word, being only "foresight" again in Latin; but we have no other good English word for the sense into which it has been warped.

kind pleasure;—therefore, chiefly to the loveliness of the natural world.

What length and severity of labor may be ultimately found necessary for the procuring of the due comforts of life, I do not know; neither what degree of refinement it is possible to unite with the so-called servile occupations of life: but this I know, that right economy of labor will, as it is understood, assign to each man as much as will be healthy for him, and no more; and that no refinements are desirable which cannot be connected with toil.

———o———

GREATNESS AND MINUTENESS.

In one sense, and that deep, there is no such thing as magnitude. The least thing is as the greatest, and one day as a thousand years, in the eyes of the Maker of great and small things. In another sense, and that close to us and necessary, there exist both magnitude and value. Though not a sparrow falls to the ground unnoted, there are yet creatures who are of more value than many; and the same Spirit which weighs the dust of the earth in a balance, counts the isles as a little thing.

The just temper of human mind in this matter may, nevertheless, be told shortly. Greatness can only be rightly estimated when minuteness is justly reverenced. Greatness is the aggregation of minuteness; nor can its sublimity be felt truthfully by any mind unaccustomed to the affectionate watching of what is least.

I have noticed lately, that some lightly-budding philosophers have depreciated true greatness; confusing the relations of scale, as they bear upon human instinct and morality;

reasoning as if a mountain were no nobler than a grain of sand, or as if many souls were not of mightier interest than one. To whom it must be shortly answered that the Lord of power and life knew which were his noblest works, when He bade His servant watch the play of the Leviathan, rather than dissect the spawn of the minnow; and that when it comes to practical question whether a single soul is to be jeoparded for many, and this Leonidas, or Curtius, or Winkelried shall abolish—so far as abolishable—his own spirit, that he may save more numerous spirits, such question is to be solved by the simple human instinct respecting number and magnitude, not by reasonings on infinity.

———o———

THE ANGEL OF THE SEA.

The great Angel of the Sea—rain;—the Angel observe, the messenger sent to a special place on a special errand. Not the diffused perpetual presence of the burden of mist, but the going and returning of intermittent cloud. All turns upon that intermittence. Soft moss on stone and rock;—cave-fern of tangled glen;—wayside well—perennial, patient, silent, clear; stealing through its square font of rough-hewn stone; ever thus deep—no more—which the winter wreck sullies not, the summer thirst wastes not, incapable of stain as of decline—where the fallen leaf floats undecayed, and th insect darts undefiling. Cressed brook and ever-eddying river, lifted even in flood scarcely over its stepping-stones,—but through all sweet summer keeping tremulous music with harp-strings of dark water among the silver fingering of the pebbles. Far away in the south the strong river Gods have all hasted, and gone down to the sea. Wasted and burning, white furnaces of blasting sand, their broad beds lie ghastly and bare; but here the soft wings of the Sea Angel droop still with dew, and the shadows of their plumes falter on the hills: strange laughings, and glitterings of silver streamlets, born suddenly, and twined about the mossy heights in trickling tinsel, answering to them as they wave.

Nor are those wings colorless. We habitually think of the rain-cloud only as dark and gray; not knowing that we owe to it perhaps the fairest, though not the most dazzling of the hues of heaven. Often in our English mornings, the rain-clouds in the dawn form soft level fields, which melt imperceptibly into the blue; or when of less extent, gather into apparent bars, crossing the sheets of broader cloud above; and all these bathed throughout in an unspeakable light of pure rose-color, and purple, and amber, and blue; not shining, but misty-soft; the barred masses, when seen nearer, composed of clusters or tresses of cloud, like floss silk; looking as if each knot were a little swathe or sheaf of lighted rain. No clouds form such skies, none are so tender, various, inimitable.

For these are the robes of love of the Angel of the Sea. To these that name is chiefly given, the "spreadings of the clouds," from their extent, their gentleness, their fulness of rain. Note how they are spoken of in Job, xxxvi. v. 29–31. "By them judgeth he the people; he giveth meat in abundance. With clouds he covereth the light. He hath hidden the light in his hands, and commanded that it should return. He speaks of it to his friend; that it is his possession, and that he may ascend thereto."

That, then, is the Sea Angel's message to God's friends; *that*, the meaning of those strange golden lights and purple flushes before the morning rain. The rain is sent to judge, and feed us; but the light is the possession of the friends of

God, and they may ascend thereto,—where the tabernacle veil will cross and part its rays no more.

———o———

PINE TREES.

Magnificent!—nay, sometimes, almost terrible. Other trees, tufting crag or hill, yield to the form and sway of the ground, clothe it with soft compliance, are partly its subjects, partly its flatterers, partly its comforters. But the pine rises in serene resistance, self-contained; nor can I ever without awe stay long under a great Alpine cliff, far from all house or work of men, looking up to its companies of pine, as they stand on the inaccessible juts and perilous ledges of the enormous wall, in quiet multitudes, each like the shadow of the one beside it—upright, fixed, spectral, as troops of ghosts standing on the walls of Hades, not knowing each other—dumb for ever. You cannot reach them, cannot cry to them;—those trees never heard human voice; they are far above all sound but of the winds. No foot ever stirred fallen leaf of theirs. All comfortless they stand, between the two eternities of the Vacancy and the Rock: yet with such iron will, that the rock itself looks bent and shattered beside them—fragile, weak, inconsistent, compared to their dark energy of delicate life, and monotony of enchanted pride:—unnumbered, unconquerable.

———o———

LESSONS FROM LEAVES.

We men, sometimes, in what we presume to be humility, compare ourselves with leaves; but we have as yet no right to do so. The leaves may well scorn the comparison. We who live for ourselves, and neither know how to use nor keep the work of past time, may humbly learn,—as from the ant, foresight,—from the leaf, reverence. The power of every great people, as of every living tree, depends on its not effacing, but confirming and concluding, the labors of its ancestors. Looking back to the history of nations, we may date the beginning of their decline from the moment when they ceased to be reverent in heart, and accumulative in hand and brain; from the moment when the redundant fruit of age hid in them the hollowness of heart, whence the simplicities of custom and sinews of tradition had withered away. Had men but guarded the righteous laws, and protected the precious works of their fathers, with half the industry they have given to change and to ravage, they would not now have been seeking vainly, in millennial visions and mechanic servitudes, the accomplishment of the promise made to them so long ago: "As the days of a tree are the days of my people, and mine elect shall long enjoy the work of their hands; they shall not labor in vain, nor bring forth for trouble; for they are the seed of the blessed of the Lord, and their offspring with them."

This lesson we have to take from the leaf's life. One more we may receive from its death. If ever in autumn, a pensiveness falls upon us as the leaves drift by in their fading, may we not wisely look up in hope to their mighty monuments? Behold how fair, how far prolonged, in arch and aisle, the avenues of the valleys; the fringes of the hills! So stately,—so eternal; the joy of man, the comfort of all living creatures, the glory of the earth,—they are but the monuments of those poor leaves that flit faintly past us to die. Let them not pass, without our understanding their last counsel and example: that we also, careless of monument by the grave, may build it in the world—monument by which men may be taught to remember, not where we died, but where we lived.

———o———

MYSTERY AND UNITY.

This system of braided or woven ornament was not confined to the Arabs; it is universally pleasing to the instinct of mankind. I believe that nearly all early ornamentation is full of it,—more especially, perhaps, Scandinavian and Anglo-Saxon; and illuminated manuscripts depend upon it for their loveliest effects of intricate color, up to the close of the thirteenth century. There are several very interesting metaphysical reasons for this strange and unfailing delight, felt in a thing so simple. It is not often that any idea of utility has power to enhance the true impressions of beauty; but it is possible that the enormous importance of the art of weaving to mankind may give some interest, if not actual attractiveness, to any type or image of the invention to which we owe, at once, our comfort and our pride. But the more profound reason lies in the innate love of mystery and unity; in the joy that the human mind has in contemplating any kind of maze or entanglement, so long as it can discern, through its confusion, any guiding clue or connecting plan: a pleasure increased and solemnized by some dim feeling of the setting forth, by such symbols, of the intricacy, and alternate rise and fall, subjection and supremacy, of human fortune; the

"Weave the warp, and weave the woof,"

of Fate and Time.

IMPERFECTION.

Imperfection is in some sort essential to all that we know of life. It is the sign of life in a mortal body, that is to say, of a state of progress and change. Nothing that lives is, or can be, rigidly perfect; part of it is decaying, part nascent. The foxglove blossom,—a third part bud, a third part past, a third part in full bloom,—is a type of the life of this world. And in all things that live there are certain irregularities and deficiencies which are not only signs of life, but sources of beauty. No human face is exactly the same in its lines on each side, no leaf perfect in its lobes, no branch in its symmetry. All admit irregularity as they imply change; and to banish imperfection is to destroy expression, to check exertion, to paralyse vitality. All things are literally better, lovelier, and more beloved for the imperfections which have been divinely appointed, that the law of human life may be Effort, and the law of human judgment, Mercy.

———o———

SUBLIMITY.

Impressions of awe and sorrow being at the root of the sensation of sublimity, and the beauty of separate flowers not being of the kind which connects itself with such sensation, there is a wide distinction, in general, between flower-loving minds and minds of the highest order.

———o———

THE HUMBLEST OF THE EARTH-CHILDREN.

Lichen, and mosses (though these last in their luxuriance are deep and rich as herbage, yet both for the most part humblest of the green things that live),—how of these? Meek creatures! the first mercy of the earth, veiling with hushed softness its dintless rocks; creatures full of pity, covering with strange and tender honor the scarred disgrace of ruin,—laying quiet finger on the trembling stones, to teach them rest. No words, that I know of, will say what these mosses are. None are delicate enough, none perfect enough, none rich enough. How is one to tell of the rounded bosses of furred and beaming green,—the starred divisions of rubied bloom, fine-filmed, as if the Rock Spirits could spin porphyry as we do glass,—the traceries of intricate silver, and fringes of amber, lustrous, arborescent, burnished through every fibre into fitful brightness and glossy traverses of silken change, yet all subdued and pensive, and framed for simplest, sweetest offices of grace. They will not be gathered, like the flowers, for chaplet or love-token; but of these the wild bird will make its nest, and the wearied child his pillow.

And, as the earth's first mercy, so they are its last gift to us. When all other service is vain, from plant and tree, the soft mosses and grey lichen take up their watch by the head-stone. The woods, the blossoms, the gift-bearing grasses, have done their parts for a time, but these do service for ever. Trees for the builder's yard, flowers for the bride's chamber, corn for the granary, moss for the grave.

Yet as in one sense the humblest, in another they are the most honored of the earth-children. Unfading, as motionless, the worm frets them not, and the autumn wastes not. Strong in lowliness, they neither blanch in heat nor pine in frost. To them slow-fingered, constant-hearted, is entrusted the weaving of the dark, eternal, tapestries of the hills; to them, slow-pencilled, iris-dyed, the tender framing of their endless imagery. Sharing the stillness of the unimpassioned rock, they share also its endurance; and while the winds of departing spring scatter the white hawthorn blossom like drifted snow, and summer dims on the parched meadow the drooping of its cowslip-gold,—far above, among the mountains, the silver lichen spots rest, star-like on the stone, and the gathering orange-stain upon the edge of yonder western peak, reflects the sunsets of a thousand years.

———o———

JUDGMENT, MERCY, AND TRUTH.

When people read, "the law came by Moses, but grace and truth by Christ," do they suppose that the law was ungracious and untrue? The law was given for a foundation; the grace (or mercy) and truth for fulfilment;—the whole forming one glorious Trinity of judgment, mercy, and truth. And if people would but read the text of their Bibles with heartier purpose of understanding it, instead of superstitiously, they would see that throughout the parts which they are intended to make most personally their own (the Psalms) it is always the Law which is spoken of with chief joy. The Psalms respecting mercy are often sorrowful, as in thought of what it cost; but those respecting the law are always full of delight. David cannot contain himself for joy in thinking of it,—he is never weary of its praise:—"How love I thy law! it is my meditation all the day. Thy testimonies are my delight and my counsellers; sweeter, also, than honey and the honeycomb."

DOERS.

Men in their several professed employments, looked at broadly, may be properly arranged under five classes:—

1. Persons who see. These in modern language are sometimes called sight-seers, that being an occupation coming more and more into vogue every day. Anciently they used to be called, simply, seers.

2. Persons who talk. These, in modern language, are usually called talkers, or speakers, as in the House of Commons, and elsewhere. They used to be called prophets.

3. Persons who make. These, in modern language, are usually called manufacturers. Anciently they were called poets.

4. Persons who think. There seems to be no very distinct modern title for this kind of person, anciently called philosophers; nevertheless we have a few of them among us.

Of the first two classes I have only this to note,—that we ought neither to say that a person sees, if he sees falsely, nor speaks, if he speaks falsely. For seeing falsely is worse than blindness, and speaking falsely, than silence. A man who is too dim-sighted to discern the road from the ditch, may feel which is which;—but if the ditch appears manifestly to him to be the road, and the road to be the ditch, what shall become of him? False seeing is unseeing,—on the negative side of blindness; and false speaking, unspeaking,—on the negative side of silence.

To the persons who think, also, the same test applies very shrewdly. Theirs is a dangerous profession; and from the time of the Aristophanes thought-shop to the great German establishment, or thought-manufactory, whose productions have, unhappily, taken in part the place of the older and more serviceable commodities of Nuremberg toys and Berlin wool, it has been often harmful enough to mankind. It should not be so, for a false thought is more distinctly and visibly no thought than a false saying is no saying. But it is touching the two great productive classes of the doers and makers, that we have one or two important points to note here.

Has the reader ever considered, carefully, what is the meaning of the word "doing?" When, accidentally or mechanically, events take place without a purpose, we have indeed effects or results, and agents or causes, but neither deeds nor doers.

Now it so happens, as we all well know, that by far the largest part of things happening in practical life *are* brought about with no deliberate purpose. There are always a number of people who have the nature of stones; they fall on other persons and crush them. Some again have the nature of weeds, and twist about other people's feet and entangle them. More have the nature of logs, and lie in the way, so that every one falls over them. And most of all have the nature of thorns, and set themselves by waysides, so that every passer-by must be torn, and all good seed choked; or perhaps make wonderful crackling under various pots, even to the extent of practically boiling water and working pistons. All these people produce immense and sorrowful effect in the world. Yet none of them are doers: it is their nature to crush, impede, and prick: but deed is not in them.*

And farther, observe, that even when some effect is finally

* We may, perhaps, expediently recollect as much of our botany as to teach us that there may be sharp and rough persons, like spines, who yet have good in them, and are essentially branches, and can bud. But the true thorny person is no spine, only an excrescence; rootless evermore,—leafless evermore. No crown made of such can ever meet glory of Angel's hand. (In Memoriam, lxviii.)

intended, you cannot call it the person's deed, unless it is *what* he intended.

If an ignorant person, purposing evil, accidentally does good (as if a thief's disturbing a family should lead them to discover in time that their house was on fire); or *vice versâ* if an ignorant person intending good, accidentally does evil (as if a child should give hemlock to his companions for celery), in neither case do you call them the doers of what may result. So that in order to a true deed, it is necessary that the effect of it should be foreseen. Which, ultimately, it cannot be, but by a person who knows, and in his deed obeys, the laws of the universe, and of its Maker. And this knowledge is in its highest form, respecting the will of the Ruling Spirit, called Trust. For it is not the knowledge that a thing is, but that, according to the promise and nature of the Ruling Spirit, a thing will be. Also obedience in its highest form is not obedience to a constant and compulsory law, but a persuaded or voluntary yielded obedience to an issued command.

And because in His doing always certain, and in His speaking always true, His name who leads the armies of Heaven is "Faithful and True," and all deeds which are done in alliance with those armies, be they small or great, are essentially deeds of *faith*, which therefore, and in this one stern, eternal sense, subdues all kingdoms, and turns to flight the armies of the aliens, and is at once the source and substance of all human deed, rightly so-called.

What, let us ask next, is the ruling character of the person who produces—the creator or maker, anciently called the poet?

We have seen what a deed is. What then is a "creation?" Nay, it may be replied, to "create" cannot be said of man's labor.

On the contrary, it not only can be said, but is and must be said continually. You certainly do not talk of creating a watch, or creating a shoe; nevertheless you *do* talk of creating a feeling. Why is this?

Look back to the greatest of all creation, that of the world. Suppose the trees had been ever so well or so ingeniously put together, stem and leaf, yet if they had not been able to grow, would they have been well created? Or suppose the fish had been cut and stitched finely out of skin and whalebone; yet, cast upon the waters, had not been able to swim? Or suppose Adam and Eve had been made in the softest clay, ever so neatly, and set at the foot of the tree of knowledge, fastened up to it, quite unable to fall, or do anything else, would they have been well created, or in any true sense created at all?

It will, perhaps, appear to you, after a little farther thought, that to create anything in reality is to put life into it.

A poet, or creator, is therefore a person who puts things together, not as a watchmaker steel, or a shoemaker leather, but who puts life into them.

His work is essentially this: it is the gathering and arranging of material by imagination, so as to have in it at last the harmony or helpfulness of life, and the passion or emotion of life. Mere fitting and adjustment of material is nothing; that is watchmaking. But helpful and passionate harmony, essentially choral harmony, so-called from the Greek word "rejoicing," is the harmony of Apollo and the Muses; the word Muse and Mother being derived from the same root, meaning "passionate seeking," or love, of which the issue is passionate finding, or sacred INVENTION. For which reason I could not bear to use any baser word than this of invention And if the reader will think over all these things, and follow them out, as I think he may easily with this much of clue given him, he will not any more think it wrong in me to place invention so high among the powers of man, or any more think it strange that the "last act of the life of Socrates should have been to purify himself from the sin of having negligently listened to the voice within him, which, through all his past life, had bid him labor, and make harmony."

———o———

THE HELPFUL, OR THE HOLY ONE.

When matter is either consistent, or living, we call it pure, or clean; when inconsistent, or corrupting (unhelpful), we call it impure, or unclean. The greatest uncleanliness being that which is essentially most opposite to life.

Life and consistency, then, both expressing one character (namely, helpfulness, of a higher or lower order), the Maker of all creatures and things, "by whom all creatures live, and all things consist," is essentially and for ever the Helpful One, or in softer Saxon, the "Holy" One.

The word has no other ultimate meaning: Helpful, harmless, undefiled: "living" or "Lord of Life."

The idea is clear and mighty in the cherubim's cry: "Helpful, helpful, helpful, Lord God of Hosts;" *i. e.* of all the hosts, armies, and creatures of the earth.

A pure or holy state of anything, therefore, is that in which all its parts are helpful or consistent. They may or may not be homogeneous. The highest or organic purities are composed of many elements in an entirely helpful state. The highest and first law of the universe—and the other name of life, is, therefore, "help." The other name of death is "separation." Government and co-operation are in all things and eternally the laws of life. Anarchy and competition eternally, and in all things, the laws of death.

———o———

ST. MARK.

"And so Barnabas took Mark, and sailed unto Cyprus." If as the shores of Asia lessened upon his sight, the spirit of prophecy had entered into the heart of the weak disciple who had turned back when his hand was on the plough, and who had been judged, by the chiefest of Christ's captains, unworthy thenceforward to go forth with him to the work,* how wonderful would he have thought it, that by the lion symbol in future ages he was to be represented among men! how woful, that the war-cry of his name should so often reanimate the rage of the soldier, on those very plains where he himself had failed in the courage of the Christian, and so often dye with fruitless blood that very Cypriot Sea, over whose waves, in repentance and shame, he was following the Son of Consolation!

———o———

THE MYSTERY OF CLEARNESS.

In an Italian twilight, when, sixty or eighty miles away, the ridge of the Western Alps rises in its dark and serrated blue against the crystalline vermilion, there is still unsearchableness, but an unsearchableness without cloud or concealment,—an infinite unknown, but no sense of any veil or inter

* Acts, xiii. 13; xv. 38, 39.

ference between us and it: we are separated from it not by any anger or storm, not by any vain and fading vapor, but only by the deep infinity of the thing itself. I find that the great religious painters rejoiced in that kind of unknowableness, and in that only; and I feel that even if they had had all the power to do so, still they would not have put rosy mists and blue shadows behind their sacred figures, but only the far-away sky and cloudless mountains. Probably the right conclusion is that the clear and cloudy mysteries are alike noble; but that the beauty of the wreaths of frost mist, folded over banks of greensward deep in dew, and of the purple clouds of evening, and the wreaths of fitful vapor gliding through groves of pine, and irised around the pillars of waterfalls, is more or less typical of the kind of joy which we should take in the imperfect knowledge granted to the earthly life, while the serene and cloudless mysteries set forth that belonging to the redeemed life.

PARTIAL KNOWLEDGE.

Our happiness as thinking beings must depend on our being content to accept only partial knowledge, even in those matters which chiefly concern us. If we insist upon perfect intelligibility and complete declaration in every moral subject, we shall instantly fall into misery of unbelief. Our whole happiness and power of energetic action depend upon our being able to breathe and live in the cloud; content to see it opening here and closing there; rejoicing to catch, through the thinnest films of it, glimpses of stable and substantial things; but yet perceiving a nobleness even in the concealment, and rejoicing that the kindly veil is spread where the untempered light might have scorched us, or the infinite clearness wearied.

JUST CRITICISM.

Men have commonly more pleasure in the criticism which hurts than in that which is innocuous, and are more tolerant of the severity which breaks hearts and ruins fortunes, than of that which falls impotently on the grave.

And thus well says the good and deep-minded Richard Hooker: "To the best and wisest, while they live, the world is continually a froward opposite; and a curious observer of their defects and imperfections, their virtues afterwards it as much admireth. And for this cause, many times that which deserveth admiration would hardly be able to find favor, if they which propose it were not content to profess themselves therein scholars and followers of the ancient. For the world will not endure to hear that we are wiser than any have been which went before."—Book v. ch. vii. 3. He therefore who would maintain the cause of contemporary excellence against that of elder time, must have almost every class of men arrayed against him. The generous, because they would not find matter of accusation against established dignities; the envious, because they like not the sound of a living man's praise; the wise, because they prefer the opinion of centuries to that of days; and the foolish, because they are incapable of forming an opinion of their own. Obloquy so universal is not lightly to be risked, and the few who make an effort to stem the torrent, as it is made commonly in favor of their own works, deserve the contempt which is their only reward.

THE NEBUCHADNEZZAR CURSE.

Though God "hath made everything beautiful in his time, also he hath set the world in their heart, so that no man can find out the work that God maketh from the beginning to the end."

This Nebuchadnezzar curse, that sends us to grass like oxen, seems to follow but too closely on the excess or continuance of national power and peace. In the perplexities of nations, in their struggles for existence, in their infancy, their impotence, or even their disorganization, they have higher hopes and nobler passions. Out of the suffering comes the serious mind; out of the salvation, the grateful heart; out of the endurance, the fortitude; out of the deliverance, the faith; but now when they have learned to live under providence of laws, and with decency and justice of regard for each other; and when they have done away with violent and external sources of suffering, worse evils seem arising out of their rest, evils that vex less and mortify more, that suck the blood though they do not shed it, and ossify the heart though they do not torture it.

———o———

OPPRESSION OF THE POOR.

You cannot but have noticed how often in those parts of the Bible which are likely to be oftenest opened when people look for guidance, comfort, or help in the affairs of daily life, namely, the Psalms and Proverbs, mention is made of the guilt attaching to the *Oppression* of the poor. Observe: not the neglect of them, but the *Oppression* of them; the word is as frequent as it is strange. You can hardly open either of those books, but somewhere in their pages you will find a description of the wicked man's attempts against the poor, such as—"He doth ravish the poor when he getteth him into his net."

"His mouth is full of deceit and fraud; in the secret places doth he murder the innocent."

"They are corrupt, and speak wickedly concerning oppression."

"Their poison is like the poison of a serpent. Ye weigh the violence of your hands in the earth."

Yes: "Ye weigh the violence of your hands;" weigh these words as well. The last things we usually think of weighing are Bible words. We like to dream and dispute over them, but to weigh them and see what their true contents are—anything but that! Yet weigh them; for I have purposely taken these verses, perhaps more strikingly to you read in this connexion, than separately in their places out of the Psalms, because, for all people belonging to the Established Church of this country these Psalms are appointed lessons, portioned out to them by their clergy to be read once through every month. Presumably, therefore, whatever portions of Scripture we may pass by or forget, these, at all events, must be brought continually to our observance as useful for direction of daily life. Now, do we ever ask ourselves what the real meaning of these passages may be, and who these wicked people are, who are "murdering the innocent?" You know it is rather singular language this!—rather strong language, we might, perhaps, call it—hearing it for the first time. Murder! and murder of innocent people!—nay, even a sort of cannibalism. Eating people,—yes, and God's people, too—eating *My* people as if they were bread! swords drawn, bows bent, poison of serpents mixed! violence of hands weighed, measured, and trafficked with as so much coin! where is all this going on? Do you suppose it was only going on in the time of David, and that nobody but Jews ever murder the poor? If so, it would surely be wiser not to mutter and mumble for our daily lessons what does not concern us; but if there be any chance that it may concern us, and if this description, in the Psalms, of human guilt is at all generally applicable, as the descriptions in the Psalms of human sorrow are, may it not be advisable to know wherein this guilt is being committed round about us, or by ourselves? and when we take the words of the Bible into our mouths in a congregational way, to be sure whether we mean sincerely to chant a piece of melodious poetry relating to other people (we know not exactly whom)—or to assert our belief in facts bearing somewhat astringently on ourselves and our daily business And if you make up your minds to do this no longer, and take pains to examine into the matter, you will find that these strange words, occurring as they do, not in a few places only, but almost in every alternate psalm, and every alternate chapter of Proverbs or prophecy, with tremendous reiteration, were not written for one nation or one time only, but for all nations and languages, for all places and all centuries; and it is as true of the wicked man now as ever it was of Nabal or Dives, that "his eyes are set against the poor."

WHO ARE THE POOR?

May we not advisedly look into this matter a little, and ask, Who are the poor?

No country is, or ever will be, without them: that is to

2

say, without the class which cannot, on the average, do more by its labour than provide for its subsistence, and which has no accumulations of property laid by on any considerable scale. Now there are a certain number of this class whom we cannot oppress with much severity. An able-bodied and intelligent workman—sober, honest, and industrious, will almost always command a fair price for his work, and lay by enough in a few years to enable him to hold his own in the labour market. But all men are not able-bodied, nor intelligent, nor industrious; and you cannot expect them to be. Nothing appears to me at once more ludicrous and more melancholy than the way the people of the present age usually talk about the morals of labourers. You hardly ever address a labouring man upon his prospects in life, without quietly assuming that he is to possess, at starting, as a small moral capital to begin with, the virtue of Socrates, the philosophy of Plato, and the heroism of Epaminondas. "Be assured, my good man,"—you say to him,—"that if you work steadily for ten hours a day all your life long, and if you drink nothing but water, or the very mildest beer, and live on very plain food, and never lose your temper, and go to church every Sunday, and always remain content in the position in which Providence has placed you, and never grumble, nor swear, and always keep your clothes decent, and rise early, and use every opportunity of improving yourself, you will get on very well, and never come to the parish."

All this is exceedingly true; but before giving the advice so confidently, it would be well if we sometimes tried it practically ourselves, and spent a year or so at some hard manual labour, not of an entertaining kind—ploughing or digging, for instance, with a very moderate allowance of beer; nothing but bread and cheese for dinner; no papers nor muffins in the morning; no sofas nor magazines at night; one small room for parlour and kitchen ; and a large family of children always in the middle of the floor. If we think we could, under these circumstances, enact Socrates or Epaminondas entirely to our own satisfaction, we shall be somewhat justified in requiring the same behaviour from our poorer neighbours; but if not, we should surely consider whether among the various forms of oppression of the poor, we may not rank as one of the first and likeliest—the oppression of expecting too much from them.

But there will always be some in the world who are not altogether intelligent and exemplary, and *occasionally* drunk on Saturday night, and who like sleep on Sunday morning better than prayers, and of unnatural parents who send their children out to beg instead of to go to school.

Now these are the kind of people whom you *can* oppress, and whom you do oppress, and that to purpose,—and with all the more cruelty and the greater sting, because it is just their own fault that puts them into your power. You know the words about wicked people are, "He doth ravish the poor when he getteth him *into his net.*" This getting into the net is constantly the fault or folly of the sufferer—his own heedlessness or his own indolence; but after he is once in the net, the oppression of him, and making the most of his distress, are ours. The nets which we use against the poor are just those worldly embarrassments which either their ignorance or their improvidence are almost certain at some time or other to bring them into : then, just at the time when we ought to hasten to help them, and disentangle them, and teach them how to manage better in future, we rush forward to *pillage* them, and force all we can out of them in their adversity. For, to take one instance only, remember this is literally and simply what we do, whenever we buy, or try to buy, cheap goods—goods offered at a price which we know cannot be remunerative for the labour involved in them Whenever we buy such goods, remember we are stealing somebody's labour. Don't let us mince the matter. I say, in plain Saxon, STEALING—taking from him the proper reward of his work, and putting it into our own pocket. You know well enough that the thing could not have been offered you at that price, unless distress of some kind had forced the producer to part with it. You take advantage of this distress, and you force as much out of him as you can under the circumstances. The old barons of the middle ages used, in general, the thumb-screw to extort property; we moderns hunger, or domestic affliction, but the fact of extortion remains precisely the same. Whether we force the man's property by pinching his stomach or pinching his fingers, makes some difference anatomically; morally, none whatever. We use a form of torture of some sort in order to make him give up his property.

———o———

MERCANTILE PANICS.

No merchant deserving the name ought to be more liable to a "panic" than a soldier should; for his name should never be on more paper than he could at any instant meet the call of, happen what will. I do not say this without feeling at the same time how difficult it is to mark, in existing commerce, the just limits between the spirit of enterprise and of speculation. Something of the same temper which makes the English soldier do always all that is possible, and attempt more than is possible, joins its influence with that of mere avarice in tempting the English merchant into risks which he cannot justify, and efforts which he cannot sustain; and the same passion for adventure which our travellers gratify every summer on perilous snow wreaths, and cloud-encompassed precipices, surrounds with a romantic fascination the glittering of a hollow investment, and gilds the clouds that curl round gulfs of ruin. Nay, a higher and a more serious feeling frequently mingles in the motley temptation; and men apply themselves to the task of growing rich, as to a labour of providential appointment, from which they cannot pause without culpability, nor retire without dishonour. Our large trading cities bear to me very nearly the aspect of monastic establishments in which the roar of the mill-wheel and the crane takes the place of other devotional music: and in which the worship of Mammon and Moloch is conducted with a tender reverence and an exact propriety: the merchant rising to his Mammon matins with the self-denial of an anchorite, and expiating the frivolities into which he may be beguiled in the course of the day by late attendance at Mammon vespers. But, with every allowance that can be made for these conscientious and romantic persons, the fact remains the same, that by far the greater number of the transactions which lead to these times of commercial embarrassment may be ranged simply under two great heads,—gambling and stealing; and both of these in their most culpable form, namely, gambling with money which is not ours, and stealing from those who trust us. I have sometimes thought a day might come, when the nation would perceive that a well-educated man who steals a hundred thousand pounds, involving the entire means of subsistence of a hundred families, deserves, on the whole, as severe a punishment as an ill-educated man who steals a purse from a pocket, or a mug from a pantry.

———o———

DIVINE LAWS.

I am very sure that no reader who has given any attention to the tendency of what I have written, will suppose me to underrate the importance, or dispute the authority, of law It has been necessary for me to allege these again and again, nor can they ever be too often or too energetically alleged, against the vast masses of men who now disturb or retard the advance of civilisation; heady and high-minded, despisers of discipline, and refusers of correction. But law, so far as it can be reduced to form and system, and is not written upon the heart,—as it is, in a Divine loyalty, upon the hearts of the great hierarchies who serve and wait about the throne of the Eternal Lawgiver,—this lower and formally expressible law has, I say, two objects. It is either for the definition and restraint of sin, or the guidance of simplicity; it either explains, forbids, and punishes wickedness, or it guides the movements and actions both of lifeless things and of the more simple and untaught among responsible agents. And so long, therefore, as sin and foolishness are in the world, so long it will be necessary for men to submit themselves painfully to this lower law, in proportion to their need of being corrected, and to the degree of childishness or simplicity by which they approach more nearly to the condition of the unthinking and inanimate things which are governed by law altogether; yet yielding, in the manner of their submission to it, a singular lesson to the pride of man,—being obedient more perfectly in proportion to their greatness. But, so far as men become good and wise, and rise above the state of children, so far they become emancipated from this written law, and invested with the perfect freedom which consists in the fulness and joyfulness of compliance with a higher and unwritten law;

a law so universal, so subtle, so glorious, that nothing but the heart can keep it.

Now pride opposes itself to the observance of this Divine law in two opposite ways: either by brute resistance, which is the way of the rabble and its leaders, denying or defying law altogether, or by formal compliance, which is the way of the Pharisee,—exalting himself while he pretends to obedience, and making void the infinite and spiritual commandment by the finite and lettered commandment. And it is easy to know which law we are obeying: for any law which we magnify and keep through pride, is always the law of the letter; but that which we love and keep through humility, is the law of the Spirit. And the letter killeth, but the Spirit giveth life.

———o———

THE CHURCH.

The Church is a body to be taught and fed, not to teach and feed: and of all sheep that are fed on the earth, Christ's Sheep are the most simple (the children of this generation are wiser): always losing themselves; doing little else in this world *but* lose themselves;—never finding themselves; always found by Some One else; getting perpetually into sloughs, and snows, and bramble thickets, like to die there, but for their Shepherd, who is for ever finding them and bearing them back, with torn fleeces and eyes full of fear.

———o———

CLERGYMEN.

As to the mode in which the officers of the Church should be elected or appointed, I do not feel it my business to say anything at present, nor much respecting the extent of their authority, either over each other or over the congregation, this being a most difficult question, the right solution of which evidently lies between two most dangerous extremes —insubordination and radicalism on one hand, and ecclesiastical tyranny and heresy on the other: of the two, insubordination is far the least to be dreaded—for this reason, that nearly all real Christians are more on the watch against their pride than their indolence, and would sooner obey their clergyman, if possible, than contend with him; while the very pride they suppose conquered often returns masked, and causes them to make a merit of their humility and their abstract obedience, however unreasonable: but they cannot so easily persuade themselves there is a merit in abstract *dis*obedience.

———o———

THE KING'S MESSENGERS.

The word ambassador has a peculiar ambiguity about it, owing to its use in modern political affairs; and these clergymen assume that the word, as used by St. Paul, means an Ambassador Plenipotentiary; representative of his King, and capable of acting for his King. What right have they to assume that St. Paul meant this? St. Paul never uses the word ambassador at all. He says, simply, "We are in embassage from Christ; and Christ beseeches you through us."

Most true. And let it further be granted, that every word that the clergyman speaks is literally dictated to him by Christ; that he can make no mistake in delivering his message; and that, therefore, it is indeed Christ himself who speaks to us the word of life through the messenger's lips. Does, therefore, the messenger represent Christ? Does the channel which conveys the waters of the Fountain represent the Fountain itself? Suppose, when we went to draw water at a cistern, that all at once the Leaden Spout should become animated, and open its mouth and say to us, See, I am Vicarious for the Fountain. Whatever respect you show to the Fountain, show some part of it to me. Should we not answer the Spout, and say, Spout, you were set there for our service, and may be taken away and thrown aside if anything goes wrong with you. But the Fountain will flow for ever.

Observe, I do not deny a most solemn authority vested in every Christian messenger from God to men. I am prepared to grant this to the uttermost; and all that George Herbert says, in the end of the Church-porch, I would enforce, at another time than this, to the uttermost. But the Authority is simply that of a King's *messenger;* not of a King's *Representative.* There is a wide difference; all the difference between humble service and blasphemous usurpation.

———o———

ILLUSTRATIONS FROM THE BIBLE.

You are not philosophers of the kind who suppose that the Bible is a superannuated book; neither are you of those who think the Bible is dishonoured by being referred to for judgment in small matters. The very divinity of the Book seems to me, on the contrary, to justify us in referring *every* thing to it, with respect to which any conclusion can be gathered from its pages. Assuming then that the Bible is neither superannuated now, nor ever likely to be so, it will follow that the illustrations which the Bible employs are likely to be *clear and intelligible illustrations* to the end of time. I do not mean that everything spoken of in the Bible histories must continue to endure for all time, but that the things which the Bible uses for illustration of eternal truths are likely to remain eternally intelligible illustrations.

———o———

THE DISSECTORS AND THE DREAMERS.

All experience goes to teach us, that among men of average intellect the most useful members of society are the dissectors, not the dreamers. It is not that they love nature or beauty less, but that they love result, effect, and progress more; and when we glance broadly along the starry crowd of benefactors to the human race, and guides of human thought, we shall find that this dreaming love of natural beauty—or at least its expression—has been more or less checked by them all, and subordinated either to hard work or watching of *human* nature.

———o———

ASSOCIATIONS OF BEAUTY.

Beauty has been appointed by the Deity to be one of the elements by which the human soul is continually sustained; it is therefore to be found more or less in all natural objects, but in order that we may not satiate ourselves with it, and weary of it, it is rarely granted to us in its utmost degrees. When we see it in those utmost degrees, we are attracted to it strongly, and remember it long, as in the case of singularly beautiful scenery, or a beautiful countenance. On the other hand, absolute ugliness is admitted as rarely as perfect beauty; but degrees of it more or less distinct are associated with whatever has the nature of death and sin, just as beauty is associated with what has the nature of virtue and of life.

———o———

RESPECTABILITY OF ARTISTS.

I believe that there is no chance of art's truly flourishing in any country, until you make it a simple and plain business, providing its masters with an easy competence, but rarely with anything more. And I say this, not because I despise the great painter, but because I honour him; and I should no more think of adding to his respectability or happiness by giving him riches, than, if Shakspeare or Milton were alive, I should think we added to *their* respectability, or were likely to get better work from them, by making them millionaires.

———o———

OPINIONS.

In many matters of opinion, our first and last coincide, though on different grounds; it is the middle stage which is farthest from the truth. Childhood often holds a truth with its feeble fingers, which the grasp of manhood cannot retain, —which it is the pride of utmost age to recover.

THE NECESSITY OF WORK.

By far the greater part of the suffering and crime which exist at this moment in civilized Europe, arises simply from people not understanding this truism—not knowing that produce or wealth is eternally connected by the laws of heaven and earth with resolute labour; but hoping in some way to cheat or abrogate this everlasting law of life, and to feed where they have not furrowed, and be warm where they have not woven.

I repeat, nearly all our misery and crime result from this one misapprehension. The law of nature is, that a certain quantity of work is necessary to produce a certain quantity of good, of any kind whatever. If you want knowledge, you must toil for it: if food, you must toil for it; and if pleasure, you must toil for it. But men do not acknowledge this law, or strive to evade it, hoping to get their knowledge, and food, and pleasure for nothing; and in this effort they either fail of getting them, and remain ignorant and miserable, or they obtain them by making other men work for their benefit; and then they are tyrants and robbers. Yes, and worse than robbers. I am not one who in the least doubts or disputes the progress of this century in many things useful to mankind; but it seems to me a very dark sign respecting us that we look with so much indifference upon dishonesty and cruelty in the pursuit of wealth. In the dream of Nebuchadnezzar it was only the *feet* that were part of iron and part of clay; but many of us are now getting so cruel in our avarice, that it seems as if, in us, the *heart* were part of iron, and part of clay.

———o———

WAR.

Wherever there is war, there *must* be injustice on one side or the other, or on both. There have been wars which were little more than trials of strength between friendly nations, and in which the injustice was not to each other, but to the God who gave them life. But in a malignant war of these present ages there is injustice of ignobler kind, at once to God and man, which *must* be stemmed for both their sakes. It may, indeed, be so involved with national prejudices, or ignorances, that neither of the contending nations can conceive it as attaching to their cause; nay, the constitution of their governments, and the clumsy crookedness of their political dealings with each other, may be such as to prevent either of them from knowing the actual cause for which they have gone to war.

For the cause of this quarrel is no dim, half-avoidable involution of mean interests and errors, as some would have us believe. There never was a great war caused by such things. There never can be. The historian may trace it, with ingenious trifling, to a courtier's jest or a woman's glance; but he does not ask—(and it is the sum of questions)—how the warring nations had come to found their destinies on the course of the sneer, or the smile. If they have so based them, it is time for them to learn, through suffering, how to build on other foundations;—for great, accumulated, and most righteous cause, their foot slides in due time; and against the torpor, or the turpitude, of their myriads, there is loosed the haste of the devouring sword and the thirsty arrow.

But it is not altogether thus: we have not been cast into this war by mere political misapprehensions, or popular ignorances. It is quite possible that neither we nor our rulers may clearly understand the nature of the conflict; and that we may be dealing blows in the dark, confusedly, and as a soldier suddenly awakened from slumber by an unknown adversary. But I believe the struggle was inevitable, and that the sooner it came, the more easily it was to be met, and the more nobly concluded.

———o———

THE ADVANTAGES OF WAR.

I believe that war is at present productive of good more than of evil. I will not argue this hardly and coldly, as I might, by tracing in past history some of the abundant evidence that nations have always reached their highest virtue, and wrought their most accomplished works, in times of straitening and battle; as, on the other hand, no nation ever yet enjoyed a protracted and triumphant peace without receiving in its own bosom ineradicable seeds of future decline. I will not so argue this matter; but I will appeal at once to the testimony of those whom the war has cost the dearest. I know what would be told me, by those who have suffered nothing; whose domestic happiness has been unbroken, whose daily comfort undisturbed; whose experience of calamity consists, at its utmost, in the incertitude of a speculation, the dearness of a luxury, or the increase of demands upon their fortune which they could meet fourfold without inconvenience.

They are bound by new fidelities to all that they have saved,—by new love to all for whom they have suffered; every affection which seemed to sink with those dim life-stains into the dust, has been delegated, by those who need it no more, to the cause for which they have expired; and every mouldering arm, which will never more embrace the beloved ones, has bequeathed to them its strength and its faithfulness.

———o———

MEN OF GROSS MINDS.

During the last age lived certain men of high intellect who had *no* love of nature whatever. They do not appear ever to have received the smallest sensation of ocular delight from any natural scene, but would have lived happily all their lives in drawing-rooms or studies. And, therefore, in these men we shall be able to determine, with the greatest chance of accuracy, what the real influence of natural beauty is, and what the character of a mind destitute of its love. Take, as conspicuous instances, Le Sage and Smollett, and you will find, in meditating over their works, that they are utterly incapable of conceiving a human soul as endowed with any nobleness whatever; their heroes are simply beasts endowed with some degree of human intellect;—cunning, false, passionate, reckless, ungrateful, and abominable, incapable of noble joy, of noble sorrow, of any spiritual perception or hope. I said, "beasts with human intellect;" but neither Gil Blas nor Roderick Random reach, morally, anything near the level of dogs.

———o———

PEDESTRIANS.

To any person who has all his senses about him, a quiet walk along not more than ten or twelve miles of road a day, is the most amusing of all travelling; and all travelling becomes dull in exact proportion to its rapidity. Going by railroad I do not consider as travelling at all; it is merely "being sent" to a place, and very little different from becoming a parcel; the next step to it would of course be telegraphic transport, of which, however, I suppose it has been truly said by Octave Feuillet,

"*Il y aurait des gens assez bêtes* pour trouver ça amusant."

———o———

WEALTH.

Wealth is simply one of the greatest powers which can be entrusted to human hands: a power, not indeed to be envied, because it seldom makes us happy; but still less to be abdicated or despised: while, in these days, and in this country, it has become a power all the more notable, in that the possessions of a rich man are not represented, as they used to be, by wedges of gold or coffers of jewels, but by masses of men variously employed, over whose bodies and minds the wealth, according to its direction, exercises harmful or helpful influence, and becomes, in that alternative, Mammon either of Unrighteousness or of Righteousness.

———o———

LABOR IN LITTLE THINGS.

We have no right at once to pronounce ourselves the wisest people because we like to do all things in the best way. There are many little things which to do admirably is to waste both time and cost; and the real question is not so much whether we have done a given thing as well as possible, as whether we have turned a given quantity of labonr to the best account.

---o---

THE MEMORY OF UNKINDNESS.

He who has once stood beside the grave, to look back upon the companionship which has been forever closed, feeling how impotent *there* are the wild love, or the keen sorrow, to give one instant's pleasure to the pulseless heart, or atone in the lowest measure to the departed spirit for the hour of unkindness, will scarcely for the future incur that debt to the heart, which can only be discharged to the dust.

---o---

DARK SIGNS OF THE TIMES.

Indeed it is woeful, when the young usurp the place, or despise the wisdom, of the aged; and among the many dark signs of these times, the disobedience and insolence of youth are among the darkest. But with whom is the fault? Youth never yet lost its modesty where age had not lost its honour; nor did childhood ever refuse its reverence, except where age had forgotten correction. The cry, "Go up thou bald head," will never be heard in the land which remembers the precept, "See that ye despise not one of these little ones;" and although indeed youth *may* become despicable, when its eager hope is changed into presumption, and its progressive power into arrested pride, there is something more despicable still, in the old age which has learned neither judgment nor gentleness, which is weak without charity, and cold without discretion.

———o———

VULGAR FRACTIONS.

If you will not amuse, nor inform, nor help anybody; you will not amuse, nor better, nor inform yourselves; you will sink into a state in which you can neither show, nor feel, nor see, anything, but that one is to two as three is to six. And in that state what should we call ourselves? Men? I think not. The right name for us would be—numerators and denominators. Vulgar Fractions.

May we not accept this great principle—that, as our bodies, to be in health, must be *generally* exercised, so our minds, to be in health, must be *generally* cultivated? You would not call a man healthy who had strong arms but was paralytic in his feet; nor one who could walk well, but had no use of his hands; nor one who could see well, if he could not hear. You would not voluntarily reduce your bodies to any such partially developed state. Much more, then, you would not, if you could help it, reduce your minds to it. Now, your minds are endowed with a vast number of gifts of totally different uses—limbs of mind as it were, which, if you don't exercise, you cripple. One is curiosity; that is a gift, a capacity of pleasure in knowing; which if you destroy, you make yourselves cold and dull. Another is sympathy; the power of sharing in the feelings of living creatures, which if you destroy, you make yourselves hard and cruel. Another of your limbs of mind is admiration; the power of enjoying beauty or ingenuity, which, if you destroy, you make yourselves base and irreverent. Another is wit; or the power of playing with the lights on the many sides of truth; which if you destroy, you make yourselves gloomy, and less useful and cheering to others than you might be. So that in choosing your way of work it should be your aim, as far as possible, to bring out all these faculties, as far as they exist in you; not one merely, nor another, but all of them. And the way to bring them out, is simply to concern yourselves attentively with the subjects of each faculty. To cultivate sympathy you must be among living creatures, and thinking about them; and to cultivate admiration, you must be among beautiful things and looking at them.

———o———

LOVE OF NATURE.

Though the absence of the love of nature is not an assured condemnation, its presence is an invariable sign of goodness of heart and justness of moral *perception*, though by no means of moral *practice;* that in proportion to the degree in which it is felt, will *probably* be the degree in which all nobleness and beauty of character will also be felt; that when it is originally absent from any mind, that mind is in many other respects hard, worldly, and degraded; that where, having been originally present, it is repressed by art or education, that repression appears to have been detrimental to the person suffering it; and that wherever the feeling exists, it acts for good on the character to which it belongs, though, as it may often belong to characters weak in other respects, it may carelessly be mistaken for a source of evil in them.

———o———

MODERN EDUCATION.

What do you suppose was the substance of good education, the education of a knight, in the Middle Ages? What was taught to a boy as soon as he was able to learn anything? First, to keep under his body, and bring it into subjection and perfect strength; then to take Christ for his captain, to live as always in his presence and, finally, to do his *devoir*—mark the word—to all men? Now, consider first, the difference in their influence over the armies of France, between the ancient word "devoir," and modern word "gloire." And, again, ask yourselves what you expect your own children to be taught at your great schools and universities. Is it Christian history, or the histories of Pan and Silenus? Your present education, to all intents and purposes, denies Christ, and that is intensely and peculiarly modernism.

Or, again, what do you suppose was the proclaimed and understood principle of all Christian *governments* in the middle ages? I do not say it was a principle acted up to, or that the cunning and violence of wicked men had not too often their full sway then, as now; but on what principles were that cunning and violence, so far as was possible, restrained? By the *confessed* fear of God, and *confessed* authority of his law. You will find that all treaties, laws, transactions whatsoever, in the middle ages, are based on a confession of Christianity as the leading rule of life; that a text of Scripture is held, in all public assemblies, strong enough to be set against an appearance of expediency; and although, in the end, the expediency might triumph, yet it was never without a distinct allowance of Christian principle, as an efficient element in the consultation. Whatever error might be committed, at least Christ was openly confessed. Now what is the custom of your British Parliament in these days? You know that nothing would excite greater manifestations of contempt and disgust than the slightest attempt to introduce the authority of Scripture in a political consultation. That is denying Christ. It is intensely and peculiarly modernism.

———o———

WANT OF SELF-KNOWLEDGE.

Half the evil in this world comes from people not knowing what they do like, not deliberately setting themselves to find out what they really enjoy. All people enjoy giving away money, for instance: they don't know *that*,—they rather think they like keeping it; and they *do* keep it under this false impression, often to their great discomfort. Every body likes to do good; but not one in a hundred finds *this* out.

———o———

THE RESPONSIBILITY OF A RICH MAN.

A rich man ought to be continually examining how he may spend his money for the advantage of others; at present, others are continually plotting how they may beguile him into spending it apparently for his own. The aspect which he presents to the eyes of the world is generally that of a person holding a bag of money with a staunch grasp, and resolved to part with none of it unless he is forced, and all the people about him are plotting how they may force him; that is to say, how they may persuade him that he wants this thing or that; or how they may produce things that he will covet and buy. One man tries to persuade him that he wants perfumes; another that he wants jewellery; another that he wants sugarplums; another that he wants roses at Christmas. Anybody who can invent a new want for him is supposed to be a benefactor to society; and thus the energies of the poorer people about him are continually directed to the production of covetable, instead of serviceable things; and the rich man has the general aspect of a fool, plotted against by all the world. Whereas the real aspect which he ought to have is that of a person wiser than others, entrusted with the management of a larger quantity of capital, which he administers for the profit of all, directing each man to the labour which is most healthy for him, and most serviceable for the community.

———o———

THE WANTS OF MODERN ART.

We don't want either the life or the decorations of the thirteenth century back again; and the circumstances with which you must surround your workmen are those simply of happy modern English life, because the designs you have now to ask for from your workmen are such as will make modern English life beautiful. All that gorgeousness of the middle ages, beautiful as it sounds in description, noble as in many respects it was in reality, had, nevertheless, for foundation and for end, nothing but the pride of life—the pride of the so-called superior classes; a pride which supported itself by violence and robbery, and led in the end to the destruction both of the arts themselves and the States in which they flourished.

The great lesson of history is, that all the fine arts hitherto

—having been supported by the selfish power of the noblesse, and never having extended their range to the comfort or the relief of the mass of the people—the arts, I say, thus practised, and thus matured, have only accelerated the ruin of the States they adorned; and at the moment when, in any kingdom, you point to the triumphs of its greatest artists, you point also to the determined hour of the kingdom's decline. The names of great painters are like passing bells; in the name of Velasquez, you hear sounded the fall of Spain; in the name of Titian, that of Venice; in the name of Leonardo, that of Milan; in the name of Raphael, that of Rome. And there is profound justice in this; for in proportion to the nobleness of the power is the guilt of its use for purposes vain or vile; and hitherto the greater the art, the more surely has it been used, and used solely, for the decoration of pride, or the provoking of sensuality. Another course lies open to us. We may abandon the hope—or if you like the words better—we may disdain the temptation, of the pomp and grace of Italy in her youth. For us there can be no more the throne of marble—for us no more the vault of gold—but for us there is the loftier and lovelier privilege of bringing the power and charm of art within the reach of the humble and the poor; and as the magnificence of past ages failed by its narrowness and its pride, ours may prevail and continue, by its universality and its lowliness.

We want now, no more feasts of the gods, nor martyrdoms of the saints; we have no need of sensuality, no place for superstition, or for costly insolence. Let us have learned and faithful historical paintings; touching and thoughtful representations of human nature in dramatic paintings; poetical and familiar renderings of natural objects, and of landscape; and rational, deeply-felt realizations of the events which are the subjects of our religious faith. And let these things we want, as far as possible, be scattered abroad, and made accessible to all men.

———o———

MANUAL LABOUR.

How wide the separation is between original and second-hand execution, I shall endeavour to show elsewhere; it is not so much to our purpose here as to mark the other and more fatal error of despising manual labour when governed by intellect; for it is no less fatal an error to despise it when thus regulated by intellect, than to value it for its own sake. We are always in these days endeavouring to separate the two; we want one man to be always thinking, and another to be always working, and we call one a gentleman, and the other an operative; whereas the workman ought often to be thinking, and the thinker often to be working, and both should be gentlemen, in the best sense. As it is, we make both ungentle, the one envying, the other despising, his brother; and the mass of society is made up of morbid thinkers, and miserable workers. Now it is only by labour that thought can be made healthy, and only by thought that labour can be made happy, and the two cannot be separated with impunity. It would be well if all of us were good handicraftsmen in some kind, and the dishonour of manual labour done away with altogether; so that though there should still be a trenchant distinction of race between nobles and commoners, there should not, among the latter, be a trenchant distinction of employment, as between idle and working men, or between men of liberal and illiberal professions. All professions should be liberal, and there should be less pride felt in peculiarity of employment, and more in excellence of achievement. And yet more, in each several profession, no master should be too proud to do its hardest work. The painter should grind his own colours; the architect work in the mason's yard with his men; the master-manufacturer be himself a more skilful operative than any man in his mills; and the distinction between one man and another be only in experience and skill, and the authority and wealth which these must naturally and justly obtain.

———o———

PRACTICAL KNOWLEDGE.

In literary and scientific teaching, the great point of economy is to give the discipline of it through knowledge which will immediately bear on practical life. Our literary work has long been economically useless to us because too much concerned with dead languages; and our scientific work will yet, for some time, be a good deal lost, because scientific men are too fond or too vain of their systems, and waste the student's time in endeavouring to give him large views, and make him perceive interesting connections of facts; when there is not one student, no, nor one man, in a thousand, who can feel the beauty of a system, or even take it clearly into his head; but nearly all men can understand, and most will be interested in, the facts which bear on daily life. Botanists have discovered some wonderful connection between nettles and figs, which a cowboy who will never see a ripe fig in his life need not be at all troubled about; but it will be interesting to him to know what effect nettles have on hay, and what taste they will give to porridge; and it will give him nearly a new life if he can be got but once, in a spring-time, to look well at the beautiful circlet of the white nettle blossom, and work out with his schoolmaster the curves of its petals, and the way it is set on its central mast. So, the principle of chemical equivalents, beautiful as it is, matters far less to a peasant boy, and even to most sons of gentlemen, than their knowing how to find whether the water is wholesome in the back-kitchen cistern, or whether the seven-acre field wants sand or chalk.

———o———

BASE CRITICISM.

It may perhaps be said that I attach too much importance to the evil of base criticism; but those who think so have never rightly understood its scope, nor the reach of that stern saying of Johnson's (Idler, No. 3, April 29, 1758): "Little does he (who assumes the character of a critic) think how many harmless men he involves in his own guilt, by teaching them to be noxious without malignity, and to repeat objections which they do not understand." And truly, not in this kind only, but in all things whatsoever, there is not, to my mind, a more woful or wonderful matter of thought than the power of a fool. In the world's affairs there is no design so great or good but it will take twenty wise men to help it forward a few inches, and a single fool can stop it; there is no evil so great or so terrible but that, after a multitude of counsellors have taken means to avert it, a single fool will bring it down. Pestilence, famine, and the sword, are given into the fool's hand as the arrows into the hand of the giant: and if he were fairly set forth in the right motley, the web of it should be sackcloth and sable; the bells on his cap, passing bells; his badge, a bear robbed of her whelps; and his bauble, a sexton's spade.

PUBLIC FAVOUR.

There is great difficulty in making any short or general statement of the difference between great and ignoble minds in their behaviour to the "public." It is by no means *uni versally* the case that a mean mind, as stated in the text, will bend itself to what you ask of it; on the contrary, there is one kind of mind, the meanest of all, which perpetually complains of the public, contemplates and proclaims itself as a "genius," refuses all wholesome discipline or humble office, and ends in miserable and revengeful ruin; also, the greatest minds are marked by nothing more distinctly than an inconceivable humility, and acceptance of work or instruction in any form, and from any quarter. They will learn from everybody, and do anything that anybody asks of them, so long as it involves only toil, or what other men would think degradation. But the point of quarrel, nevertheless, assuredly rises some day between the public and them, respecting some matter, not of humiliation, but of Fact. Your great man always at last comes to see something the public don't see. This something he will assuredly persist in asserting, whether with tongue or pencil, to be as *he* sees it, not as *they* see it; and all the world in a heap on the other side, will not get him to say otherwise. Then, if the world objects to the saying, he may happen to get stoned or burnt for it, but that does not in the least matter to him: if the world has no particular objection to the saying, he may get leave to mutter it to himself till he dies, and be merely taken for an idiot; that also does not matter to him—mutter it he will, according to what he perceives to be fact, and not at all according to the roar ing of the walls of Red sea on the right hand or left of him Hence the quarrel, sure at some time or other, to be started between the public and him; while your mean man, though he will spit and scratch spiritedly at the public, while it does not attend to him, will bow to it for its clap in any direction, and say anything when he has got its ear, which he thinks will bring him another clap; and thus, as stated in the text, he and it go on smoothly together.

There are, however, times when the obstinacy of the mean man looks very like the obstinacy of the great one; but if you look closely into the matter, you will always see that the obstinacy of the first is in the pronunciation of "I;" and of the second, in the pronunciation of "It."

———o———

POLITICAL ECONOMY.

A nation's labour, well applied, should be amply sufficient to provide its whole population with good food and comfortable habitation; and not with those only, but with good education besides, and objects of luxury, art treasures, such as these you have around you now. But by those same laws of Nature and Providence, if the labour of the nation or of the individual be misapplied, and much more if it be insufficient,—if the nation or man be indolent and unwise,—suffering and want result, exactly in proportion to the indolence and improvidence,—to the refusal of labour, or to the misapplication of it. Wherever you see want, or misery, or degradation, in this world about you, there, be sure, either industry has been wanting, or industry has been in error. It is not accident, it is not Heaven-commanded calamity, it is not the original and inevitable evil of man's nature, which fill your streets with lamentation, and your graves with prey. It is only that, when there should have been providence, there has been waste; when there should have been labour, there has been lasciviousness; and wilfulness, when there should have been subordination.*

———o———

"THE CHURCH" IN THE NEW TESTAMENT.

The word occurs in the New Testament, one hundred and fourteen times. In every one of those occurrences, it bears one and the same grand sense: that of a congregation or assembly of men. But it bears this sense under four different modifications, giving four separate meanings to the word. These are—

I. The entire Multitude of the Elect; otherwise called the Body of Christ; and sometimes the Bride, the Lamb's Wife; including the Faithful in all ages; Adam, and the children of Adam, yet unborn.

In this sense it is used in Ephesians v. 25, 27, 32; Colossians i. 18, and several other passages.

II. The entire multitude of professing believers in Christ, existing on earth at a given moment; including false brethren, wolves in sheep's clothing, goats, and tares, as well as sheep and wheat, and other forms of bad fish with good in the net.

In this sense it is used in 1 Cor. x. 32; xv. 9; Galatians i. 13; 1 Tim. iii. 5, &c.

III. The multitude of professed believers, living in a certain city, place, or house. This is the most frequent sense in which the word occurs, as in Acts vii. 38; xiii. 1; 1 Cor. i. 2; xvi. 19, &c.

IV. Any assembly of men: as in Acts xix. 32, 41.

* Proverbs xiii. 23, "Much food is in the tillage of the poor, but there is that is destroyed for want of judgment."

That in a hundred and twelve out of the hundred and fourteen texts, the word bears some one of these four meanings, is indisputable. But there are two texts in which, if the word had alone occurred, its meaning might have been doubtful. These are Matt. xvi. 18, and xviii. 17.

———o———

SPECULATIONS.

There are some speculations that are fair and honest—speculations made with our own money, and which do not involve in their success the loss, by others, of what we gain. But generally modern speculation involves much risk to others, with chance of profit only to ourselves: even in its best conditions it is merely one of the forms of gambling or treasure-hunting; it is either leaving the steady plough and the steady pilgrimage of life, to look for silver mines beside the way; or else it is the full stop beside the dice-tables in Vanity Fair—investing all the thoughts and passions of the soul in the fall of the cards, and choosing rather the wild accidents of idle fortune than the calm and accumulative rewards of toil. And this is destructive enough, at least to our peace and virtue. But it is usually destructive of far more than *our* peace, or *our* virtue. Have you ever deliberately set yourselves to imagine and measure the suffering, the guilt, and the mortality caused necessarily by the failure of any large-dealing merchant, or largely-branched bank? Take it at the lowest possible supposition—count, at the fewest you choose, the families whose means of support have been involved in the catastrophe. Then, on the morning after the intelligence of ruin, let us go forth amongst them in earnest thought; let us use that imagination which we waste so often on fictitious sorrow, to measure the stern facts of that multitudinous distress; strike open the private doors of their chambers, and enter silently into the midst of the domestic misery; look upon the old men who had reserved for their failing strength some remainder of rest in the evening-tide of life, cast helplessly back into trouble and tumult; look upon the active strength of middle age suddenly blasted into incapacity—its hopes crushed and its hardly-earned rewards snatched away in the same instant—at once the heart withered and the right arm snapped; look upon the piteous children, delicately nurtured, whose soft eyes, now large with wonder at their parents' grief, must soon be set in the dimness of famine; and far more than all this, look forward to the length of sorrow beyond—to the hardest labour of life now to be undergone, either in all the severity of unexpected and inexperienced trial, or else, more bitter still, to be begun again, and endured for the second time, amidst the ruins of cherished hopes and the feebleness of advancing years, embittered by the continual sting and taunt of the inner feeling that it has all been brought about, not by the fair course of appointed circumstance, but by miserable chance and wanton treachery; and, last of all, look beyond this—to the shattered destinies of those who have faltered under the trial, and sunk past recovery to despair. And then consider whether the hand which has poured this poison into all the springs of life be one whit less guiltily red with human blood than that which literally pours the hemlock into the cup, or guides the dagger to the heart? We read with horror of the crimes of a Borgia or a Tophana; but there never lived Borgias such as live now in the midst of us. The cruel lady of Ferrara slew only in the strength of passion—she slew only a few, those who thwarted her purposes or who vexed her soul; she slew sharply and suddenly, embittering the fate of her victims with no foretastes of destruction, no prolongations of pain; and, finally and chiefly, she slew, not without remorse, nor without pity. But *we*, in no storm of passion—in no blindness of wrath,—we, in calm and clear and untempted selfishness, pour our poison—not for a few only but for multitudes;—not for those who have wronged us, or resisted,—but for those who have trusted us and aided;—we, not with sudden gift of merciful and unconscious death, but with slow waste of hunger and weary rack of disappointment and despair;—we, last and chiefly, do our murdering, not with any pauses of pity or scorching of conscience, but in facile and forgetful calm of mind,—and so, forsooth, read day by day, complacently, as if they meant any one else than ourselves, the words that forever describe the wicked: "The *poison of asps* is under their lips, and their feet are swift to shed blood."

---o---

BE WHAT NATURE INTENDED.

Pure history and pure topography are most precious things; in many cases more useful to the human race than high imaginative work; and assuredly it is intended that a large majority of all who are employed in art should never aim at anything higher. It is *only* vanity, never love, nor any other noble feeling, which prompts men to desert their allegiance to the simple truth, in vain pursuit of the imaginative truth which has been appointed to be for evermore sealed to them.

Nor let it be supposed that artists who possess minor degrees of imaginative gift need be embarrassed by the doubtful sense of their own powers. In general, when the imagination is at all noble, it is irresistible, and therefore those who can at all resist it *ought* to resist it. Be a plain topographer if you possibly can; if Nature meant you to be anything else, she will force you to it; but never try to be a prophet; go on quietly with your hard camp-work, and the spirit will come to you in the camp, as it did to Eldad and Medad, if you are appointed to have it; but try above all things to be quickly perceptive of the noble spirit in others, and to discern in an instant between its true utterance and the diseased mimicries of it. In a general way, remember it is a far better thing to find out other great men, than to become one yourself: for you can but become *one* at best, but you may bring others to light in numbers.

SAILORS' SUPERSTITIONS.

It is one notable effect of a life passed on shipboard to destroy weak beliefs in appointed forms of religion. A sailor may be grossly superstitious, but his superstitions will be connected with amulets and omens, not cast in systems. He must accustom himself, if he prays at all, to pray anywhere and anyhow. Candlesticks and incense not being portable into the maintop, he perceives those decorations to be, on the whole, inessential to a maintop mass. Sails must be set and cables bent, be it never so strict a saint's day, and it is found that no harm comes of it. Absolution on a lee-shore must be had of the breakers, it appears, if at all, and they give it plenary and brief, without listening to confession.

———o———

SANCTITY OF COLOUR.

I do not think that there is anything more necessary to the progress of European art in the present day than the complete understanding of this sanctity of Colour. I had much pleasure in finding it, the other day, fully understood and thus sweetly expressed in a little volume of poems by a Miss Maynard:

"For still in every land, though to Thy name
Arose no temple,—still in every age,
Though heedless man had quite forgot Thy praise,
We praise Thee; and at rise and set of sun
Did we assemble duly, and intone
A choral hymn that all the lands might hear.
In heaven, on earth, and in the deep we praised Thee,
Singly, or mingled in sweet sisterhood.
But now, acknowledged ministrants, we come,
Co-worshippers with man in this Thy house,
We, the Seven Daughters of the Light, to praise
Thee, Light of Light! Thee, God of very God!"

A Dream of Fair Colours.

These poems seem to be otherwise remarkable for a very unobtrusive and pure religious feeling in subjects connected with art.

———o———

HUMAN ASSOCIATIONS.

Put the fine dresses and jewelled girdles into the best group you can; paint them with all Veronese's skill: will they satisfy you?

Not so. As long as they are in their due services and

subjection—while their folds are formed by the motion of men, and their lustre adorns the nobleness of men—so long the lustre and the folds are lovely. But cast them from the human limbs;—golden circlet and silken tissue are withered; the dead leaves of autumn are more precious than they.

This is just as true, but in a far deeper sense, of the weaving of the natural robe of man's soul. Fragrant tissue of flowers, golden circlets of clouds, are only fair when they meet the fondness of human thoughts, and glorify human visions of heaven.

———o———

"THY KINGDOM COME."

So far as in it lay, this century has caused every one of its great men, whose hearts were kindest, and whose spirits most perceptive of the work of God, to die without hope:—Scott, Keats, Byron, Shelley, Turner. Great England, of the Iron-heart now, not of the Lion-heart; for these souls of her children an account may perhaps be one day required of her.

She has not yet read often enough that old story of the Samaritan's mercy. He whom he saved was going down from Jerusalem to Jericho—to the accursed city (so the old Church used to understand it). He should not have left Jerusalem; it was his own fault that he went out into the desert, and fell among the thieves, and was left for dead. Every one of these English children, in their day, took the desert bypath as he did, and fell among fiends—took to making bread out of stones at their bidding, and then died, torn and famished; careful England, in her pure, priestly dress, passing by on the other side. So far as we are concerned, that is the account *we* have to give of them.*

So far as *they* are concerned, I do not fear for them;—there being one Priest who never passes by. The longer I live, the more clearly I see how all souls are in His hand—the mean and the great. Fallen on the earth in their baseness, or fading as the mist of morning in their goodness; still in the hand of the potter as the clay, and in the temple of their master as the cloud. It was not the mere bodily death that He conquered—that death had no sting. It was this spiritual death which He conquered, so that at last it should be swallowed up—mark the word—not in life; but in victory. As the dead body shall be raised to life, so also the defeated soul to victory, if only it has been fighting on its Master's side, has made no covenant with death; nor itself bowed its forehead for his seal. Blind from the prison-house, maimed from the battle, or mad from the tombs, their souls shall surely yet sit, astonished, at His feet who giveth peace.

Who *giveth* peace? Many a peace we have made and named for ourselves, but the falsest is in that marvellous thought that we, of all generations of the earth, only know the right; and that to us, at last,—and us alone,—all the schemes of God, about the salvation of men, has been shown. "This is the light in which *we* are walking. Those vain Greeks are gone down to their Persephone for ever—Egypt and Assyria, Elam and her multitude,—uncircumcised, their graves are round about them—Pathros and careless Ethiopia—filled with the slain. Rome, with her thirsty sword, and poison wine, how did she walk in her darkness! We only

* It is strange that the last words Turner ever attached to a picture should have been these:—

"The priest held the poisoned cup."

Compare the words of 1798 with those of 1850.

have no idolatries—ours are the seeing eyes; in our pure hands at last, the seven-sealed book is laid; to our true tongues entrusted the preaching of a perfect gospel. Who shall come after us? Is it not peace? The poor Jew, Zimri, who slew his master, there is no peace for him: but, for us? tiara on head, may we not look out of the windows of heaven?"

Another kind of peace I look for than this, though I hear it said of me that I am hopeless.

I am not hopeless, though my hope may be as Veronese's: the dark-veiled.

Veiled, not because sorrowful, but because blind. I do not know what my England desires, or how long she will choose to do as she is doing now;—with her right hand casting away the souls of men, and with her left the gifts of God.

In the prayers which she dictates to her children, she tells them to fight against the world, the flesh, and the devil. Some day, perhaps, it may also occur to her as desirable to tell those children what she means by this. What is the world which they are to "fight with," and how does it differ from the world which they are to "get on in?" The explanation seems to me the more needful, because I do not, in the book we profess to live by, find anything very distinct about fighting with the world. I find something about fighting with the rulers of its darkness, and something also about overcoming it; but it does not follow that this conquest is to be by hostility, since evil may be overcome with good. But I find it written very distinctly that God loved the world, and that Christ is the light of it.

What the much used words, therefore, mean, I cannot tell. But this, I believe, they *should* mean. That there is, indeed, one world which is full of care, and desire, and hatred: a world of war, of which Christ is not the light, which indeed is without light, and has never heard the great "Let there be." Which is, therefore, in truth, as yet no world; but chaos, on the face of which, moving, the Spirit of God yet causes men to hope that a world will come. The better one, they call it: perhaps they might, more wisely, call it the real one. Also, I hear them speak continually of going to it, rather than of its coming to them; which, again, is strange, for in that prayer which they had straight from the lips of the Light of the world, and which He apparently thought sufficient prayer for them, there is not anything about going to another world; only something of another government coming into this; or rather, not another, but the only government,—that government which will constitute it a world indeed. New heavens and new earth. Earth, no more without form and void, but sown with fruit of righteousness. Firmament, no more of passing cloud, but of cloud risen out of the crystal sea—cloud in which, as He was once received up, so He shall again come with power, and every eye shall see Him, and all kindreds of the earth shall wail because of Him.

Kindreds of the earth, or tribes of it! *—the "earth begotten," the Chaos children—children of this present world, with its desolate seas and its Medusa clouds: the Dragon children, merciless: they who dealt as clouds without water: serpent clouds, by whose sight men were turned into stone; —the time must surely come for their wailing.

"Thy kingdom come," we are bid to ask then! But how shall it come? With power and great glory, it is written; and yet not with observation, it is also written. Strange kingdom! Yet its strangeness is renewed to us with every dawn.

* Compare Matt. xxiv. 30.

When the time comes for us to wake out of the world's sleep, why should it be otherwise than out of the dreams of the night? Singing of birds, first, broken and low, as, not to dying eyes, but eyes that wake to life, "the casement slowly grows a glimmering square;" and then the gray, and then the rose of dawn; and last the light, whose going forth is to the ends of heaven.

This kingdom it is not in our power to bring; but it is, to receive. Nay, it has come already, in part; but not received, because men love chaos best; and the Night, with her daughters. That is still the only question for us, as in the old Elias days, "If ye will receive it." With pains it may be shut out still from many a dark place of cruelty; by sloth it may be still unseen for many a glorious hour. But the pain of shutting it out must grow greater and greater:—harder, every day, that struggle of man with man in the abyss, and shorter wages for the fiend's work. But it is still at our choice; the simoom-dragon may still be served if we will, in the fiery desert, or else God walking in the garden, at cool of day. Coolness now, not of Hesperus over Atlas, stooped endurer of toil; but of Heosphorus over Sion, the joy of the earth.* The choice is no vague or doubtful one. High on the desert mountain, full descried, sits throned the tempter, with his old promise—the kingdoms of this world, and the glory of them. He still calls you to your labour, as Christ to your rest;—labour and sorrow, base desire, and cruel hope. So far as you desire to possess, rather than to give; so far as you look for power to command, instead of to bless; so far as your own prosperity seems to you to issue out of contest or rivalry, of any kind, with other men, or other nations; so long as the

* Ps. xlviii. 2.—This joy it is to receive and to give, because its officers (governors of its acts) are to be Peace, and its exactors (governors of its dealings), Righteousness —Is. lx. 17.

hope before you is for supremacy instead of love; and your desire is to be greatest, instead of least;—first, instead of last;—so long you are serving the Lord of all that is last, and least;—the last enemy that shall be destroyed—Death; and you shall have death's crown, with the worm coiled in it; and death's wages, with the worm feeding on them; kindred of the earth shall you yourself become; saying to the grave, "Thou art my father;" and to the worm, "Thou art my mother, and my sister."

I leave you to judge, and to choose, between this labour, and the bequeathed peace; this wages, and the gift of the Morning Star; this obedience, and the doing of the will which shall enable you to claim another kindred than of the earth, and to hear another voice than that of the grave, saying, "My brother, and sister, and mother."

———o———

VULGARITY.

There is, indeed, perhaps, no greater sign of innate and *real* vulgarity of mind or defective education than the want of power to understand the universality of the ideal truth; the absence of sympathy with the colossal grasp of those intellects, which have in them so much of divine, that nothing is small to them, and nothing large; but with equal and unoffended vision they take in the sum of the world,—Straw Street and the seventh heavens,—in the same instant. A certain portion of this divine spirit is visible even in the lower examples of all the true men; it is, indeed, perhaps, the clearest test of their belonging to the true and great group, that they are continually touching what to the multitude appear vulgarities. The higher a man stands, the more the word "vulgar" becomes unintelligible to him.

We may dismiss this matter of vulgarity in plain and few words, at least as far as regards art. There is never vulgarity in a *whole* truth, however commonplace. It may be unimportant or painful. It cannot be vulgar. Vulgarity is only in concealment of truth, or in affectation.

———o———

SCIENCE.

The common consent of men proves and accepts the proposition, that whatever part of any pursuit ministers to the bodily comforts, and admits of material uses, is ignoble, and whatsoever part is addressed to the mind only, is noble; and that geology does better in reclothing dry bones and revealing lost creations, than in tracing veins of lead and beds of iron; astronomy better in opening to us the houses of heaven than in teaching navigation; botany better in displaying structure than in expressing juices; surgery better in investigating organization than in setting limbs; only it is ordained that, for our encouragement, every step we make in the more exalted range of science adds something also to its practical applicabilities; that all the great phenomena of nature, the knowledge of which is desired by the angels only, by us partly, as it reveals to farther vision the being and the glory of Him in whom they rejoice and we live, dispense yet such kind influences and so much of material blessing as to be joyfully felt by all inferior creatures, and to be desired by them with such single desire as the imperfection of their nature may admit; that the strong torrents which in their own gladness fill the hills with hollow thunder and the vales with winding light, have yet their bounden charge of field to feed and barge to bear; that the fierce flames to which the Alp owes its upheaval and the volcano its terror, temper for us the metal vein and quickening spring; and that for our incitement, I say not our reward, for knowledge is its own reward, herbs have their healing, stones their preciousness, and stars their times.

———o———

INFINITY.

That which we foolishly call vastness is, rightly considered, not more wonderful, not more impressive, than that which we insolently call littleness, and the infinity of God is not mysterious, it is only unfathomable, not concealed, but incomprehensible: it is a clear infinity, the darkness of the pure unsearchable sea.

———o———

NEARNESS AND DISTANCE.

Are not all natural things, it may be asked, as lovely near as far away? Nay, not so. Look at the clouds, and watch the delicate sculpture of their alabaster sides, and the rounded lustre of their magnificent rolling. They are meant to be beheld far away; they were shaped for their place, high above your head; approach them, and they fuse into vague mists, or whirl away in fierce fragments of thunderous vapour. Look at the crest of the Alp, from the far-away plains over which its light is cast, whence human souls have communion with it by their myriads. The child looks up to it in the dawn, and the husbandman in the burden and heat of the day, and the old man in the going down of the sun, and it is to them all as the celestial city on the world's horizon; dyed with the depth of heaven, and clothed with the calm of eternity. There was it set, for holy dominion, by Him who marked for the sun his journey, and bade the moon know her going down. It was built for its place in the far-off sky; approach it, and as the sound of the voice of man dies away about its foundations, and the tide of human life, shallowed upon the vast aërial shore, is at last met by the Eternal "Here shall thy waves be stayed," the glory of its aspect fades into blanched fearfulness; its purple walls are rent into grisly rocks, its silver fretwork saddened into wasting snow; the storm-brands of ages are on its breast, the ashes of its own ruin lie solemnly on its white raiment.

———o———

NOVELTY.

"Custom hangs upon us, with a weight
Heavy as frost, and deep almost as life."

And if we grow impatient under it, and seek to recover the mental energy by more quickly repeated and brighter novelty, it is all over with our enjoyment. There is no cure for this evil, any more than for the weariness of the imagination already described, but in patience and rest: if we try to obtain perpetual change, change itself will become monotonous: and then we are reduced to that old despair, "If water chokes, what will you drink after it?" And the two points of practical wisdom in this matter are, first, to be content with as little novelty as possible at a time; and, secondly, tc preserve, as much as possible in the world, the sources of novelty.

---o---

EXCITEMENT OF THE IMAGINATION.

Remember that when the imagination and feelings are strongly excited, they will not only bear with strange things, but they will *look* into *minute* things with a delight quite unknown in hours of tranquillity. You surely must remember moments of your lives in which, under some strong excitement of feeling, all the details of visible objects presented themselves with a strange intensity and insistance, whether you would or no; urging themselves upon the mind, and thrust upon the eye, with a force of fascination which you could not refuse. Now, to a certain extent, the senses get into this state whenever the imagination is strongly excited. Things trivial at other times assume a dignity or significance which we cannot explain; but which is only the more attractive because inexplicable: and the powers of attention, quickened by the feverish excitement, fasten and feed upon the minutest circumstances of detail, and remotest traces of intention.

---o---

PEACE AND WAR.

Both peace and war are noble or ignoble according to their kind and occasion. No man has a profounder sense of the horror and guilt of ignoble war than I have. I have personally seen its effects, upon nations, of unmitigated evil, on soul and body, with perhaps as much pity, and as much bitterness of indignation, as any of those whom you will hear continually declaiming in the cause of peace. But peace may be sought in two ways. One way is as Gideon sought it, wher he built his altar in Ophrah, naming it, "God send peace," yet sought this peace that he loved, as he was ordered to seek it, and the peace was sent, in God's way:—"the country was in quietness forty years in the days of Gideon." And the other way of seeking peace is as Menahem sought it when he gave the King of Assyria a thousand talents of silver, that "his hand might be with him." That is, you may either win your peace, or buy it:—win it, by resistance to evil;—buy it, by compromise with evil. You may buy your peace, with silenced consciences;—you may buy it, with broken vows,—buy it, with lying words,—buy it, with base connivances,—buy it, with the blood of the slain, and the cry of the captive, and the silence of lost souls—over hemispheres of the earth, while you sit smiling at your serene hearths, lisping comfortable prayers evening and morning, and counting your pretty Protestant beads (which are flat, and of gold, instead of round, and of ebony, as the monks' once were), and so mutter continually to yourselves, "Peace, peace," when there is No peace; but only captivity and death, for you, as well as for those you leave unsaved;—and yours darker than theirs.

I cannot utter to you what I would in this matter; we all see too dimly, as yet, what our great world-duties are, to allow any of us to try to outline their enlarging shadows. But think over what I *have* said, and in your quiet homes reflect that their peace was not won for you by your own hands; but by theirs who long ago jeoparded their lives for you, their children; and remember that neither this inherited peace, nor any other, can be kept, but through the same jeopardy. No peace was ever won from Fate by subterfuge or agreement; no peace is ever in store for any of us, but that which we shall win by victory over shame or sin;—victory over the sin that oppresses, as well as over that which corrupts. For many a year to come, the sword of every righteous nation must be whetted to save or to subdue; nor will it be by patience of others' suffering, but by the offering of your own, that you will ever draw nearer to the time when the great change shall pass upon the iron of the earth;—when men shall beat their swords into ploughshares, and their spears into pruning-hooks; neither shall they learn war any more.

———o———

THE PLEASURES OF SIGHT.

Had it been ordained by the Almighty that the highest pleasures of sight should be those of most difficult attainment, and that to arrive at them it should be necessary to accumulate gilded palaces tower over tower, and pile artificial mountains around insinuated lakes, there would have been a direct contradiction between the unselfish duties and inherent desires of every individual. But no such contradiction exists in the system of Divine Providence, which, leaving it open to us, if we will, as creatures in probation, to abuse this sense like every other, and pamper it with selfish and thoughtless vanities as we pamper the palate with deadly meats, until the appetite of tasteful cruelty is lost in its sickened satiety, incapable of pleasure unless, Caligula-like, it concentrate the labour of a million of lives into the sensation of an hour, leaves it also open to us, by humble and loving ways, to make ourselves susceptible of deep delight from the meanest objects of creation, and of a delight which shall not separate us from our fellows, nor require the sacrifice of any duty or occupation, but which shall bind us closer to men and to God, and be with us always, harmonized with every action, consistent with every claim, unchanging and eternal.

———o———

PRIDE.

Pride is base from the necessary foolishness of it, because at its best, that is when grounded on a just estimation of our own elevation or superiority above certain others, it cannot but imply that our eyes look downward only, and have never been raised above our own measure, for there is not the man so lofty in his standing nor capacity but he must be humble in thinking of the cloud habitation and far sight of the angelic intelligences above him, and in perceiving what infinity there is of things he cannot know nor even reach unto, as it stands compared with that little body of things he can reach, and of which nevertheless he can altogether understand not one: not to speak of that wicked and fond attributing of such excellency as he may have to himself, and thinking of it as his own getting, which is the real essence and criminality of pride, nor of those viler forms of it, founded on false estimation of things beneath us and irrational contemning of them: but taken at its best, it is still base to that degree that there is no grandeur of feature which it cannot destroy and make despicable.

———o———

TRUE LIBERTY

Wise laws and just restraints are to a noble nation not chains, but chain mail—strength and defence, though something also of an incumbrance. And this necessity of restraint, remember, is just as honourable to man as the necessity of labour. You hear every day greater numbers of foolish people speaking about liberty, as if it were such an honourable thing: so far from being that, it is, on the whole, and in the broadest sense, dishonourable, and an attribute of the lower creatures. No human being, however great or powerful, was ever so free as a fish. There is always something that he must, or must not do; while the fish may do whatever he likes. All the kingdoms of the world put together are not half so large as the sea, and all the railroads and wheels that ever were, or will be, invented are not so easy as fins. You will find, on fairly thinking of it, that it is his Restraint which is honourable to man, not his Liberty; and, what is more, it is restraint which is honourable even in the lower animals. A butterfly is much more free than a bee; but you honour the bee more, just because it is subject to certain laws which fit it for orderly function in bee society. And throughout the world, of the two abstract things, liberty and restraint, restraint is always the more honourable. It is true, indeed, that in these and all other matters you never can reason finally from the abstraction, for both liberty and restraint are good when they are nobly chosen, and both are bad when they are basely chosen; but of the two, I repeat, it is restraint which characterizes the higher creature, and betters the lower creature: and, from the ministering of the archangel to the labour of the insect,—from the poising of the planets to the gravitation of a grain of dust,—the power and glory of all creatures, and all matter, consist in their obedience, not in their freedom. The Sun has no liberty--a dead leaf has much. The dust of which you are formed has no liberty. Its liberty will come—with its corruption.

———o———

WEAK THINGS MADE STRONG.

Is not this a strange type, in the very heart and height of these mysterious Alps—these wrinkled hills in their snowy, cold, grey-haired old age, at first so silent, then, as we keep quiet at their feet, muttering and whispering to us garrulously, in broken and dreaming fits, as it were, about their childhood—is it not a strange type of the things which "out of weakness are made strong!" If one of those little flakes of mica-sand, hurried in tremulous spangling along the bottom of the ancient river, too light to sink, too faint to float, almost too small for sight, could have had a mind given to it as it was at last borne down with its kindred dust into the abysses of the stream, and laid (would it not have thought?) for a hopeless eternity in the dark ooze, the most despised, forgotten, and feeble of all earth's atoms; incapable of any use or change; not fit, down there in the diluvial darkness, so much as to help an earth-wasp to build its nest, or feed the first fibre of a lichen;—what would it have thought, had it been told that one day, knitted into a strength as of imperishable iron, rustless by the air, infusible by the flame, out of the substance of it, with its fellows, the axe of God should hew that Alpine tower; that against *it*—poor, helpless, mica flake!—the wild north winds should rage in vain; beneath *it*—low-fallen mica flake!—the snowy hills should lie bowed like flocks of sheep, and the kingdoms of the earth fade away in unregarded blue; and around it—weak, wave-drifted mica flake!—the great war of the firmament should burst in thun der, and yet stir it not; and the fiery arrows and angry meteors of the night fall blunted back from it into the air; and all the stars in the clear heaven should light, one by one as they rose, new cressets upon the points of snow that fringed its abiding-place on the imperishable spire!

———o———

THE TRUTH OF TRUTHS.

Truth is to be discovered, and Pardon to be won for every man by himself. This is evident from innumerable texts of Scripture, but chiefly from those which exhort every man to seek after Truth, and which connect knowing with doing. We are to seek after knowledge as silver, and search for her as for hid treasures; therefore, from every man she must be naturally hid, and the discovery of her is to be the reward only of personal search. The kingdom of God is as treasure hid in a field; and of those who profess to help us to seek for it, we are not to put confidence in those who say,—Here is the treasure, we have found it, and have it, and will give you some of it; but to those who say,—We think that is a good place to dig, and you will dig most easily in such and such a way.

Farther, it has been promised that if such earnest search be made, Truth shall be discovered: as much truth, that is, as is necessary for the person seeking. These, therefore, I hold, for two fundamental principles of religion,—that, without seeking, truth cannot be known at all; and that, by seeking, it may be discovered by the simplest. I say, without seeking it cannot be known at all. It can neither be declared from pulpits, nor set down in Articles, nor in any wise "prepared and sold" in packages, ready for use. Truth must be ground for every man by himself out of its husk, with such help as he can get, indeed, but not without stern labour of his own. In what science is knowledge to be had cheap? or truth to be told over a velvet cushion, in half an hour's talk every seventh day? Can you learn chemistry so?—zoology? —anatomy? and do you expect to penetrate the secret of all secrets, and to know that whose price is above rubies; and of which the depth saith,—It is not in me, in so easy fashion? There are doubts in this matter which evil spirits darken with their wings, and that is true of all such doubts which we were told long ago—they can "be ended by action alone."

As surely as we live, this truth of truths can only so be discerned: to those who act on what they know, more shall be revealed; and thus, if any man will do His will, he shall know the doctrine whether it be of God. Any man:—not the man who has most means of knowing, who has the subtlest brains, or sits under the most orthodox preacher, or has his library fullest of most orthodox books—but the man who strives to know, who takes God at His word, and sets himself to dig up the heavenly mystery, roots and all, before sunset, and the night come, when no man can work. Beside such a man, God stands in more and more visible presence as he toils, and teaches him that which no preacher can teach—no earthly authority gainsay. By such a man, the preacher must himself be judged.

———o———

GOD'S PLACE IN THE HUMAN HEART.

Anything which makes religion its second object, makes religion *no* object. God will put up with a great many things in the human heart, but there is one thing He will not put up with in it—a second place. He who offers God a second place, offers Him *no* place

———o———

MEMBERS OF THE CHURCH.

Men not in office in the Church suppose themselves, on that ground, in a sort unholy; and that, therefore, they may sin with more excuse, and be idle or impious with less danger, than the Clergy: especially they consider themselves relieved from all ministerial function, and as permitted to devote their whole time and energy to the business of this world. No mistake can possibly be greater. Every member of the Church is equally bound to the service of the Head of the Church; and that service is preëminently the saving of souls. There is not a moment of a man's active life in which he may not be indirectly preaching; and throughout a great part of his life he ought to be *directly* preaching, and teaching both strangers and friends; his children, his servants, and all who in any way are put under him, being given to him as especial objects of his ministration.

———o———

DISCERNMENT OF CHRISTIAN CHARACTER.

If we hear a man profess himself a believer in God and in Christ, and detect him in no glaring and wilful violation of God's law, we speak of him as a Christian; and, on the other hand, if we hear him or see him denying Christ, either in his words or conduct, we tacitly assume him not to be a Christian. A mawkish charity prevents us from outspeaking in this matter, and from earnestly endeavouring to discern who are Christians and who are not; and this I hold to be one of the chief sins of the Church in the present day; for thus wicked men are put to no shame; and better men are encouraged in their failings, or caused to hesitate in their virtues, by the example of those whom, in false charity, they choose to call Christians.

———o———

PATRONAGE OF ART.

As you examine into the career of historical painting, you will be more and more struck with the fact I have stated to you,—that none was ever truly great but that which represented the living forms and daily deeds of the people among whom it arose;—that all precious historical work records, not the past but the present. Remember, therefore, that it is not so much in *buying* pictures, as in *being* pictures, that you can encourage a noble school. The best patronage of art is not that which seeks for the pleasures of sentiment in a vague ideality, nor for beauty of form in a marble image; but that which educates your children into living heroes, and binds down the flights and the fondnesses of the heart into practical duty and faithful devotion.

———o———

COMPANIONSHIP WITH NATURE.

To the mediæval knight, from Scottish moor to Syrian sand, the world was one great exercise ground, or field of adventure; the staunch pacing of his charger penetrated the pathlessness of outmost forest, and sustained the sultriness of the most secret desert. Frequently alone,—or, if accompanied, for the most part only by retainers of lower rank, incapable of entering into complete sympathy with any of his thoughts,—he must have been compelled often to enter into dim companionship with the silent nature around him, and must assuredly sometimes have talked to the wayside flowers of his love, and to the fading clouds of his ambition.

———o———

ALL CARVING AND NO MEAT.

The divisions of a church are much like the divisions of a sermon; they are always right so long as they are necessary to edification, and always wrong when they are thrust upon the attention as divisions only. There may be neatness in carving when there is richness in feasting; but I have heard many a discourse, and seen many a church wall, in which it was all carving and no meat.

———o———

THE TRUE CHURCH.

The Church which is composed of Faithful men, is the one true, indivisible and indiscernible Church, built on the foundation of Apostles and Prophets, Jesus Christ himself being the chief corner-stone. It includes all who have ever fallen asleep in Christ, and all yet unborn, who are to be saved in Him; its Body is as yet imperfect; it will not be perfected till the last saved human spirit is gathered to its God.

A man becomes a member of this Church only by believing in Christ with all his heart; nor is he positively recognizable for a member of it, when he has become so, by any one but God, not even by himself. Nevertheless, there are certain signs by which Christ's sheep may be guessed at. Not by their being in any definite Fold—for many are lost sheep at times: but by their sheep-like behaviour; and a great many are indeed sheep which, on the far mountain side, in their peacefulness, we take for stones. To themselves, the best proof of their being Christ's sheep is to find themselves on Christ's shoulders; and, between them, there are certain sympathies (expressed in the Apostles' Creed by the term "communion of Saints"), by which they may in a sort recognise each other, and so become verily visible to each other for mutual comfort.

———o———

FLOWERS.

Flowers seem intended for the solace of ordinary humanity; children love them; quiet, tender, contented ordinary people love them as they grow; luxurious and disorderly people rejoice in them gathered: They are the cottager's treasure; and in the crowded town, mark, as with a little broken fragment of rainbow, the windows of the workers in whose heart rests the covenant of peace. Passionate or religious minds contemplate them with fond, feverish intensity; the affection is seen severely calm in the works of many old religious painters, and mixed with more open and true country sentiment in those of our own pre-Raphaelites. To the child and the girl, the peasant and the manufacturing operative, to the grisette and the nun, the lover and monk, they are precious always. But to the men of supreme power and thoughtfulness, precious only at times; symbolically and pathetically often to the poets, but rarely for their own sake. They fall forgotten from the great workmen's and soldiers' hands. Such men will take, in thankfulness, crowns of leaves, or crowns of thorns—not crowns of flowers.

———o———

THE CLOUD-BALANCINGS.

When the earth had to be prepared for the habitation of man, a veil, as it were, of intermediate being was spread between him and its darkness, in which were joined, in a subdued measure, the stability and insensibility of the earth, and the passion and perishing of mankind.

But the heavens, also, had to be prepared for his habitation.

Between their burning light,—their deep vacuity, and man, as between the earth's gloom of iron substance, and man, a veil had to be spread of intermediate being; which should appease the unendurable glory to the level of human feebleness, and sign the changeless motion of the heavens with a semblance of human vicissitude.

Between earth and man arose the leaf. Between the heaven and man came the cloud. His life being partly as the falling leaf, and partly as the flying vapor.

Has the reader any distinct idea of what clouds are? We had some talk about them long ago, and perhaps thought their nature, though at that time not clear to us, would be easily enough understandable when we put ourselves seriously to make it out. Shall we begin with one or two easiest questions?

That mist which lies in the morning so softly in the valley, level and white, through which the tops of the trees rise as if through an inundation—why is *it* so heavy? and why does it lie so low, being yet so thin and frail that it will melt away utterly into splendour of morning, when the sun has shone on it but a few moments more. Those colossal pyramids, huge and firm, with outlines as of rocks, and strength to bear the beating of the high sun full on their fiery flanks—why are *they* so light,—their bases high over our heads, high over the heads of Alps? why will these melt away, not as the sun rises, but as he descends, and leave the stars of twilight clear, while the valley vapour gains again upon the earth like a shroud?

Or that ghost of a cloud, which steals by yonder clump of pines; nay, which does *not* steal by them, but haunts them, wreathing yet round them, and yet—and yet, slowly: now falling in a fair waved line like a woman's veil; now fading, now gone: we look away for an instant, and look back, and it is again there. What has it to do with that clump of pines, that it broods by them and weaves itself among their branches, to and fro? Has it hidden a cloudy treasure among the moss at their roots, which it watches thus? Or has some strong enchanter charmed it into fond returning, or bound it fast within those bars of bough? And yonder filmy crescent, bent like an archer's bow above the snowy summit, the highest of all the hill,—that white arch which never forms but over the supreme crest,—how is it stayed there, repelled pparently from the snow—nowhere touching it, the clear sky seen between it and the mountain edge, yet never leaving it—poised as a white bird hovers over its nest?

Or those war-clouds that gather on the horizon, dragon-crested, tongued with fire;—how is their barbed strength bridled? what bits are these they are champing with their vaporous lips; flinging off flakes of black foam? Leagued leviathans of the Sea of Heaven, out of their nostrils goeth smoke, and their eyes are like the eyelids of the morning. The sword of him that layeth at them cannot hold the spear, the dart, nor the habergeon. Where ride the captains of their armies? Where are set the measures of their march? Fierce murmurers, answering each other from morning until evening—what rebuke is this which has awed them into peace? what hand has reined them back by the way by which they came.

I know not if the reader will think at first that questions like these are easily answered. So far from it, I rather believe that some of the mysteries of the clouds never will be understood by us at all. "Knowest thou the balancings of the clouds?" Is the answer ever to be one of pride? "The wondrous works of Him which is perfect in knowledge?" Is *our* knowledge ever to be so?

It is one of the most discouraging consequences of the varied character of this work of mine, that I am wholly unable to take note of the advance of modern science. What has conclusively been discovered or observed about clouds, I know not; but by the chance inquiry possible to me I find no book which fairly states the difficulties of accounting for even the ordinary aspects of the sky. I shall, therefore, be able in this section to do little more than suggest inquiries to the reader, putting the subject in a clear form for him. All men accustomed to investigation will confirm me in saying that it is a great step when we are personally quite certain what we do *not* know.

First, then, I believe we do not know what makes clouds float. Clouds are water, in some fine form or another: but water is heavier than air, and the finest form you can give a heavy thing will not make it float in a light thing. *On* it, yes; as a boat: but *in* it, no. Clouds are not boats, nor boat-shaped, and they float in the air, not on the top of it "Nay, but though unlike boats, may they not be like feathers? If out of quill substance there may be constructed eider down, and out of vegetable tissue, thistle-down, both buoyant enough for a time, surely of water-tissue may be constructed also water-down, which will be buoyant enough for all cloudy purposes." Not so. Throw out your eider plumage in a calm day, and it will all come settling to the ground: slowly indeed, to aspect; but practically so fast that all our finest clouds would be here in a heap about our ears in an hour or two, if they were only made of water feathers. "But may they not be quill feathers, and have air inside them? May not all their particles be minute little balloons?"

A balloon only floats when the air inside it is either specifically, or by heating, lighter than the air it floats in. If the cloud-feathers had warm air inside their quills, a cloud would be warmer than the air about it, which it is not (I believe). And if the cloud-feathers had hydrogen inside their quills, a cloud would be unwholesome for breathing, which it is not—at least so it seems to me.

"But may they not have nothing inside their quills?" Then they would rise, as bubbles do through water, just as certainly as, if they were solid feathers, they would fall. All our clouds would go up to the top of the air, and swim in eddies of cloud-foam.

"But is not that just what they do?" No. They float at different heights, and with definite forms, in the body of the air itself. If they rose like foam, the sky on a cloudy day would look like a very large flat glass of champagne seen from below, with a stream of bubbles (or clouds) going up as fast as they could to a flat foam-ceiling.

"But may they not be just so nicely mixed out of some thing and nothing, as to float where they are wanted?"

Yes: that is just what they not only may, but must be: only this way of mixing something and nothing is the very thing I want to explain or have explained, and cannot do it, nor get it done.

Except thus far. It is conceivable that minute hollow spherical globes might be formed of water, in which the enclosed vacuity just balanced the weight of the enclosing water, and that the arched sphere formed by the watery film was strong enough to prevent the pressure of the atmosphere from breaking it in. Such a globule would float like a balloon at the height in the atmosphere where the equipoise between the vacuum it enclosed, and its own excess of weight above that of the air, was exact. It would, probably, approach its companion globules by reciprocal attraction, and form aggregations which might be visible.

This is, I believe, the view usually taken by meteorologists. I state it as a possibility, to be taken into account in examining the question—a possibility confirmed by the scriptural words which I have taken for the title of this chapter.

Nevertheless, I state it as a possibility only, not seeing how any known operation of physical law could explain the formation of such molecules. This, however, is not the only difficulty. Whatever shape the water is thrown into, it seems at first improbable that it should lose its property of wetness. Minute division of rain, as in "Scotch mist," makes it capable of floating farther, or floating up and down a little, just as dust will float, though pebbles will not; or gold-leaf, though a sovereign will not; but minutely divided rain wets as much as any other kind, whereas a cloud, partially always, sometimes entirely, loses its power of moistening. Some low clouds look, when you are in them, as if they were made of specks of dust, like short hairs; and these clouds are entirely dry. And also many clouds will wet some substances, but not others. So that we must grant farther, if we are to be happy in our theory, that the spherical molecules are held together by an attraction which prevents their adhering to any foreign body, or perhaps ceases only under some peculiar electric conditions.

The question remains, even supposing their production accounted for,—What intermediate states of water may exist between these spherical hollow molecules and pure vapor?

Has the reader ever considered the relations of commonest forms of volatile substance? The invisible particles which cause the scent of a rose-leaf, how minute, how multitudinous, passing richly away into the air continually! The visible cloud of frankincense—why visible? Is it in consequence of the greater quantity, or larger size of the particles, and how does the heat act in throwing them off in this quantity, or of this size?

Ask the same questions respecting water. It dries, that is, becomes volatile, invisibly, at (any?) temperature. Snow dries, as water does. Under increase of heat, it volatilizes faster, so as to become dimly visible in large mass, as a heat-haze. It reaches boiling point, then becomes entirely visible. But compress it, so that no air shall get between the watery particles—it is invisible again. At the first issuing from the steam-pipe the steam is transparent; but opaque, or visible, as it diffuses itself. The water is indeed closer, because cooler, in that diffusion; but more air is between its particles. Then this very question of visibility is an endless one, wavering between form of substance and action of light. The clearest (or least visible) stream becomes brightly opaque by more minute division in its foam, and the clearest dew in hoar-frost. Dust, unperceived in shade, becomes constantly visible in sunbeam; and watery vapor in the atmosphere, which is itself opaque, when there is promise of fine weather, becomes exquisitely transparent; and (questionably) blue, when it is going to rain.

Questionably blue: for besides knowing very little about water, we know what, except by courtesy, must, I think, be called Nothing—about air. Is it the watery vapor, or the air itself, which is blue? Are neither blue, but only white, producing blue when seen over dark spaces? If either blue, or white, why, when crimson is their commanded dress, are the most distant clouds crimsonest? Clouds close to us may be blue, but far off golden,—a strange result, if the air is blue. And again, if blue, why are rays that come through large spaces of it red; and that Alp, or anything else that catches far-away light, why colored red at dawn and sunset? No one knows, I believe. It is true that many substances, as opal, are blue, or green, by reflected light, yellow by transmitted; but air, if blue at all, is blue always by transmitted light. I hear of a wonderful solution of nettles, or other unlovely herb, which is green when shallow,—red when deep. Perhaps some day, as the motion of the heavenly bodies by help of an apple, their light by help of a nettle, may be explained to mankind.

But farther: these questions of volatility, and visibility, and hue, are all complicated with those of shape. How is a cloud outlined? Granted whatever you choose to ask, concerning its material, or its aspect, its loftiness and luminousness,—how of its limitation? What hews it into a heap, or spins it into a web? Cold is usually shapeless, I suppose, extending over large spaces equally, or with gradual diminution. You cannot have, in the open air, angles, and wedges, and coils, and cliffs of cold. Yet the vapor stops suddenly, sharp and steep as a rock, or thrusts itself across the gates of heaven in likeness of a brazen bar; or braids itself in and out, and across and across, like a tissue of tapestry; or falls into ripples, like sand; or into waving shreds and tongues, as fire. On what anvils and wheels is the vapor pointed, twisted, hammered, whirled, as the potter's clay? By what hands is the incense of the sea built up into domes of marble?

And, lastly, all these questions respecting substance, and aspect, and shape, and line, and division, are involved with others as inscrutable, concerning action. The curves in which clouds move are unknown;—nay, the very method of their motion, or apparent motion, how far it is by change of place, how far by appearance in one place and vanishing from another. And these questions about movement lead partly far away into high mathematics, where I cannot follow them, and partly into theories concerning electricity and infinite space, where I suppose at present no one can follow them.

What, then, is the use of asking the questions?

For my own part, I enjoy the mystery, and perhaps the reader may. I think he ought. He should not be less grateful for summer rain, or see less beauty in the clouds of morning, because they come to prove him with hard questions; to which, perhaps, if we look close at the heavenly scroll,* we may find also a syllable or two of answer illuminated here and there.

* There is a beautiful passage in *Sartor Resartus* concerning this old Hebrew scroll, in its deeper meanings, and the child's watching it, though long illegible for him, yet "with an eye to the gilding." It signifies in a word or two nearly all that is to be said about clouds.

———o———

FEAR OF DEATH.

For, exactly in proportion as the pride of life became more insolent, the fear of death became more servile; and the difference in the manner in which the men of early and later days adorned the sepulchre, confesses a still greater difference in their manner of regarding death. To those he came as the comforter and the friend, rest in his right hand, hope in his left; to these as the humiliator, the spoiler, and the avenger. And, therefore, we find the early tombs at once simple and lovely in adornment, severe and solemn in their expression; confessing the power, and accepting the peace, of death, openly and joyfully; and in all their symbols marking that the hope of resurrection lay only in Christ's righteousness; signed always with this simple utterance of the dead, "I will lay me down in peace, and take my rest; for it is thou, Lord, only that makest me dwell in safety." But the tombs of the later ages are a ghastly struggle of mean pride and miserable terror: the one mustering the statues of the Virtues about the tomb, disguising the sarcophagus with delicate sculpture, polishing the false periods of the elaborate epitaph, and filling with strained animation the features of the portrait statue; and the other summoning underneath, out of the niche or from behind the curtain, the frowning skull, or scythed skeleton, or some other more terrible image of the enemy in whose defiance the whiteness of the sepulchre had been set to shine above the whiteness of the ashes.

———o———

RECREATION.

It is one thing to indulge in playful rest, and another to be devoted to the pursuit of pleasure: and gaiety of heart during the reaction after hard labour, and quickened by satisfaction in the accomplished duty or perfected result, is altogether compatible with, nay, even in some sort arises naturally out of, a deep internal seriousness of disposition.

---o---

TYPES.

I trust that some day the language of Types will be more read and understood by us than it has been for centuries; and when this language, a better one than either Greek or Latin, is again recognized amongst us, we shall find, or remember, that as the other visible elements of the universe —its air, its water, and its flame—set forth, in their pure energies, the life-giving, purifying, and sanctifying influences of the Deity upon His creatures, so the earth, in its purity, sets forth His eternity and His TRUTH. I have dwelt above on the historical language of stones; let us not forget this, which is their theological language; and, as we would not wantonly pollute the fresh waters when they issue forth in their clear glory from the rock, nor stay the mountain winds into pestilential stagnancy, nor mock the sunbeams with artificial and ineffective light; so let us not by our own base and barren falsehoods, replace the crystalline strength and burning colour of the earth from which we were born, and to which we must return; the earth which, like our own bodies, though dust in its degradation, is full of splendour when God's hand gathers its atoms; and which was for ever sanctified by Him, as the symbol no less of His love than of His truth, when He bade the high priest bear the names of the Children of Israel on the clear stones of the Breastplate of Judgment.

---o---

EXPLAINING NATURE.

The sea was meant to be irregular! Yes, and were not also the leaves, and the blades of grass; and, in a sort, as far as may be without mark of sin, even the countenance of man? Or would it be pleasanter and better to have us all alike, and numbered on our foreheads, that we might be known one from the other?

Is there, then, nothing to be done by man's art? Have we only to copy, and again copy, for ever, the imagery of the universe? Not so. We have work to do upon it; there is not any one of us so simple, nor so feeble, but he has work to do upon it. But the work is not to improve, but to explain. This infinite universe is unfathomable, inconceivable, in its whole; every human creature must slowly spell out, and long contemplate, such part of it as may be possible for him to reach; then set forth what he has learned of it for those beneath him; extricating it from infinity, as one gathers a violet out of grass; one does not improve either violet or grass in gathering it, but one makes the flower visible; and then the human being has to make its power upon his own heart visible also, and to give it the honour of the good thoughts it has raised up in him, and to write upon it the history of his own soul. And sometimes he may be able to do more than this, and to set it in strange lights, and display it in a thousand ways before unknown: ways especially directed to necessary and noble purposes, for which he had to choose instruments out of the wide armoury of God. All this he may do: and in this he is only doing what every Christian has to do with the written, as well as the created word, "rightly *dividing* the word of truth." Out of the infinity of the written word, he has also to gather and set forth things new and old, to choose them for the season and the work that are before him, to explain and manifest them to others, with such illustration and enforcement as may be in his power, and to crown them with the history of what, by them, God has done for his soul. And, in doing this, is he improving the Word of God?

THE LOVE OF FLOWERS.

Perhaps it may be thought, if we understood flowers better, we might love them less.

We do not love them much, as it is. Few people care about flowers. Many, indeed, are fond of finding a new shape of blossom, caring for it as a child cares about a kaleidoscope. Many, also, like a fair service of flowers in the greenhouse, as a fair service of plate on the table. Many are scientifically interested in them, though even these in the nomenclature rather than the flowers. And a few enjoy their gardens; but I have never heard of a piece of land, which would let well on a building lease, remaining unlet because it was a flowery piece. I have never heard of parks being kept for wild hyacinths, though often of their being kept for wild beasts. And the blossoming time of the year being principally spring, I perceive it to be the mind of most people, during that period, to stay in towns.

A year or two ago, a keen-sighted and eccentrically minded friend of mine, having taken it into his head to violate this national custom, and go to the Tyrol in spring, was passing through a valley near Landech, with several similarly headstrong companions. A strange mountain appeared in the distance, belted about its breast with a zone of blue, like our English Queen. Was it a blue cloud? A blue horizontal bar of the air that Titian breathed in youth, seen now far away, which mortal might never breathe again? Was it a mirage—a meteor? Would it stay to be approached? (ten miles of winding road yet between them and the foot of its mountain.) Such questioning had they concerning it. My keen-sighted friend alone maintained it to be substantial: whatever it might be, it was not air, and would not vanish. The ten miles of road were overpassed, the carriage left, the mountain climbed. It stayed patiently, expanding still into richer breadth and heavenlier glow—a belt of gentians. Such things may verily be seen among the Alps in spring, and in spring only. Which being so, I observe most people prefer going in autumn.

———o———

THE EARTH-VEIL.

"To dress it and to keep it."

That, then, was to be our work. Alas! what work have we set ourselves upon instead! How have we ravaged the garden instead of kept it—feeding our war-horses with its flowers, and splintering its trees into spear-shafts!

"And at the East a flaming sword."

Is its flame quenchless? and are those gates that keep the

way indeed passable no more? or is it not rather that we no more desire to enter? For what can we conceive of that first Eden which we might not yet win back, if we chose? It was a place full of flowers, we say. Well: the flowers are always striving to grow wherever we suffer them; and the fairer, the closer. There may indeed have been a Fall of Flowers, as a Fall of Man; but assuredly creatures such as we are can now fancy nothing lovelier than roses and lilies, which would grow for us side by side, leaf overlapping leaf, till the Earth was white and red with them, if we cared to have it so. And Paradise was full of pleasant shades and fruitful avenues. Well: what hinders us from covering as much of the world as we like with pleasant shade and pure blossom, and goodly fruit? Who forbids its valleys to be covered over with corn, till they laugh and sing? Who prevents its dark forests, ghostly and uninhabitable, from being changed into infinite orchards, wreathing the hills with frail-floretted snow, far away to the half-lighted horizon of April, and flushing the face of all the autumnal earth with glow of clustered food? But Paradise was a place of peace, we say, and all the animals were gentle servants to us. Well: the world would yet be a place of peace if we were all peacemakers, and gentle service should we have of its creatures if we gave them gentle mastery. But so long as we make sport of slaying bird and beast, so long as we choose to contend rather with our fellows than with our faults, and make battle-field of our meadows instead of pasture—so long, truly, the Flaming Sword will still turn every way, and the gates of Eden remain barred close enough, till we have sheathed the sharper flame of our own passions, and broken down the closer gates of our own hearts.

I have been led to see and feel this more and more, as I considered the service which the flowers and trees, which man was at first appointed to keep, were intended tc render to him in return for his care; and the services they still render to him, as far as he allows their influence, or fulfils his own task towards them. For what infinite wonderfulness there is in this vegetation, considered, as indeed it is, as the means by which the earth becomes the companion of man—his friend and his teacher! In the conditions which we have traced in its rocks, there could only be seen preparation for his existence;—the characters which enable him to live on it safely, and to work with it easily—in all these it has been inanimate and passive; but vegetation is to it as an imperfect soul, given to meet the soul of man. The earth in its depths must remain dead and cold, incapable except of slow crystalline change; but at its surface, which human beings look upon and deal with, it ministers to them through a veil of strange intermediate being; which breathes, but has no voice; moves, but cannot leave its appointed place; passes through life without consciousness, to death without bitterness; wears the beauty of youth, without its passion; and declines to the weakness of age, without its regret.

And in this mystery of intermediate being, entirely subordinate to us, with which we can deal as we choose, having just the greater power as we have the less responsibility for our treatment of the unsuffering creature, most of the pleasures which we need from the external world are gathered, and most of the lessons we need are written, all kinds of precious grace and teaching being united in this link between the Earth and Man: wonderful in universal adaptation to his need, desire, and discipline; God's daily preparation of the earth for him, with beautiful means of life. First a carpet to make it soft for him; then, a colored fantasy of embroidery thereon; then, tall spreading of foliage to shade him from sun-heat, and shade also the fallen rain, that it may not dry quickly back into the clouds, but stay to nourish the springs among the moss. Stout wood to bear this leafage: easily to be cut, yet tough and light, to make houses for him, or instruments (lance-shaft, or plough-handle, according to his temper); useless it had been, if harder; useless, if less fibrous; useless, if less elastic. Winter comes, and the shade of leaf age falls away, to let the sun warm the earth; the strong boughs remain, breaking the strength of winter winds. The seeds which are to prolong the race, innumerable according to the need, are made beautiful and palatable, varied into infinitude of appeal to the fancy of man, or provision for his service; cold juice, or glowing spice, or balm, or incense, softening oil, preserving resin, medicine of styptic, febrifuge, or lulling charm: and all these presented in forms of endless change. Fragility or force, softness and strength, in all degrees and aspects; unerring uprightness, as of temple pillars, or undivided wandering of feeble tendrils on the ground; mighty resistances of rigid arm and limb to the storms of ages, or wavings to and fro with faintest pulse of summer streamlet. Roots cleaving the strength of rock, or binding the transience of the sand; crests basking in sunshine of the desert, or hiding by dripping spring and lightless cave; foliage far tossing in entangled fields beneath every wave of ocean—clothing with variegated, everlasting films, the peaks of the trackless mountains, or ministering at cottage doors to every gentlest passion and simplest joy of humanity.

Being thus prepared for us in all ways, and made beautiful, and good for food, and for building, and for instruments of our hands, this race of plants, deserving boundless affection and admiration from us, become, in proportion to their obtaining it, a nearly perfect test of our being in right temper of mind and way of life; so that no one can be far wrong in either who loves the trees enough, and every one is assured ly wrong in both, who does not love them, if his life has brought them in his way. It is clearly possible to do without them, for the great companionship of the sea and sky are all that sailors need; and many a noble heart has been taught the best it had to learn between dark stone walls. Still if human life be cast among trees at all, the love borne to them is a sure test of its purity. And it is a sorrowful proof of the mistaken ways of the world that the "country," in the simple sense of a place of fields and trees, has hitherto been the source of reproach to its inhabitants, and that the words "countryman, rustic, clown, paysan, villager," still signify a rude and untaught person, as opposed to the words "townsman," and "citizen." We accept this usage of words, or the evil which it signifies, somewhat too quietly; as if it were quite necessary and natural that country-people should be rude, and towns-people gentle. Whereas I believe that the result of each mode of life may, in some stages of the world's progress, be the exact reverse; and that another use of words may be forced upon us by a new aspect of facts, so that we may find ourselves saying: "Such and such a person is very gentle and kind—he is quite rustic; and such and such another person is very rude and ill-taught—he is quite urbane."

At all events, cities have hitherto gained the better part of their good report through our evil ways of going on in the world generally;—chiefly and eminently through our bad habit of fighting with each other. No field, in the middle ages, being safe from devastation, and every country lane yielding easier passage to the marauders, peacefully-minded men necessarily congregated in cities, and walled themselves in, making as few cross-country roads as possible: while the men who sowed and reaped the harvests of Europe were only the servants or slaves of the barons. The disdain of all agricultural pursuits by the nobility, and of all plain facts by the monks, kept educated Europe in a state of mind over which natural phenomena could have no power; body and intellect being lost in the practice of war without purpose, and the meditation of words without meaning. Men learned the dexterity with sword and syllogism, which they mistook for education, within cloister and tilt-yard; and looked on all the broad space of the world of God mainly as a place for exer cise of horses, or for growth of food.

There is a beautiful type of this neglect of the perfectness of the Earth's beauty, by reason of the passions of men, in that picture of Paul Uccello's of the battle of Sant' Egidio, in which the armies meet on a country road beside a hedge of wild roses; the tender red flowers tossing above the helmets, and glowing between the lowered lances. For in like manner the whole of Nature only shone hitherto for man between the tossing of helmet-crests; and sometimes I cannot but think of the trees of the earth as capable of a kind of sorrow, in that imperfect life of theirs, as they opened their innocent leaves in the warm spring-time, in vain for men; and all along the dells of England her beeches cast their dappled shade only where the outlaw drew his bow, and the king rode his careless chase; and by the sweet French rivers their long ranks of poplar waved in the twilight, only to show the flames of burning cities, on the horizon, through the tracery of their stems; amidst the fair defiles of the Apennines, the twisted olive-trunks hid the ambushes of treachery; and on their valley meadows, day by day, the lilies which were white at the dawn were washed with crimson at sunset.

And indeed I had once purposed, in this work, to show what kind of evidence existed respecting the possible influence of country life on men; it seeming to me, then, likely that here and there a reader would perceive this to be a grave question, more than most which we contend about, political or social, and might care to follow it out with me earnestly.

The day will assuredly come when men will see that it *is* a grave question; at which period, also, I doubt not, there will arise persons able to investigate it.

THE INFLUENCE OF CUSTOM.

Custom has a twofold operation: the one to deaden the frequency and force of repeated impressions, the other to endear the familiar object to the affections. Commonly, where the mind is vigorous, and the power of sensation very perfect, it has rather the last operation than the first; with meaner minds, the first takes place in the higher degree, so that they are commonly characterized by a desire of excitement, and the want of the loving, fixed, theoretic power. But both take place in some degree with all men, so that as life advances, impressions of all kinds become less rapturous owing to their repetition. It is however beneficently ordained that repulsiveness shall be diminished by custom in a far greater degree than the sensation of beauty, so that the anatomist in a little time loses all sense of horror in the torn flesh and carious bone, while the sculptor ceases not to feel to the close of his life, the deliciousness of every line of the outward frame. So then as in that with which we are made familiar, the repulsiveness is constantly diminishing, and such claims as it may be able to put forth on the affections are daily becoming stronger, while in what is submitted to us of new or strange, that which may be repulsive is felt in its full force, while no hold is as yet laid on the affections, there is a very strong preference induced in most minds for that to which they are accustomed over that they know not, and this is strongest in those which are least open to sensations of positive beauty. But however far this operation may be carried, its utmost effect is but the deadening and approximating the sensations of beauty and ugliness. It never mixes nor crosses, nor in any way alters them; it has not the slightest connection with nor power over their nature. By tasting two wines alternately, we may deaden our perception of their flavour; nay, we may even do more than can ever be done in the case of sight, we may confound the two flavours together. But it will hardly be argued therefore that custom is the cause of either flavour. And so, though by habit we may deaden the effect of ugliness or beauty, it is not for that reason to be affirmed that habit is the cause of either sensation. We may keep a skull beside us as long as we please, we may overcome its repulsiveness, we may render ourselves capable of perceiving many qualities of beauty about its lines, we may contemplate it for years together if we will, it and nothing else, but we shall not get ourselves to think as well of it as of a child's fair face.

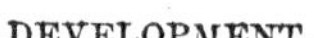

DEVELOPMENT.

I believe an immense gain in the bodily health and happiness of the upper classes would follow on their steadily endeavouring, however clumsily, to make the physical exertion they now necessarily take in amusements, definitely serviceable. It would be far better, for instance, that a gentleman should mow his own fields than ride over other people's.

Again, respecting degrees of possible refinement, I cannot

yet speak positively, because no effort has yet been made to teach refined habits to persons of simple life.

The idea of such refinement has been made to appear absurd, partly by the foolish ambition of vulgar persons in low life, but more by the worse than foolish assumption, acted on so often by modern advocates of improvement, that "education" means teaching Latin, or algebra, or music, or drawing, instead of developing or "drawing out" the human soul.

It may not be the least necessary that a peasant should know algebra, or Greek, or drawing. But it may, perhaps, be both possible and expedient that he should be able to arrange his thoughts clearly, to speak his own language intelligibly, to discern between right and wrong, to govern his passions, and to receive such pleasures of ear or sight as his life may render accessible to him. I would not have him taught the science of music; but most assuredly I would have him taught to sing. I would not teach him the science of drawing; but certainly I would teach him to see; without learning a single term of botany, he should know accurately the habits and uses of every leaf and flower in his fields; and unencumbered by any theories of moral or political philosophy, he should help his neighbour, and disdain a bribe.

———o———

THE REAL USE OF SCIENCE AND ART.

All effort in social improvement is paralyzed, because no one has been bold or clear-sighted enough to put and press home this radical question: "What is indeed the noblest tone and reach of life for men; and how can the possibility of it be extended to the greatest numbers?" It is answered broadly and rashly, that wealth is good; that knowledge is good; that art is good; that luxury is good. Whereas none of them are good in the abstract, but good only if rightly received. Nor have any steps whatever been yet securely taken,—nor otherwise than in the resultless rhapsody of moralists,—to ascertain what luxuries and what learning it is either kind to bestow, or wise to desire. This, however, at least we know, shown clearly by the history of all time, that the arts and sciences, ministering to the pride of nations, have invariably hastened their ruin; and this, also, without venturing to say that I know, I nevertheless firmly believe, that the same arts and sciences will tend as distinctly to exalt the strength and quicken the soul of every nation which employs them to increase the comfort of lowly life, and grace with happy intelligence the unambitious courses of honourable toil.

———o———

THE SYMBOL OF FEAR.

I might devote half a volume to a description of the fantastic and incomprehensible arrangement of the rocks and their veins; but all that is necessary for the general reader to know or remember, is this broad fact of the *undulation* of their whole substance. For there is something, it seems to me inexpressibly marvellous in this phenomenon, largely looked at. They have nothing of the look of dried earth about them, nothing petty or limited in the display of their bulk. Where they are, they seem to form the world; no mere bank of a river here, or of a lane there peeping out among the hedges or forests: but from the lowest valley to the highest clouds, all is theirs—one adamantine dominion and rigid authority of rock. We yield ourselves to the impression of their eternal, unconquerable stubbornness of strength; their mass seems the least yielding, least to be softened, or in any-wise dealt with by external force, of all earthly substance. And, behold, as we look farther into it, it is all touched and troubled, like waves by a summer breeze; rippled, far more delicately than seas or lakes are rippled; *they* only undulate along their surfaces—this rock trembles through its every fibre, like the chords of an Eolian harp—like the stillest air of spring with the echoes of a child's voice. Into the heart of all those great mountains, through every tossing of their boundless crests, and deep beneath all their unfathomable defiles, flows that strange quivering of their substance. Other and weaker things seem to express their subjection to an Infinite power only by momentary terrors: as the weeds bow down before the feverish wind, and the sound of the going in the tops of the taller trees passes on before the clouds, and the fitful opening of pale spaces on the dark water as if some invisible hand were casting dust abroad upon it, gives warning of the anger that is to come, we may well imagine that there is indeed a fear passing upon the grass, and leaves, and waters, at the presence of some great spirit commissioned to let the tempest loose; but the terror passes, and their sweet rest is perpetually restored to the pastures and the waves. Not so to the mountains. They, which at first seem strengthened beyond the dread of any violence or change, are yet also ordained to bear upon them the symbol of a perpetual Fear: the tremor which fades from the soft lake and gliding river is sealed, to all eternity, upon the rock; and while things that pass visibly from birth to death may sometimes forget their feebleness, the mountains are made to possess a perpetual memorial of their infancy,—that infancy which the prophet saw in his vision: "I beheld the earth, and lo, it was without form and void, and the heavens, and they had no light. I beheld the mountains, and lo, they *trembled;* and all the hills *moved lightly.*"

———o———

GRADATION.

There is a marked likeness between the virtue of man and the enlightenment of the globe he inhabits—the same diminishing gradation in vigor up to the limits of their domains, the same essential separation from their contraries—the same twilight at the meeting of the two: a something wider belt than the line where the world rolls into night, that strange twilight of the virtues; that dusky debateable land, wherein zeal becomes impatience, and temperance becomes severity, and justice becomes cruelty, and faith superstition, and each and all vanish into gloom.

Nevertheless, with the greater number of them, though their dimness increases gradually, we may mark the moment of their sunset; and, happily, may turn the shadow back by the way by which it had gone down: but for one, the line of the horizon is irregular and undefined; and this, too, the very equator and girdle of them all—Truth; that only one of which there are no degrees, but breaks and rents continually; that pillar of the earth, yet a cloudy pillar; that golden and narrow line, which the very powers and virtues that lean upon it bend, which policy and prudence conceal, which kindness and courtesy modify, which courage overshadows with his shield, imagination covers with her wings, and charity dims with her tears. How difficult must the maintenance of that authority be, which, while it has to restrain the hostility of all the worst principles of man, has also to restrain the dis orders of his best—which is continually assaulted by the one and betrayed by the other, and which regards with the same severity the lightest and the boldest violations of its law!

———o———

LOVE AND TRUST.

My dear friend and teacher, Lowell, right as he is in almost everything, is for once wrong in these lines, though with a noble wrongness:—

> "Disappointment's dry and bitter root,
> Envy's harsh berries, and the choking pool
> Of the world's scorn, are the right mother-milk
> To the tough hearts that pioneer their kind."

They are not so; love and trust are the only mother-milk of any man's soul. So far as he is hated and mistrusted, his powers are destroyed. Do not think that with impunity you can follow the eyeless fool, and shout with the shouting charlatan; and that the men you thrust aside with gibe and blow, are thus sneered and crushed into the best service they can do you. I have told you they *will* not serve you for pay. They *cannot* serve you for scorn. Even from Balaam, money-lover though he be, no useful prophecy is to be had for silver or gold. From Elisha, savior of life though he be, no saving of life—even of children's, who "knew no better,"—is to be got by the cry, Go up, thou bald-head. No man can serve you either for purse or curse; neither kind of pay will answer. No pay is, indeed, receivable by any true man; but power is receivable by him, in the love and faith you give him. So far only as you give him these can he serve you; that is the meaning of the question which his Master asks always,

"Believest thou that I am able?" And from every one of His servants—to the end of time—if you give them the Caper naum measure of faith, you shall have from them Capernaum measure of works, and no more.

Do not think that I am irreverently comparing great and small things. The system of the world is entirely one; small things and great are alike part of one mighty whole. As the flower is gnawed by frost, so every human heart is gnawed by faithlessness. And as surely,—as irrevocably,—as the fruit-bud falls before the east wind, so fails the power of the kindest human heart, if you meet it with poison.

———o———

INFIDELITY IN ENGLAND.

The form which the infidelity of England, especially, has taken, is one hitherto unheard of in human history. No nation ever before declared boldly, by print and word of mouth, that its religion was good for show, but "would not work." Over and over again it has happened that nations have denied their gods, but they denied them bravely. The Greeks in their decline jested at their religion, and frittered it away in flatteries and fine arts; the French refused theirs fiercely, tore down their altars and brake their carven images. The question about God with both these nations was still, even in their decline, fairly put, though falsely answered. "Either there is or is not a Supreme Ruler; we consider of it, declare there is not, and proceed accordingly." But we English have put the matter in an entirely new light: "There *is* a Supreme Ruler, no question of it, only He cannot rule. His orders won't work. He will be quite satisfied with euphonious and respectful repetition of them. Execution would be too dangerous under existing circumstances, which He certainly never contemplated."

---o---

THE NOBLENESS OF COLOUR.

The fact is, we none of us enough appreciate the nobleness and sacredness of colour. Nothing is more common than to hear it spoken of as a subordinate beauty,—nay, even as the mere source of a sensual pleasure; and we might almost believe that we were daily among men who

> "Could strip, for aught the prospect yields
> To them, their verdure from the fields;
> And take the radiance from the clouds
> With which the sun his setting shrouds."

But it is not so. Such expressions are used for the most part in thoughtlessness; and if the speakers would only take the pains to imagine what the world and their own existence would become, if the blue were taken from the sky, and the gold from the sunshine, and the verdure from the leaves, and the crimson from the blood which is the life of man, the flush from the cheek, the darkness from the eye, the radiance from the hair,—if they could but see for an instant, white human creatures living in a white world,—they would soon feel what they owe to colour. The fact is, that, of all God's gifts to the sight of man, colour is the holiest, the most divine, the most solemn. We speak rashly of gay colour, and sad colour, for colour cannot at once be good and gay. All good colour is in some degree pensive, the loveliest is melancholy, and the purest and most thoughtful minds are those which love colour the most.

THE RAINBOW.

In that heavenly circle which binds the statutes of colour upon the front of the sky, when it became the sign of the covenant of peace, the pure hues of divided light were sanctified to the human heart for ever; nor this, it would seem, by mere arbitrary appointment, but in consequence of the fore-ordained and marvellous constitution of those hues into a sevenfold, or, more strictly still, a threefold order, typical of the Divine nature itself. Observe also, the name Shem, or Splendour, given to that son of Noah in whom this covenant with mankind was to be fulfilled, and see how that name was justified by every one of the Asiatic races which descended from him. Not without meaning was the love of Israel to his chosen son expressed by the coat "of many colours;" not without deep sense of the sacredness of that symbol of purity, did the lost daughter of David tear it from her breast:—"With such robes were the king's daughters that were virgins apparelled."* We know it to have been by Divine command that the Israelite, rescued from servitude, veiled the tabernacle with its rain of purple and scarlet, while the under sunshine flashed through the fall of the colour from its tenons of gold.

———o———

BROTHERHOOD.

Whether, indeed, derived from the quarterings of the knights' shields, or from what other source, I know not; but there is one magnificent attribute of the colouring of the late twelfth, the whole thirteenth, and the early fourteenth

* 2 Samuel xiii. 18.

century, which I do not find definitely in any previous work, nor afterwards in general art, though constantly, and necessarily, in that of great colourists, namely, the union of one colour with another by reciprocal interference: that is to say, if a mass of red is to be set beside a mass of blue, a piece of the red will be carried into the blue, and a piece of the blue carried into the red; sometimes in nearly equal portions, as in a shield divided into four quarters, of which the uppermost on one side will be of the same colour as the lowermost on the other; sometimes in smaller fragments, but, in the periods above named, always definitely and grandly, though in a thousand various ways. And I call it a magnificent principle, for it is an eternal and universal one, not in art only, but in human life. It is the great principle of Brotherhood, not by equality, nor by likeness, but by giving and receiving; the souls that are unlike, and the nations that are unlike, and the natures that are unlike, being bound into one noble whole by each receiving something from, and of, the others' gifts and the others' glory. I have not space to follow out this thought,—it is of infinite extent and application,—but I note it for the reader's pursuit, because I have long believed, and the whole second volume of "Modern Painters" was written to prove, that in whatever has been made by the Deity externally delightful to the human sense of beauty, there is some type of God's nature or of God's laws; nor are any of His laws, in one sense, greater than the appointment that the most lovely and perfect unity shall be obtained by the taking of one nature into another. I trespass upon too high ground; and yet I cannot fully show the reader the extent of this law, but by leading him thus far. And it is just because it is so vast and so awful a law, that it has rule over the smallest things; and there is not a vein of colour on the lightest leaf which the spring winds are at this moment unfolding in the fields around us, but it is an illustration of an ordainment to which the earth and its creatures owe their continuance, and their Redemption.

———o———

THE HARVEST IS RIPE.

"Put ye in the sickle, for the harvest is ripe." The word is spoken in our ears continually to other reapers than the angels—to the busy skeletons that never tire for stooping. When the measure of iniquity is full, and it seems that another day might bring repentance and redemption,—"Put ye in the sickle." When the young life has been wasted all away, and the eyes are just opening upon the tracks of ruin, and faint resolution rising in the heart for nobler things,—"Put ye in the sickle." When the roughest blows of fortune have been borne long and bravely, and the hand is just stretched to grasp its goal,—"Put ye in the sickle." And when there are but a few in the midst of a nation, to save it, or to teach, or to cherish; and all its life is bound up in those few golden ears,—"Put ye in the sickle, pale reapers, and pour hemlock for your feast of harvest home."

———o———

MISSING THE MARK.

Perhaps, some day, people will again begin to remember the force of the old Greek word for sin; and to learn that all sin is in essence—"Missing the mark;" losing sight or consciousness of heaven; and that this loss may be various in its guilt: it cannot be judged by us. It is this of which the words are spoken so sternly, "Judge not;" which words people always quote, I observe, when they are called upon to "do judgment and justice." For it is truly a pleasant thing to condemn men for their wanderings; but it is a bitter thing to acknowledge a truth, or to take any bold share in working out an equity. So that the habitual modern practical application of the precept, "Judge not," is to avoid the trouble of pronouncing verdict, by taking, of any matter, the pleasantest malicious view which first comes to hand; and to obtain licence for our own convenient iniquities, by being indulgent to those of others.

These two methods of obedience being just the two which are most directly opposite to the law of mercy and truth.

"Bind them about thy neck." I said, but now, that of an evil tree men never gathered good fruit.

———o———

LIFE AND LOVE.

I must not enter here into the solemn and far-reaching fields of thought which it would be necessary to traverse, in order to detect the mystical connection between life and love set forth in that Hebrew system of sacrificial religion to which we may trace most of the received ideas respecting sanctity, consecration, and purification. This only I must hint to the reader—for his own following out—that if he earnestly examines the original sources from which our heedless popular language respecting the washing away of sins has been borrowed, he will find that the fountain in which sins are indeed to be washed away, is that of love, not of agony.

But, without approaching the presence of this deeper meaning of the sign, the reader may rest satisfied with the connection given him directly in written words, between the cloud and its bow. The cloud, or firmament, as we have seen, signifies the ministration of the heavens to man. That ministration may be in judgment or mercy—in the lightning, or the dew. But the bow, or colour, of the cloud, signifies always mercy, the sparing of life; such ministry of the heaven, as shall feed and prolong life. And as the sunlight, undivided, is the type of the wisdom and righteousness of God, so divided, and softened into colour by means of the firmamental ministry, fitted to every need of man, as to every delight, and becoming one chief source of human beauty, by being made part of the flesh of man;—thus divided, the sunlight is the type of the wisdom of God, becoming sanctification and redemption. Various in work—various in beauty—various in power.

Colour is, therefore, in brief terms, the type of love. Hence it is especially connected with the blossoming of the earth; and again, with its fruits; also, with the spring and fall of the leaf, and with the morning and evening of the day, in order to show the waiting of love about the birth and death of man.

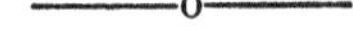

SYMBOLS OF TRUTH.

The fact seems to be that strength of religious feeling is capable of supplying for itself whatever is wanting in the rudest suggestions of art, and will either, on the one hand, purify what is coarse into inoffensiveness, or, on the other, raise what is feeble into impressiveness. Probably all art, as such, is unsatisfactory to it; and the effort which it makes to supply the void will be induced rather by association and accident than by the real merit of the work submitted to it. The likeness to a beloved friend, the correspondence with a habitual conception, the freedom from any strange or offensive particularity, and, above all, an interesting choice of incident, will win admiration for a picture when the noblest efforts of religious imagination would otherwise fail of power. How much more, when to the quick capacity of emotion is joined a childish trust that the picture does indeed represent a fact! It matters little whether the fact be well or ill told; the moment we believe the picture to be true, we complain little of its being ill-painted. Let it be considered for a moment, whether the child, with its coloured print, inquiring eagerly and gravely which is Joseph, and which is Benjamin, is not more capable of receiving a strong, even a sublime, impression from the rude symbol which it invests with reality by its own effort, than the connoisseur who admires the grouping of the three figures in Raphael's "Telling of the Dreams;" and whether also, when the human mind is in right religious tone, it has not always this childish power—I speak advisedly, this power—a noble one, and possessed more in youth than at any period of after life, but always, I think, restored in a measure by religion—of raising into sublimity and reality the rudest symbol which is given to it of accredited truth.

———o———

STRIVING AFTER PERFECTION.

The modern English mind has this much in common with that of the Greek, that it intensely desires, in all things, the utmost completion or perfection compatible with their nature. This is a noble character in the abstract, but becomes ignoble when it causes us to forget the relative dignities of that nature itself, and to prefer the perfectness of the lower nature to the imperfection of the higher; not considering that as, judged by such a rule, all the brute animals would be preferable to man, because more perfect in their functions and kind, and yet are always held inferior to him, so also in the works of man, those which are more perfect in their kind are always inferior to those which are, in their nature, liable to more faults and shortcomings. For the finer the nature, the more flaws it will show through the clearness of it; and it is a law of this universe, that the best things shall be seldomest seen in their best form. The wild grass grows well and strongly, one year with another; but the wheat is, according to the greater nobleness of its nature, liable to the bitterer blight. And therefore, while in all things that we see, or do, we are to desire perfection, and strive for it, we are nevertheless not to set the meaner thing, in its narrow accomplishment, above the nobler thing, in its mighty progress; not to esteem smooth minuteness above shattered majesty; not to prefer mean victory to honourable defeat; not to lower the level of our aim, that we may the more surely enjoy the complacency of success. But, above all, in our dealings with the souls of other men, we are to take care how we check by severe requirement or narrow caution, efforts which might otherwise lead to a noble issue; and, still more, how we withhold our admiration from great excellences, because they are mingled with rough faults.

———o———

THE PINES AND THE SWISS.

Amidst the delicate delight of cottage and field, the young pines stand delicatest of all, scented as with frankincense, their slender stems straight as arrows, and crystal white, looking as if they would break with a touch, like needles; and their arabesques of dark leaf pierced through and through, by the pale radiance of clear sky, opal blue, where they follow each other along the soft hill-ridges, up and down.

I have watched them in such scenes with the deeper interest, because of all trees they have hitherto had most influence on human character. The effect of other vegetation, however great, has been divided by mingled species; elm and oak in England, poplar in France, birch in Scotland, olive in Italy and Spain, share their power with inferior trees, and with all the changing charm of successive agriculture. But the tremendous unity of the pine absorbs and moulds the life of a race. The pine shadows rest upon a nation. The Northern peoples, century after century, lived under one or other of the two great powers of the Pine and the Sea, both infinite. They dwelt amidst the forests, as they wandered on the waves, and saw no end, nor any other horizon;—still the dark green trees, or the dark green waters, jagged the dawn with their fringe, or their foam. And whatever elements of imagination, or of warrior strength, or of domestic justice, were brought down by the Norwegian and the Goth against the dissoluteness or degradation of the South of Europe, were taught them under the green roofs and wild penetralia of the pine.

I do not attempt, delightful as the task would be, to trace this influence (mixed with superstition) in Scandinavia, or North Germany; but let us at least note it in the instance which we speak of so frequently, yet so seldom take to heart.

There has been much dispute respecting the character of the Swiss, arising out of the difficulty which other nations had to understand their simplicity. They were assumed to be either romantically virtuous, or basely mercenary, when in fact they were neither heroic nor base, but were true-hearted men, stubborn with more than any recorded stubbornness; not much regarding their lives, yet not casting them causelessly away; forming no high ideal of improvement, but never relaxing their grasp of a good they had once gained; devoid of all romantic sentiment, yet loving with a practical and patient love that neither wearied nor forsook; little given to enthusiasm in religion, but maintaining their faith in a purity which no worldliness deadened and no hypocrisy soiled; neither chivalrously generous nor pathetically humane, yet never pursuing their defeated enemies, nor suffering their poor to perish: proud, yet not allowing their pride to prick them into unwary or unworthy quarrel; avaricious, yet contentedly rendering to their neighbour his due; dull, but clear-sighted to all the principles of justice; and patient, without ever allowing delay to be prolonged by sloth, or forbearance by fear.

This temper of Swiss mind, while it animated the whole confederacy, was rooted chiefly in one small district which formed the heart of their country, yet lay not among its highest mountains. Beneath the glaciers of Zermatt and Evolena, and on the scorching slopes of the Valais, the peasants remained in an aimless torpor, unheard of but as the obedient vassals of the great Bishopric of Sion. But where the lower ledges of calcareous rock were broken by the inlets of the Lake Lucerne, and bracing winds penetrating from the north forbade the growth of the vine, compelling the peasantry to adopt an entirely pastoral life, was reared another race of men. Their narrow domain should be marked by a small green spot on every map of Europe. It is about forty miles from east to west; as many from north to south: yet on that shred of rugged ground, while every kingdom of the world around it rose or fell in fatal change, and every multitudinous race mingled or wasted itself in various dispersion and decline, the simple shepherd dynasty remained changeless. There is no record of their origin. They are neither Goths, Burgundians, Romans, nor Germans. They have been for ever Helvetii, and for ever free. Voluntarily placing themselves under the protection of the House of Hapsburg, they acknowledged its supremacy, but resisted its oppression; and rose against the unjust governors it appointed over them, not to gain, but to redeem their liberties. Victorious in the struggle by the Lake of Egeri, they stood the foremost standard-bearers among the nations of Europe in the cause of loyalty and life—loyalty in its highest sense, to the laws of God's helpful justice, and of man's faithful and brotherly fortitude.

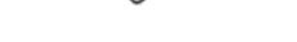

PRECIPICES.

Precipices are among the most impressive as well as the most really dangerous of mountain ranges; in many spots inaccessible with safety either from below or from above; dark in colour, robed with everlasting mourning, for ever tottering like a great fortress shaken by war, fearful as much in their weakness as in their strength, and yet gathered after every fall into darker frowns and unhumiliated threatening; for ever incapable of comfort or of healing from herb or flower, nourishing no root in their crevices, touched by no hue of life on buttress or ledge, but, to the utmost, desolate;

knowing no shaking of leaves in the wind, nor of grass beside the stream,—no motion but their own mortal shivering, the deathful crumbling of atom from atom in their corrupting stones; knowing no sound of living voice or living tread cheered neither by the kid's bleat nor the marmot's cry; haunted only by uninterpreted echoes from far off, wandering hither and thither among their walls, unable to escape, and by the hiss of angry torrents, and sometimes the shriek of a bird that flits near the face of them, and sweeps frightened back from under their shadow into the gulf of air: and, sometimes, when the echo has fainted, and the wind has carried the sound of the torrent away, and the bird has vanished, and the mouldering stones are still for a little time,—a brown moth, opening and shutting its wings upon a grain of dust, may be the only thing that moves, or feels, in all the waste of weary precipice, darkening five thousand feet of the blue depth of heaven.

It will not be thought that there is nothing in a scene such as this deserving our contemplation, or capable of conveying useful lessons, if it were fitly rendered by art.

———o———

THE USE OF PICTURES.

We should use pictures not as authorities, but as comments on nature, just as we use divines, not as authorities, but as comments on the Bible. Constable, in his dread of saint-worship, excommunicates himself from all benefit of the Church, and deprives himself of much instruction from the Scripture to which he holds, because he will not accept aid in the reading of it from the learning of other men. Sir George Beaumont, on the contrary, furnishes, in the anecdotes given of him in Constable's life, a melancholy instance of the degradation into which the human mind may fall, when it suffers human works to interfere between it and its Master. The recommending the colour of an old Cremona fiddle for the prevailing tone of everything, and the vapid inquiry of the conventionalist, "Where do you put your brown tree?" show a prostration of intellect so laughable and lamentable, that they are at once, on all, and to all, students of the gallery, a satire and a warning. Art so followed is the most servile indolence in which life can be wasted. There are then two dangerous extremes to be shunned,—forgetfulness of the Scripture, and scorn of the divine—slavery on the one hand, free-thinking on the other. The mean is nearly as difficult to determine or keep in art as in religion, but the great danger is on the side of superstition. He who walks humbly with Nature will seldom be in danger of losing sight of Art. He will commonly find in all that is truly great of man's works, something of their original, for which he will regard them with gratitude, and sometimes follow them with respect; while he who takes Art for his authority may entirely lose sight of all that it interprets, and sink at once into the sin of an idolater, and the degradation of a slave.

———o———

SANCTIFICATION.

All the divisions of humanity are noble or brutal, immortal or mortal, according to the degree of their sanctification; and there is no part of the man which is not immortal and divine when it is once given to God, and no part of him which is not mortal by the second death, and brutal before the first, when it is withdrawn from God For to what shall we trust for our distinction from the beasts that perish? To our higher intellect?—yet are we not bidden to be wise as the serpent, and to consider the ways of the ant?—or to our affections? nay; these are more shared by the lower animals than our intelligence. Hamlet leaps into the grave of his beloved, and leaves it,—a dog had stayed. Humanity and immortality consist neither in reason, nor in love; not in the body, nor in the animation of the heart of it, nor in the thoughts and stirrings of the brain of it,—but in the dedication of them all to Him who will raise them up at the last day.

———o———

HOW TO LIVE.

It surely is a subject for serious thought, whether it might not be better for many of us, if, on attaining a certain position in life, we determined, with God's permission, to choose a home in which to live and die,—a home not to be increased by adding stone to stone and field to field, but which, being enough for all our wishes at that period, we should resolve to be satisfied with for ever. Consider this; and also, whether we ought not to be more in the habit of seeking honour from our descendants than our ancestors; thinking it better to be nobly remembered than nobly born; and striving so to live, that our sons, and our sons' sons, for ages to come, might still lead their children reverently to the doors out of which we had been carried to the grave, saying, "Look: This was his house: This was his chamber."

———o———

MAN'S NATURE.

Now the basest thought possible concerning man is, that he has no spiritual nature; and the foolishest misunderstanding of him possible is, that he has or should have, no animal nature. For his nature is nobly animal, nobly spiritual—coherently and irrevocably so; neither part of it may, but at its peril, expel, despise, or defy the other.

———o———

SELF-GOVERNMENT.

There are more people who can forget themselves than govern themselves.

———o———

CANDID SEEING.

Some years ago, as I was talking of the curvilinear forms in a piece of rock to one of our academicians, he said to me, in a somewhat despondent accent, "If you look for curves, you will see curves; if you look for angles, you will see angles."

The saying appeared to me an infinitely sad one. It was the utterance of an experienced man; and in many ways true, for one of the most singular gifts, or, if abused, most singular weaknesses, of the human mind is its power of persuading itself to see whatever it chooses;—a great gift, if directed to the discernment of the things needful and pertinent to its own work and being; a great weakness, if directed to the discovery of things profitless or discouraging. In all things throughout the world, the men who look for the crooked will see the crooked, and the men who look for the straight will see the straight. But yet the saying was a notably sad one; for it came of the conviction in the speaker's mind that there was in reality *no* crooked and *no* straight; that all so-called discernment was fancy, and that men might, with equal rectitude of judgment, and good-deserving of their fellow-men, perceive and paint whatever was convenient to them.

Whereas things may always be seen truly by candid people, though never *completely*. No human capacity ever yet saw the whole of a thing; but we may see more and more of it the longer we look. Every individual temper will see something different in it: but supposing the tempers honest, all the differences are there. Every advance in our acuteness of perception will show us something new; but the old and first discerned thing will still be there, not falsified, only modified and enriched by the new perceptions, becoming continually more beautiful in its harmony with them and more approved as a part of the Infinite truth.

———o———

INTEMPERANCE.

Men are held intemperate (ἀκόλαστοι) only when their desires overcome or prevent the action of their reason, and they are indeed intemperate in the exact degree in which such prevention or interference takes place, and so are actually ἀκόλαστοι, in many instances, and with respect to many resolves, which lower not the world's estimation of their temperance. But when it is palpably evident that the reason cannot have erred, but that its voice has been deadened or disobeyed, and that the reasonable creature has been dragged dead round the walls of his own citadel by mere passion and impulse,—then, and then only, men are of all held intemperate. And this is evidently the case with respect to inordinate indulgence in pleasures of touch and taste, for these, being destructive in their continuance not only of all other pleasures, but of the very sensibilities by which they themselves are received, and as this penalty is actually known and experienced by those indulging in them, so that the reason cannot but pronounce right respecting their perilousness, there is no palliation of the wrong choice; and the man, as utterly incapable of will, is called intemperate, or ἀκόλαστος.

It would be well if the reader would for himself follow out this subject, which it would be irrelevant here to pursue farther, observing how a certain degree of intemperance is suspected and attributed to men with respect to higher impulses; as, for instance, in the case of anger, or any other passion criminally indulged, and yet is not so attributed, as in the case of sensual pleasures; because in anger the reason is supposed not to have had time to operate, and to be itself affected by the presence of the passion, which seizes the man involuntarily and before he is aware; whereas, in the case of the sensual pleasures, the act is deliberate, and determined on beforehand, in direct defiance of reason. Nevertheless, if no precaution be taken against immoderate anger, and the passions gain upon the man, so as to be evidently wilful and unrestrained, and admitted contrary to all reason, we begin to look upon him as, in the real sense of the word, intemperate, or ἀκόλαστος, and assign to him, in consequence, his place among the beasts, as definitely as if he had yielded to the pleasurable temptations of touch or taste.

———o———

THE 19TH PSALM.

Take up the 19th Psalm and look at it verse by verse. Perhaps to my younger readers one word may be permitted respecting their Bible-reading in general. The Bible is, indeed, a deep book, when depth is required; that is to say, for deep people! But it is not intended, particularly, for profound persons; on the contrary, much more for shallow and simple persons. And therefore the first, and generally the main and leading idea of the Bible, is on its surface, written in plainest possible Greek, Hebrew, or English, needing no penetration, nor amplification, needing nothing but what we all might give—attention.

But this, which is in every one's power, and is the only thing that God wants, is just the last thing any one will give Him.

We are delighted to ramble away into day-dreams, to repeat pet verses from other places, suggested by chance words; to snap at an expression which suits our own particular views, or to dig up a meaning from under a verse, which we should be amiably grieved to think any human being had been so happy as to find before. But the plain, intended, immediate, fruitful meaning, which every one ought to find always, and especially that which depends on our seeing the relation of the verse to those near it, and getting the force of the whole passage, in due relation—this sort of significance we do not look for;—it being, truly, not to be discovered, unless we really attend to what is said, instead of to our own feelings.

It is unfortunate also, but very certain, that in order to attend to what is said, we must go through the irksomeness of knowing the meaning of the words. And the first thing that children should be taught about their Bibles is, to distinguish clearly between words that they understand and words that they do not; and to put aside the words they do not understand, and verses connected with them, to be asked about, or for a future time; and never to think they are reading the Bible when they are merely repeating phrases of an unknown tongue.

Let us try, by way of example, this 19th Psalm, and see what plain meaning is uppermost in it.

"The heavens declare the glory of God."

What are the heavens?

The word occurring in the Lord's Prayer, and the thing expressed being what a child may, with some advantage, be led to look at, it might be supposed among a schoolmaster's first duties to explain this word clearly.

Now there can be no question that in the minds of the sacred writers, it stood naturally for the entire system of cloud, and of space beyond it, conceived by them as a vault set with stars. But there can, also, be no question, as we saw in previous inquiry, that the firmament, which is said to have been "called" heaven, at the creation, expresses, in all definite use of the word, the system of clouds, as spreading the power of the water over the earth; hence the constant expressions dew of heaven, rain of heaven, etc., where heaven is used in the singular; while the "heavens," when used plurally, and especially when in distinction as here, from the word "firmament," remained expressive of the starry space beyond.

But whatever different nations had called them, at least I would make it clear to the child's mind that in this 19th Psalm, their whole power being intended, the two words are used which express it: the Heavens, for the great vault or void, with all its planets, and stars, and ceaseless march of orbs innumerable; and the Firmament, for the ordinance of the clouds.

These heavens, then, declare "the *glory* of God;" that is, the light of God, the eternal glory, stable and changeless. As their orbs fail not, but pursue their course for ever to give light upon the earth—so God's glory surrounds man for ever —changeless, in its fulness insupportable—infinite.

"And the firmament showeth his *handiwork*." The clouds, prepared by the hands of God for the help of man, varied in their ministration—veiling the inner splendour—show, not His eternal glory, but His daily handiwork. So He dealt with Moses. I will cover thee "with my hand" as I pass by. Compare Job xxxvi. 24.

"Remember that thou magnify His work, which men behold. Every man may see it." Not so the glory—that only in part; the courses of these stars are to be seen imperfectly, and but by a few. But this firmament, every man may see it; man may behold it "afar off." "Behold, God is great, and we know him not. For he maketh small the drops of water: they pour down rain according to the vapor thereof."

"Day unto day uttereth speech, and night unto night sheweth knowledge. They have no speech nor language, yet without these their voice is heard. Their rule is gone out throughout the earth, and their words to the end of the world."

Note that. Their rule throughout the earth, whether inhabited or not—their law of right is thereon; but their words, spoken to human souls, to the end of the inhabited world.

"In them hath He set a tabernacle for the sun," etc. Literally, a tabernacle, or curtained tent, with its veil and its hangings; also of the colours of His desert tabernacle—blue, and purple, and scarlet.

Thus far the Psalm describes the manner of this great heaven's message.

Thenceforward, it comes to the matter of it.

Observe, you have the two divisions of the declaration The heavens (compare Psalm viii.) declare the eternal glory of God before men, and the firmament the daily mercy of God towards men. And the eternal glory is in this—that the law of the Lord is perfect, and His testimony sure, and His statutes right.

And the daily mercy in this—that the commandment of the Lord is pure, and His fear is clean, and His judgments true and righteous.

There are three oppositions:—

Between law and commandment.

Between testimony and fear.

Between statute and judgment.

I. Between law and commandment.

The law is fixed and everlasting; uttered once, abiding for ever, as the sun, it may not be moved. It is "perfect, converting the soul:" the whole question about the soul being, whether it has been turned from darkness to light, acknowledged this law or not,—whether it is godly or ungodly? But the commandment is given momentarily to each man, according to the need. It does not convert: it guides. It does not concern the entire purpose of the soul; but it enlightens the eyes, respecting a special act. The law is, "Do this always;" the commandment, "Do *thou* this *now*:" often mysterious enough, and through the cloud; chilling, and with strange rain of tears; yet always pure (the law converting, but the commandment cleansing): a rod not for guiding merely, but for strengthening, and tasting honey with. "Look how mine eyes have been enlightened, because I tasted a little of this honey."

II. Between testimony and fear.

The testimony is everlasting: the true promise of salvation.

Bright as the sun beyond all the earth-cloud, it makes wise the simple; all wisdom being assured in perceiving it and trusting it; all wisdom brought to nothing which does not perceive it.

But the fear of God is taught through special encouragement and special withdrawal of it, according to each man's need—by the earth-cloud—smile and frown alternately: it also, as the commandment, is clean, purging and casting out all other fear, it only remaining for ever.

III. Between statute and judgment.

The statutes are the appointments of the Eternal justice: fixed and bright, and constant as the stars; equal and balanced as their courses. They "are right, rejoicing the heart." But the judgments are special judgments of given acts of men. "True," that is to say, fulfilling the warning or promise given to each man; "righteous altogether," that is, done or executed in truth and righteousness. The statute is right, in appointment. The judgment righteous altogether, in appointment and fulfilment;—yet not always rejoicing the heart.

Then, respecting all these, comes the expression of passionate desire, and of joy; that also divided with respect to each. The glory of God, eternal in the Heavens, is future, "to be *desired* more than gold, than much fine gold"—treasure in the heavens that faileth not. But the present guidance and teaching of God are on earth; they are now possessed, sweeter than all earthly food—"sweeter than honey and the honeycomb. Moreover by them" (the law and the testimony) "is Thy servant warned"—warned of the ways of death and life.

"And in keeping them" (the commandments and the judgments) "there is great reward;" pain now and bitterness of tears, but reward unspeakable.

Thus far the Psalm has been descriptive and interpreting It ends in prayer.

"Who can understand his errors?" (wanderings from the perfect law.) "Cleanse thou me from secret faults; from all that I have done against Thy will, and far from Thy way in the darkness. Keep back Thy servant from presumptuous sins" (sins against the commandment) "against Thy will when it is seen and direct, pleading with heart and conscience. So shall I be undefiled and innocent from the great transgression,—the transgression that crucifies afresh.

"Let the words of my mouth (for I have set them to declare Thy law), and the meditation of my heart (for I have set it to keep Thy commandments), be acceptable in Thy sight, whose glory is my strength, and whose work my redemption; my Strength and my Redeemer."

———o———

SEEKING FOR FACTS.

He who habituates himself, in his daily life, to seek for the stern facts in whatever he hears or sees, will have these facts again brought before him by the involuntary imaginative power in their noblest associations; and he who seeks for frivolities and fallacies, will have frivolities and fallacies again presented to him in his dreams. Thus if, in reading history for the purpose of painting from it, the painter severely seeks for the accurate circumstances of every event; as, for instance, determining the exact spot of ground on which his hero fell, the way he must have been looking at the moment, the height the sun was at (by the hour of the day), and the way in which the light must have fallen upon his face, the actual number and individuality of the persons by him at the moment, and such other veritable details, ascertaining and dwelling upon them without the slightest care for any desira bleness or poetic propriety in them, but for their own truth's sake; then these truths will afterwards rise up and form the body of his imaginative vision, perfected and united as his inspiration may teach. But if, in reading the history, he does not regard these facts, but thinks only how it might all most prettily, and properly, and impressively have happened, then there is nothing but prettiness and propriety to form the body of his future imagination, and his whole ideal becomes false. So, in the higher or expressive part of the work, the whole virtue of it depends on his being able to quit his own personality, and enter successively into the hearts and thoughts of each person; and in all this he is still passive: in gathering the truth he is passive, not determining what the truth to be gathered shall be; and in the after vision he is passive, not determining, but as his dreams will have it, what the truth to be represented shall be; only according to his own nobleness is his power of entering into the hearts of noble persons, and the general character of his dream of them.

———o———

JUSTICE TO THE LIVING.

It would be well for us if we could quit our habit of thinking that what we say of the dead is of more weight than what we say of the living. The dead either know nothing, or know enough to despise both us and our insults, or adulation.

"Well, but," it is answered, "there will always be this weakness in our human nature; we shall for ever, in spite of reason, take pleasure in doing funereal honour to the corpse, and writing sacredness to memory upon marble.' Then, if you are to do this,—if you are to put off your kindness until death,—why not, in God's name, put off also your enmity? and if you choose to write your lingering affections upon stones, wreak also your delayed anger upon clay. This would be just, and, in the last case, little as you think it, generous. The true baseness is in the bitter reverse—the strange iniquity of our folly. Is a man to be praised, honored, pleaded for? It might do harm to praise or plead for him while he lived. Wait till he is dead. Is he to be maligned, dishonored, and discomforted? See that you do it while he is alive. It would be too ungenerous to slander him when he could feel malice no more; too contemptible to try to hurt him when he was past anguish. Make yourselves busy, ye unjust, ye lying, ye hungry for pain! Death is near. This is your hour, and the power of darkness. Wait, ye just, ye merciful, ye faithful in love! Wait but for a little while, for this is not your rest.

———o———

THE DEFENDERS OF THE DEAD.

"Is it not, indeed, ungenerous to speak ill of the dead, since they cannot defend themselves?"

Why should they? If you speak ill of them falsely, it concerns you, not them. Those lies of thine will "hurt a man as thou art," assuredly they will hurt thyself; but that clay, or the delivered soul of it, in no wise. Ajacean shield, sevenfolded, never stayed lance-thrust as that turf will, with daisies pied. What you say of those quiet ones is wholly and utterly the world's affair and yours. The lie will, indeed, cost its proper price, and work its appointed work; you may ruin living myriads by it,—you may stop the progress of centuries by it,—you may have to pay your own soul for it,—but as for ruffling one corner of the folded shroud by it, think it not. The dead have none to defend them! Nay, they have two defenders, strong enough for the need—God, and the worm.

———o———

RIGHT GENERALIZATION.

To see in all mountains nothing but similar heaps of earth, in all rocks, nothing but similar concretions of solid matter; in all trees, nothing but similar accumulations of leaves, is no sign of high feeling or extended thought. The more we know, and the more we feel, the more we separate; we separate to obtain a more perfect unity. Stones, in the thoughts of the peasant, lie as they do on his field, one is like another, and there is no connexion between any of them. The geologist distinguishes, and in distinguishing connects them. Each becomes different from its fellow, but in differing from, assumes a relation to its fellow; they are no more each the repetition of the other,—they are parts of a system, and each implies and is connected with the existence of the rest. That generalization then is right, true, and noble, which is based on the knowledge of the distinctions and observance of the relations of individual kinds. That generalization is wrong, false, and contemptible, which is based on ignorance of the one, and disturbance of the other. It is indeed no generalization, but confusion and chaos; it is the generalization of a defeated army into indistinguishable impotence—the generalization of the elements of a dead carcass into dust.

———o———

THE FORMATIVE PERIOD.

The common plea that anything does to "exercise the mind upon," is an utterly false one. The human soul, in youth, is *not* a machine of which you can polish the cogs with any kelp or brickdust near at hand; and, having got it into working order, and good, empty, and oiled serviceableness, start your immortal locomotive at twenty-five years old or thirty, express from the Strait Gate, on the Narrow Road. The whole period of youth is one essentially of formation, edification, instruction, I use the words with their weight in them; intaking of stores, establishment in vital habits, hopes, and faiths. There is not an hour of it but is trembling with destinies,—not a moment of which, once past, the appointed work can ever be done again, or the neglected blow struck on the cold iron. Take your vase of Venice glass out of the furnace, and strew chaff over it in its transparent heat, and recover *that* to its clearness and rubied glory when the north wind has blown upon it; but do not think to strew chaff over the child fresh from God's presence, and to bring the heavenly colours back to him—at least in this world.

———o———

MAKING A RIGHT CHOICE.

A single knot of quartz occurring in a flake of slate at the crest of the ridge may alter the entire destinies of the mountain form. It may turn the little rivulet of water to the right or left, and that little turn will be to the future direction of the gathering stream what the touch of a finger on the barrel of a rifle would be to the direction of a bullet. Each succeeding year increases the importance of every determined form, and arranges in masses yet more and more harmonious, the promontories shaped by the sweeping of the eternal waterfalls.

The importance of the results thus obtained by the slightest change of direction in the infant streamlets, furnishes an interesting type of the formation of human characters by habit. Every one of those notable ravines and crags is the expression, not of any sudden violence done to the mountain, but of its little *habits*, persisted in continually. It was created with one ruling instinct; but its destiny depended nevertheless, for effective result, on the direction of the small and all but invisible tricklings of water, in which the first shower of rain found its way down its sides. The feeblest, most insensible oozings of the drops of dew among its dust were in reality arbiters of its eternal form; commissioned, with a touch more tender than that of a child's finger,—as silent and slight as the fall of a half-checked tear on a maiden's cheek,—to fix for ever the forms of peak and precipice, and hew those leagues of lifted granite into the shapes that were to divide the earth and its kingdoms. Once the little stone evaded,—once the dim furrow traced,—and the peak was for ever invested with its majesty, the ravine for ever doomed to its degradation. Thenceforward, day by day, the subtle habit gained in power; the evaded stone was left with wider basement; the chosen furrow deepened with swifter-sliding wave; repentance and arrest were alike impossible, and hour after hour saw written in larger and rockier characters upon the sky, the history of the choice that had been directed by a drop of rain, and of the balance that had been turned by a grain of sand.

———o———

GOOD TEACHING.

If we have the power of teaching the right to anybody, we should teach them the right; if we have the power of showing them the best thing, we should show them the best thing; there will always, I fear, be enough want of teaching, and enough bad teaching, to bring out very curious erratical results if we want them. So, if we are to teach at all, let us teach the right thing, and ever the right thing. There are many attractive qualities inconsistent with rightness;—do not let us teach them,—let us be content to waive them. There are attractive qualities in Burns, and attractive qualities in Dickens, which neither of those writers would have possessed if the one had been educated, and the other had been studying higher nature than that of cockney London; but those attractive qualities are not such as we should seek in a school of literature. If we want to teach young men a good manner of writing, we should teach it from Shakspeare,—not from Burns; from Walter Scott,—and not from Dickens.

———o———

SERIOUSNESS AND LEVITY.

There is no essential reason, because we live after the fatal seventeenth century, that we should never again be able to confess interest in sculpture, or see brightness in embroidery; nor, because now we choose to make the night deadly with our pleasures, and the day with our labours, prolonging the dance till dawn, and the toil to twilight, that we should never again learn how rightly to employ the sacred trusts of strength, beauty, and time. Whatever external charm attaches itself to the past, would then be seen in proper subordination to the brightness of present life; and the elements of romance would exist, in the earlier ages, only in the attraction which must generally belong to whatever is unfamiliar; in the reverence which a noble nation always pays to its ancestors; and in the enchanted light which races, like individuals, must perceive in looking back to the days of their childhood.

Again: the peculiar levity with which natural scenery is regarded by a large number of modern minds cannot be considered as entirely characteristic of the age, inasmuch as it never can belong to its greatest intellects. Men of any high mental power must be serious, whether in ancient or modern days: a certain degree of reverence for fair scenery is found in all our great writers without exception,—even the one who has made us laugh oftenest, taking us to the valley of Chamouni, and to the sea beach, there to give peace after suffering, and change revenge into pity. It is only the dull, the uneducated, or the worldly, whom it is painful to meet on the hill sides; and levity, as a ruling character, cannot be ascribed to the whole nation, but only to its holiday-making apprentices, and its House of Commons.

———o———

THE ALPINE PEASANT.

A slight incident which happened to myself, is singularly illustrative of the religious character of the Alpine peasant when under favourable circumstances of teaching. I was coming down one evening from the Rochers de Naye, above Montreux, having been at work among the limestone rocks, where I could get no water, and both weary and thirsty. Coming to a spring at a turn of the path, conducted, as usual, by the herdsmen into a hollowed pine-trunk, I stooped to it and drank deeply: as I raised my head, drawing breath heavily, some one behind me said, "Celui qui boira de cette eau-ci, aura encore soif." I turned, not understanding for the moment what was meant; and saw one of the hill-peasants, probably returning to his châlet from the market-place at Vevay or Villeneuve. As I looked at him with an uncomprehending expression, he went on with the verse:—"Mais celui qui boira de l'eau que je lui donnerai, n'aura jamais soif."

I doubt if this would have been thought of, or said, by even the most intelligent lowland peasant. The thought might have occurred to him, but the frankness of address, and expectation of being at once understood without a word of preparative explanation, as if the language of the Bible were familiar to all men, mark, I think, the mountaineer.

TOWERS OF ROCK.

I can hardly conceive any one standing face to face with one of these towers of central rock, and yet not also asking himself, Is this indeed the actual first work of the Divine Master on which I gaze? Was the great precipice shaped by His finger, as Adam was shaped out of the dust? Were its clefts and ledges carved upon it by its Creator, as the letters were on the Tables of the Law, and was it thus left to bear its eternal testimony to His beneficence among these clouds of heaven? Or is it the descendant of a long race of mountains, existing under appointed laws of birth and endurance, death and decrepitude?

There can be no doubt as to the answer. The rock itself answers audibly by the murmur of some falling stone or rending pinnacle. It is *not* as it was once. Those waste leagues around its feet are loaded with the wrecks of what it was. On these, perhaps, of all mountains, the characters of decay are written most clearly; around these are spread most gloomily the memorials of their pride, and the signs of their humiliation.

"What then were they once?"

The only answer is yet again,—"Behold the cloud."

Their form, as far as human vision can trace it, is one of eternal decay. No retrospection can raise them out of their ruins, or withdraw them beyond the law of their perpetual fate. Existing science may be challenged to form, with the faintest colour of probability, any conception of the original aspect of a crystalline mountain: it cannot be followed in its elevation, nor traced in its connection with its fellows. No eyes ever "saw its substance, yet being imperfect;" its history is a monotone of endurance and destruction: all that we can certainly know of it, is that it was once greater than it is now, and it only gathers vastness, and still gathers, as it fades into the abyss of the unknown.

Yet this one piece of certain evidence ought not to be altogether unpursued; and while with all humility we shrink from endeavouring to theorize respecting processes which are concealed, we ought not to refuse to follow, as far as it will lead us, the course of thought which seems marked out by conspicuous and consistent phenomena.

———o———

LOVE OF CHANGE.

In subjects of the intellect, the chief delight they convey is dependent upon their being newly and vividly comprehended, and as they become subjects of contemplation they lose their value, and become tasteless and unregarded, except as instruments for the reaching of others, only that though they sink down into the shadowy, effectless, heap of things indifferent, which we pack, and crush down, and stand upon, to reach things new, they sparkle afresh at intervals as we stir them by throwing a new stone into the heap, and letting the newly admitted lights play upon them. And both in subjects of the intellect and the senses it is to be remembered, that the love of change is a weakness and imperfection of our nature, and implies in it the state of probation, and that it is to teach us that things about us here are not meant for our continual possession or satisfaction, that ever such passion of change was put in us as that "custom lies upon us with a weight, heavy as frost, and deep almost as life," and only such weak back and baby grasp given to our intellect as that "the best things we do are painful, and the exercise of them grievous, being continued without intermission, so as in those very actions whereby we are especially perfected in this life we are not able to persist." And so it will be found that they are the weakest-minded and the hardest-hearted men that most love variety and change, for the weakest-minded are those who both wonder most at things new, and digest worst things old, in so far that everything they have lies rusty, and loses lustre for want of use; neither do they make any stir among their possessions, nor look over them to see what may be made of them, nor keep any great store, nor are householders with storehouses of things new and old, but they catch at the new-fashioned garments, and let the moth and thief look after the rest; and the hardest-hearted men are those that least feel the endearing and binding power of custom, and hold on by no cords of affection to any shore, but drive with the waves that cast up mire and dirt.

IMAGINATION.

We all have a general and sufficient idea of imagination, and of its work with our hands and in our hearts: we understand it, I suppose, as the imaging or picturing of new things in our thoughts; and we always show an involuntary respect for this power, wherever we can recognise it, acknowledging it to be a greater power than manipulation, or calculation, or observation, or any other human faculty. If we see an old woman spinning at the fireside, and distributing her thread dexterously from the distaff, we respect her for her manipulation—if we ask her how much she expects to make in a year, and she answers quickly, we respect her for her calculation—if she is watching at the same time that none of her grandchildren fall into the fire, we respect her for her observation—yet for all this she may still be a commonplace old woman enough. But if she is all the time telling her grandchildren a fairy tale out of her head, we praise her for her imagination, and say, she must be a rather remarkable old woman.

SIR JOSHUA REYNOLDS.

Do you recollect the evidence respecting the character of this man,—the two points of bright peculiar evidence given by the sayings of the two greatest literary men of his day, Johnson and Goldsmith? Johnson, who, as you know, was always Reynolds' attached friend, had but one complaint to make against him, that he hated nobody:—"Reynolds," he said, "you hate no one living; I like a good hater!" Still more significant is the little touch in Goldsmith's "Retaliation." You recollect how in that poem he describes the vari ous persons who met at one of their dinners at St. James's Coffee-house, each person being described under the name of some appropriate dish. You will often hear the concluding lines about Reynolds quoted—

"He shifted his trumpet," &c. ;—

less often, or at least less attentively, the preceding ones, far more important—

"Still born to improve us in every part—
His pencil our faces, his *manners our heart*;"

and never, the most characteristic touch of all, near the beginning:—

"Our dean shall be venison, just fresh from the plains;
Our Burke shall be tongue, with a garnish of brains;
To make out the dinner, full certain I am,
That Rich is anchovy, and Reynolds is *lamb*."

———o———

THE THINKER AND THE PERCEIVER.

He who, having journeyed all day beside the Leman Lake, asked of his companions, at evening, where it was,* probably was not wanting in sensibility; but he was generally a thinker, not a perceiver. And this instance is only an extreme one of the effect which, in all cases, knowledge, becoming a subject of reflection, produces upon the sensitive faculties. It must be but poor and lifeless knowledge, if it has no tendency to force itself forward, and become ground for reflection, in despite of the succession of external objects. It will

* St. Bernard.

not obey their succession. The first that comes gives it food enough for its day's work; it is its habit, its duty, to cast the rest aside, and fasten upon that. The first thing that a thinking and knowing man sees in the course of the day, he will not easily quit. It is not his way to quit anything without getting to the bottom of it, if possible. But the artist is bound to receive all things on the broad, white, lucid field of his soul, not to grasp at one. For instance, as the knowing and thinking man watches the sunrise, he sees something in the colour of a ray, or the change of a cloud, that is new to him; and this he follows out forthwith into a labyrinth of optical and pneumatical laws, perceiving no more clouds nor rays all the morning. Bnt the painter must catch all the rays, all the colours that come, and see them all truly, all in their real relations and succession; therefore, everything that occupies room in his mind he must cast aside for the time, as completely as may be. The thoughtful man is gone far away to seek; but the perceiving man must sit still, and open his heart to receive. The thoughtful man is knitting and sharpening himself into a two-edged sword, wherewith to pierce. The perceiving man is stretching himself into a four-cornered sheet wherewith to catch. And all the breadth to which he can expand himself, and all the white emptiness into which he can blanch himself, will not give him the intelligence God has to give him.

---o---

A NATION'S PLACE IN HISTORY.

A nation may produce a great effect, and take up a high place in the world's history, by the temporary enthusiasm or fury of its multitudes, without being truly great; or, on the other hand, the discipline of morality and common sense may extend its physical power or exalt its well-being, while yet its creative and imaginative powers are continually diminishing. And again: a people may take so definite a lead over all the rest of the world in one direction, as to obtain a respect which is not justly due to them if judged on universal grounds. Thus the Greeks perfected the sculpture of the human body; threw their literature into a disciplined form, which has given it a peculiar power over certain conditions of modern mind; and were the most carefully educated race that the world has seen; but a few years hence, I believe, we shall no longer think them a greater people than either the Egyptians or Assyrians.

———o———

TREES AND COMMUNITIES.

There is a strange coincidence between trees and communities of men. When the community is small, people fall more easily into their places, and take, each in his place, a firmer standing than can be obtained by the individuals of a great nation. The members of a vast community are separately weaker, as an aspen or elm leaf is thin, tremulous, and directionless, compared with the spear-like setting and firm substance of a rhododendron or laurel leaf. The laurel and rhododendron are like the Athenian or Florentine republics; the aspen like England—strong-trunked enough when put to proof, and very good for making cartwheels of, but shaking pale with epidemic panic at every breeze. Nevertheless, the aspen has the better of the great nation, in that if you take it bough by bough, you shall find the gentle law of respect and room for each other truly observed by the leaves in such broken way as they can manage it; but in the nation you find every one scrambling for his neighbour's place.

THE PURIST AND THE SENSUALIST.

In saying that nearly everything presented to us in nature has mingling in it of good and evil, I do not mean that nature is conceivably improvable, or that anything that God has made could be called evil, if we could see far enough into its uses, but that, with respect to immediate effects or appearances, it may be so, just as the hard rind or bitter kernel of a fruit may be an evil to the eater, though in the one is the protection of the fruit, and in the other its continuance. The Purist, therefore, does not mend nature, but receives from nature and from God that which is good for him; while the Sensualist fills himself "with the husks that the swine did eat."

The three classes may, therefore, be likened to men reaping wheat, of which the Purists take the fine flour, and the Sensualists the chaff and straw, but the Naturalists take all home, and make their cake of the one, and their couch of the other.

For instance. We know more certainly every day that whatever appears to us harmful in the universe has some beneficent or necessary operation; that the storm which destroys a harvest brightens the sunbeams for harvests yet unsown, and that the volcano which buries a city preserves a thousand from destruction. But the evil is not for the time less fearful, because we have learned it to be necessary; and we easily understand the timidity or the tenderness of the spirit which would withdraw itself from the presence of destruction, and create in its imagination a world of which the peace should be unbroken, in which the sky should not darken nor the sea rage, in which the leaf should not change nor the blossom wither. That man is greater, however, who contemplates with an equal mind the alternations of terror and of beauty; who, not rejoicing less beneath the sunny sky, can bear also to watch the bars of twilight narrowing on the horizon; and, not less sensible to the blessing of the peace of nature, can rejoice in the magnificence of the ordinances by which that peace is protected and secured. But separated from both by an immeasurable distance would be the man who delighted in convulsion and disease for their own sake: who found his daily food in the disorder of nature mingled with the suffering of humanity; and watched joyfully at the right hand of the Angel whose appointed work is to destroy as well as to accuse, while the corners of the House of feasting were struck by the wind from the wilderness.

And far more is this true, when the subject of contemplation is humanity itself. The passions of mankind are partly protective, partly beneficent, like the chaff and grain of the corn; but none without their use, none without nobleness when seen in balanced unity with the rest of the spirit which they are charged to defend. The passions of which the end is the continuance of the race; the indignation which is to arm it against injustice, or strengthen it to resist wanton injury; and the fear* which lies at the root of prudence, reverence, and awe, are all honourable and beautiful, so long as man is regarded in his relations to the existing world. The religious Purist, striving to conceive him withdrawn from those relations, effaces from the countenance the traces of all

* Not selfish fear, caused by want of trust in God, or of resolution in the soul.

transitory passion, illumines it with holy hope and love, and seals it with the serenity of heavenly peace; he conceals the forms of the body by the deep-folded garment, or else represents them under severely chastened types, and would rather paint them emaciated by the fast, or pale from the torture, than strengthened by exertion, or flushed by emotion. But the great Naturalist takes the human being in its wholeness, in its mortal as well as its spiritual strength. Capable of sounding and sympathizing with the whole range of its passions, he brings one majestic harmony out of them all; he represents it fearlessly in all its acts and thoughts, in its haste, its anger, its sensuality, and its pride, as well as in its fortitude or faith, but makes it noble in them all; he casts aside the veil from the body, and beholds the mysteries of its form like an angel looking down on an inferior creature; there is nothing which he is reluctant to behold, nothing that he is ashamed to confess; with all that lives, triumphing, falling, or suffering, he claims kindred, either in majesty or in mercy, yet standing, in a sort, afar off, unmoved even in the deepness of his sympathy; for the spirit within him is too thoughtful to be grieved, too brave to be appalled, and too pure to be polluted.

How far beneath these two ranks of men shall we place, in the scale of being, those whose pleasure is only in sin or in suffering; who habitually contemplate humanity in poverty or decrepitude, fury or sensuality; whose works are either temptations to its weakness, or triumphs over its ruin, and recognize no other subjects for thought or admiration than the subtlety of the robber, the rage of the soldier, or the joy of the Sybarite. It seems strange, when thus definitely stated, that such a school should exist. Yet consider a little what gaps and blanks would disfigure our gallery and chamber walls, in places that we have long approached with reverence, if every picture, every statue, were removed from them, of which the subject was either the vice or the misery of mankind, portrayed without any moral purpose: consider the innumerable groups having reference merely to various forms of passion, low or high; drunken revels and brawls among peasants, gambling or fighting scenes among soldiers, amours and intrigues among every class, brutal battle-pieces, banditti subjects, gluts of torture and death in famine, wreck, or slaughter, for the sake merely of the excitement,—that quickening and suppling of the dull spirit that cannot be gained for it but by bathing it in blood, afterward to wither back into stained and stiffened apathy; and then that whole vast false heaven of sensual passion, full of nymphs, satyrs, graces, goddesses, and I know not what, from its high seventh circle in Correggio's Antiope, down to the Grecized ballet-dancers and smirking Cupids of the Parisian upholsterer. Sweep away all this, remorselessly, and see how much art we should have left.

And yet these are only the grossest manifestations of the tendency of the school. There are subtler, yet not less certain, signs of it in the works of men who stand high in the world's list of sacred painters. I doubt not that the reader was surprised when I named Murillo among the men of this third rank. Yet, go into the Dulwich Gallery, and meditate for a little over that much celebrated picture of the two beggar boys, one eating lying on the ground, the other standing beside him. We have among our own painters one who cannot indeed be set beside Murillo as a painter of Madonnas, for he is a pure Naturalist, and, never having seen a Madonna, does not paint any; but who, as a painter of beggar or peasant boys, may be set beside Murillo, or any one else,—W. Hunt. He loves peasant boys, because he finds them more roughly and picturesquely dressed, and more healthily coloured, than others. And he paints all that he sees in them fearlessly; all the health and humour, and freshness, and vitality, together with such awkwardness and stupidity, and what else of negative or positive harm there may be in the creature; but yet so that on the whole we love it, and find it perhaps even beautiful, or if not, at least we see that there is capability of good in it, rather than of evil; and all is lighted up by a sunshine and sweet colour that makes the smock frock as precious as cloth of gold. But look at those two ragged and vicious vagrants that Murillo has gathered out of the street. You smile at first, because they are eating so naturally, and their roguery is so complete. But is there anything else than roguery there, or was it well for the painter to give his time to the painting of those repulsive and wicked children? Do you feel moved with any charity towards children as you look at them? Are we the least more likely to take any interest in ragged schools, or to help the next pauper child that comes in our way, because the painter has shown us a cunning beggar feeding greedily. Mark the choice of the act. He might have shown hunger in other ways, and given interest to even this act of eating, by making the face wasted, or the eye wistful. But he did not care to do this. He delighted merely in the disgusting manner of eating, the food filling the cheek; the boy is not hungry, else he would not turn round to talk and grin as he eats.

But observe another point in the lower figure. It lies so that the sole of the foot is turned towards the spectator; not because it would have lain less easily in another attitude, but that the painter may draw, and exhibit, the grey dust engrained in the foot. Do not call this the painting of nature: it is mere delight in foulness. The lesson, if there be any, in the picture, is not one whit the stronger. We all know that a beggar's bare foot cannot be clean; there is no need to thrust its degradation into the light, as if no human imagination were vigorous enough for its conception.

———o———

THE TYPE OF STRONG AND NOBLE LIFE.

Great Art is nothing else than the type of strong and noble life; for, as the ignoble person, in his dealings with all that occurs in the world about him, first sees nothing clearly,—looks nothing fairly in the face, and then allows himself to be swept away by the trampling torrent, and unescapable force, of the things that he would not foresee, and could not understand: so the noble person, looking the facts of the world full in the face, and fathoming them with deep faculty, then deals with them in unalarmed intelligence and unhurried strength, and becomes, with his human intellect and will, no unconscious nor insignificant agent, in consummating their good, and restraining their evil.

———o———

THE VISIBLE AND THE TANGIBLE.

Of no other source than the tangible and the visible can we, by any effort in our present condition of existence, conceive. For what revelations have been made to humanity inspired, or caught up to heaven of things to the heavenly region belonging, have been either by unspeakable words which it is not lawful for a man to utter, or else by their very nature incommunicable, except in types and shadows; and ineffable by words belonging to earth, foı of things different from the visible, words appropriated to the visible can convey no image. How different from earthly gold that clear pavement of the city might have seemed to the eyes of St. John, we of unreceived sight cannot know; neither of that strange jasper and sardine can we conceive the likeness which he assumed that sat on the throne above the crystal sea; neither what seeming that was of slaying that the Root of David bore in the midst of the elders; neither what change it was upon the form of the fourth of them that walked in the furnace of Dura, that even the wrath of idolatry knew for the likeness of the Son of God.

MODERN GREATNESS.

The simple fact, that we are, in some strange way, different from all the great races that have existed before us, cannot at once be received as the proof of our own greatness; nor can it be granted, without any question, that we have a legitimate subject of complacency in being under the influence of feelings, with which neither Miltiades nor the Black Prince, neither Homer nor Dante, neither Socrates nor St. Francis, could for an instant have sympathized.

Whether, however, this fact be one to excite our pride or not, it is assuredly one to excite our deepest interest. The fact itself is certain. For nearly six thousand years the energies of man have pursued certain beaten paths, manifesting some constancy of feeling throughout all that period, and involving some fellowship at heart, among the various nations who by turns succeeded or surpassed each other in the several aims of art or policy. So that, for these thousands of years, the whole human race might be to some extent described in general terms. Man was a creature separated from all others by his instinctive sense of an Existence superior to his own, invariably manifesting this sense of the being of a God more strongly in proportion to his own perfectness of mind and body; and making enormous and self-denying efforts, in order to obtain some persuasion of the immediate presence or approval of the Divinity.

———o———

SMOKE AND THE WHIRLWIND.

Much of the love of mystery in our romances, our poetry, our art, and, above all, in our metaphysics, must come under that definition so long ago given by the great Greek, "speaking ingeniously concerning smoke." And much of the instinct, which, partially developed in painting, may be now seen throughout every mode of exertion of mind,—the easily encouraged doubt, easily excited curiosity, habitual agitation, and delight in the changing and the marvellous, as opposed to the old quiet serenity of social custom and religious faith, is again deeply defined in those few words, the "dethroning of Jupiter," the "coronation of the whirlwind."

———o———

MODERN ENTANGLEMENT.

The vain and haughty projects of youth for future life; the giddy reveries of insatiable self-exaltation; the discontented dreams of what might have been or should be, instead of the thankful understanding of what is; the casting about for sources of interest in senseless fiction, instead of the real human histories of the people round us; the prolongation from age to age of romantic historical deceptions instead of sifted truth; the pleasures taken in fanciful portraits of rural or romantic life in poetry and on the stage, without the smallest effort to rescue the living rural population of the world from its ignorance or misery; the excitement of the feelings by laboured imagination of spirits, fairies, monsters, and demons, issuing in total blindness of heart and sight to the true presences of beneficent or destructive spiritual powers around us; in fine, the constant abandonment of all the straightforward paths of sense and duty, for fear of losing some of the enticement of ghostly joys, or trampling somewhat "sopra lor vanità, che par persona;" all these various forms of false idealism have so entangled the modern mind, often called, I suppose ironically, practical, that truly I believe there never yet was idolatry of stock or staff so utterly unholy as this our idolatry of shadows; nor can I think that, of those who burnt incense under oaks, and poplars, and elms, because "the shadow thereof was good," it could in any wise be more justly or sternly declared than of us—"The wind hath bound them up in her wings, and they shall be ashamed because of their sacrifices."*

———o———

THE DIVINE GOVERNMENT.

All human government is nothing else than the executive expression of Divine authority. The moment government ceases to be the practical enforcement of Divine law, it is tyranny; and the meaning which I attach to the words, "paternal government," is in more extended terms, simply

* Hosea, chap. iv. 12, 13, and 19.

this—"The executive fulfilment, by formal human methods, of the will of the Father of mankind respecting His children."

---o---

THREE ORDERS OF HUMAN BEINGS.

The apathy which cannot perceive beauty is very different from the stern energy which disdains it; and the coldness of heart which receives no emotion from external nature, is not to be confounded with the wisdom of purpose which represses emotion in action. In the case of most men, it is neither acuteness of the reason, nor breadth of humanity, which shields them from the impressions of natural scenery, but rather low anxieties, vain discontents, and mean pleasures; and for one who is blinded to the works of God by profound abstraction or lofty purpose, tens of thousands have their eyes sealed by vulgar selfishness, and their intelligence crushed by impious care.

Observe, then: we have, among mankind in general, the three orders of being;—the lowest, sordid and selfish, which neither sees nor feels; the second, noble and sympathetic, but which sees and feels without concluding or acting; the third and highest, which loses sight in resolution, and feeling in work.

---o---

NATURAL ADMIRATION.

Examine well the channels of your admiration, and you will find that they are, in verity, as unchangeable as the channels of your heart's blood; that just as by the pressure of a bandage, or by unwholesome and perpetual action of some part of the body, that blood may be wasted or arrested, and in its stagnancy cease to nourish the frame, or in its disturbed flow affect it with incurable disease, so also admiration itself may, by the bandages of fashion, bound close over the eyes and the arteries of the soul, be arrested in its natural pulse and healthy flow; but that wherever the artificial pressure is removed, it will return into that bed which has been traced for it by the finger of God.

———o———

THE REFORMATION.

The strength of the Reformation lay entirely in its being a movement towards purity of practice.

The Catholic priesthood was hostile to it in proportion to the degree in which they had been false to their own principles of moral action, and had become corrupt or worldly in heart.

The Reformers indeed cast out many absurdities, and demonstrated many fallacies, in the teaching of the Roman Catholic Church. But they themselves introduced errors, which rent the ranks, and finally arrested the march of the Reformation, and which paralyze the Protestant Church to this day. Errors of which the fatality was increased by the controversial bent which lost accuracy of meaning in force of declamation, and turned expressions, which ought to be used only in retired depth of thought, into phrases of custom, or watchwords of attack. Owing to which habits of hot, ingenious, and unguarded controversy, the Reformed churches themselves soon forgot the meaning of the word which, of all words, was oftenest in their mouths. They forgot that πίστις is a derivative of πείθομαι, not of πιστεύω, and that "fides," closely connected with "fio" on one side, and with "confido" on the other, is but distinctly related to "credo."*

By whatever means, however, the reader may himself be disposed to admit, the Reformation *was* arrested; and got itself shut up into chancels of cathedrals in England (even those, generally too large for it), and into conventicles everywhere else. Then rising between the infancy of Reformation, and the palsy of Catholicism;—between a new shell of half-built religion on one side, daubed with untempered mortar, and a falling ruin of outworn religion on the other, lizard-crannied and ivy-grown;—rose, on its independent foundation, the faithless and materialized mind of modern Europe—ending in the rationalism of Germany, the polite formalism of England, the careless blasphemy of France, and the helpless sensualities of Italy; in the midst of which, steadily advancing science, and the charities of more and more widely extended peace, are preparing the way for a Christian church, which shall depend neither on ignorance for its continuance, nor on controversy for its progress; but shall reign at once in light and love.

* None of our present forms of opinion are more curious than those which have developed themselves from this verbal carelessness. It never seems to strike any of our religious teachers, that if a child has a father living, it either *knows* it has a father, or does not: it does not "believe" it has a father. We should be surprised to see an intelligent child standing at its garden gate, crying out to the passers-by: "I believe in my father, because he built this house;" as logical people proclaim that they believe in God, because He must have made the world.

———o———

QUIETNESS.

The refusal or reserve of a mighty painter cannot be imitated; it is only by reaching the same intellectual strength that you will be able to give an equal dignity to your self-denial. No one can tell you beforehand what to accept, or what to ignore; only remember always, in painting as in eloquence, the greater your strength, the quieter will be your manner, and the fewer your words; and in painting, as in all the arts and acts of life, the secret of high success will be found, not in a fretful and various excellence, but in a quiet singleness of justly chosen aim.

———o———

THE TRUE GENTLEMAN.

Two great errors, coloring, or rather discoloring, severally, the minds of the higher and lower classes, have sown wide dissension, and wider misfortune, through the society of modern days. These errors are in our modes of interpreting the word "gentleman."

Its primal, literal, and perpetual meaning is "a man of pure race;" well bred, in the sense that a horse or dog is well bred.

The so-called higher classes, being generally of purer race than the lower, have retained the true idea, and the convictions associated with it; but are afraid to speak it out, and equivocate about it in public; this equivocation mainly proceeding from their desire to connect another meaning with it, and a false one;—that of "a man living in idleness on other people's labor:"—with which idea the term has nothing whatever to do.

The lower classes, denying vigorously, and with reason, the notion that a gentleman means an idler, and rightly feeling that the more any one works, the more of a gentleman he becomes, and is likely to become,—have nevertheless got little of the good they otherwise might, from the truth, because, with it, they wanted to hold a falsehood,—namely, that race was of no consequence. It being precisely of as much consequence in man as it is in any other animal.

The nation cannot truly prosper till both these errors are finally got quit of. Gentlemen have to learn that it is no part of their duty or privilege to live on other people's toil. They have to learn that there is no degradation in the hardest manual, or the humblest servile, labor, when it is honest. But that there *is* degradation, and that deep, in extravagance, in bribery, in indolence, in pride, in taking places they are not fit for, or in coining places for which there is no need. It does not disgrace a gentleman to become an errand boy, or a day laborer; but it disgraces him much to become a knave, or a thief. And knavery is not the less knavery because it involves large interests, nor theft the less theft because it is countenanced by usage, or accompanied by failure in undertaken duty. It is an incomparably less guilty form of robbery to cut a purse out of a man's pocket, than to take it out of his hand on the understanding that you are to steer his ship up channel, when you do not know the soundings.

On the other hand, the lower orders, and all orders, have to learn that every vicious habit and chronic disease communicates itself by descent; and that by purity of birth the entire system of the human body and soul may be gradually elevated, or by recklessness of birth, degraded; until there shall be as much difference between the well-bred and ill-bred human creature (whatever pains be taken with their education) as between a wolf-hound and the vilest mongrel cur. And the knowledge of this great fact ought to regulate the education of our youth, and the entire conduct of the nation.*

Gentlemanliness, however, in ordinary parlance, must be taken to signify those qualities which are usually the evidence of high breeding, and which, so far as they can be acquired, it should be every man's effort to acquire; or, if he has them by nature, to preserve and exalt. Vulgarity, on the other hand, will signify qualities usually characteristic of ill-breeding, which, according to his power, it becomes every person's duty to subdue. We have briefly to note what these are.

A gentleman's first characteristic is that fineness of structure in the body, which renders it capable of the most delicate sensation; and of structure in the mind which renders it

* We ought always in pure English to use the term "good breeding" literally; and to say "good nurture" for what we usually mean by good breeding. Given the race and make of the animal, you may turn it to good or bad account; you may spoil your good dog or colt, and make him as vicious as you choose, or break his back at once by ill-usage; and you may, on the other hand, make something serviceable and respectable out of your poor cur or colt if you educate them carefully; but ill-bred they will both of them be to their lives' end; and the best you will ever be able to say of them is, that they are useful, and decently behaved ill-bred creatures. An error, which is associated with the truth, and which makes it always look weak and disputable, is the confusion of race with name; and the supposition that the blood of a family must still be good, if its genealogy be unbroken and its name not lost, though sire and son have been indulging age after age in habits involving perpetual degeneracy of race. Of course it is equally an error to suppose that, because a man's name is common, his blood must be base; since his family may have been ennobling it by pureness of moral habit for many generations, and yet may not have got any title, or other sign of nobleness attached to their names. Nevertheless, the probability is always in favour of the race which has had acknowledged supremacy, and in which every motive leads to the endeavour to preserve their true nobility.

capable of the most delicate sympathies—one may say, sim ply, "fineness of nature." This is, of course, compatible with heroic bodily strength and mental firmness; in fact heroic strength is not conceivable without such delicacy. Elephan tine strength may drive its way through a forest and feel nc touch of the boughs; but the white skin of Homer's Atrides would have felt a bent. rose-leaf, yet subdue its feelings in glow of battle, and behave itself like iron. I do not mean to call an elephant a vulgar animal; but if you think about him carefully, you will find that his non-vulgarity consists in such gentleness as is possible to elephantine nature; not in his insensitive hide, nor in his clumsy foot; but in the way he will lift his foot if a child lies in his way; and in his sensitive trunk, and still more sensitive mind, and capability of pique on points of honour.

And, though rightness of moral conduct is ultimately the great purifier of race, the sign of nobleness is not in this rightness of moral conduct, but in sensitiveness. When the make of the creature is fine, its temptations are strong, as well as its perceptions; it is liable to all kinds of impressions from without in their most violent form; liable therefore to be abused and hurt by all kinds of rough things which would do a coarser creature little harm, and thus to fall into frightful wrong if its fate will have it so. Thus David, coming of gentlest as well as royalest race, of Ruth as well as of Judah, is sensitiveness through all flesh and spirit; not that his compassion will restrain him from murder when his terror urges him to it; nay, he is driven to the murder all the more by his sensitiveness to the shame which otherwise threatens him. But when his own story is told him under a disguise, though only a lamb is now concerned, his passion about it leaves him no time for thought. "The man shall die"—note the reason —"because he had no pity." He is so eager and indignant that it never occurs to him as strange that Nathan hides the name. This is true gentleman. A vulgar man would assuredly have been cautious, and asked "who it was?"

Hence it will follow that one of the probable signs of high-breeding in men generally, will be their kindness and mercifulness; these always indicating more or less fineness of make in the mind; and miserliness and cruelty the contrary; hence that of Isaiah: "The vile person shall no more be called liberal, nor the churl said to be bountiful." But a thousand things may prevent this kindness from displaying or continuing itself; the mind of the man may be warped so as to bear mainly on his own interests, and then all his sensibilities will take the form of pride, or fastidiousness, or revengefulness; and other wicked, but not ungentlemanly tempers; or, farther, they may run into utter sensuality and covetousness, if he is bent on pleasure, accompanied with quite infinite cruelty when the pride is wounded or the passions thwarted;—until your gentleman becomes Ezzelin, and your lady, the deadly Lucrece; yet still gentleman and lady, quite incapable of making anything else of themselves, being so born.

A truer sign of breeding than mere kindness is therefore sympathy; a vulgar man may often be kind in a hard way, on principle, and because he thinks he ought to be; whereas, a highly-bred man, even when cruel, will be cruel in a softer way, understanding and feeling what he inflicts, and pitying his victim. Only we must carefully remember that the quantity of sympathy a gentleman feels can never be judged of by its outward expression, for another of his chief characteristics is apparent reserve. I say "apparent" reserve; for the sympathy is real, but the reserve not: a perfect gentleman is never reserved, but sweetly and entirely open, so far as it is good for others, or possible, that he should be. In a great many respects it is impossible that he should be open except to men of his own kind. To them, he can open himself, by a word, or syllable, or a glance; but to men not of his kind he cannot open himself, though he tried it through an eternity of clear grammatical speech. By the very acuteness of his sympathy he knows how much of himself he can give to anybody; and he gives that much frankly;—would always be glad to give more if he could, but is obliged, nevertheless, in his general intercourse with the world, to be a somewhat silent person; silence is to most people, he finds, less reserve than speech. Whatever he said, a vulgar man would misinterpret: no words that he could use would bear the same sense to the vulgar man that they do to him; if he used any, the vulgar man would go away saying, "He had said so and so, and meant so and so" (something assuredly he never meant); but he keeps silence, and the vulgar man goes away saying, "He didn't know what to make of him." Which is precisely the fact, and the only fact which he is anywise able to announce to the vulgar man concerning himself.

There is yet another quite as efficient cause of the apparent reserve of a gentleman. His sensibility being constant and intelligent, it will be seldom that a feeling touches him, however acutely, but it has touched him in the same way often before, and in some sort is touching him always. It is not that he feels little, but that he feels habitually; a vulgar man having some heart at the bottom of him, if you can by talk or by sight fairly force the pathos of anything down to his heart, will be excited about it and demonstrative; the sensation of pity being strange to him, and wonderful. But your gentleman has walked in pity all day long; the tears have never been out of his eyes; you thought the eyes were bright only; but they were wet. You tell him a sorrowful story, and his countenance does not change; the eyes can but be wet still: he does not speak neither, there being, in fact, nothing to be said, only something to be done; some vulgar person, beside you both, goes away saying, "How hard he is!" Next day he hears that the hard person has put good end to the sorrow he said nothing about;—and then he changes his wonder, and exclaims, "How reserved he is!"

Self-command is often thought a characteristic of high breeding: and to a certain extent it is so, at least it is one of the means of forming and strengthening character; but it is rather a way of imitating a gentleman than a characteristic of him; a true gentleman has no need of self-command; he simply feels rightly on all occasions: and desiring to express only so much of his feeling as it is right to express, does not need to command himself. Hence perfect ease is indeed characteristic of him; but perfect ease is inconsistent with self-restraint. Nevertheless gentlemen, so far as they fail of their own ideal, need to command themselves, and do so; while, on the contrary, to feel unwisely, and to be unable to restrain the expression of the unwise feeling, is vulgarity; and yet even then, the vulgarity, at its root, is not in the mistimed expression, but in the unseemly feeling; and when we find fault with a vulgar person for "exposing himself," it is not his openness, but clumsiness; and yet more the want of sensibility to his own failure, which we blame; so that still the vulgarity resolves itself into want of sensibility. Also, it is to be noted that great powers of self-restraint may be attained by very vulgar persons, when it suits their purposes.

Closely, but strangely, connected with this openness is that form of truthfulness which is opposed to cunning, yet not opposed to falsity absolute. And herein is a distinction of great importance.

Cunning signifies especially a habit or gift of over-reaching, accompanied with enjoyment and a sense of superiority. It is associated with small and dull conceit, and with an absolute want of sympathy or affection. Its essential connection with vulgarity may be at once exemplified by the expression of the butcher's dog in Landseer's "Low Life." Cruikshank's "Noah Claypole," in the illustrations to Oliver Twist, in the interview with the Jew, is, however, still more characteristic. It is the intensest rendering of vulgarity absolute and utter with which I am acquainted.*

The truthfulness which is opposed to cunning ought, perhaps, rather to be called the desire of truthfulness; it comes more in unwillingness to deceive than in not deceiving,—and unwillingness implying sympathy with and respect for the person deceived; and a fond observance of truth up to the possible point, as in a good soldier's mode of retaining his honour through a *ruse-de-guerre*. A cunning person seeks for opportunities to deceive; a gentleman shuns them. A cunning person triumphs in deceiving; a gentleman is humiliated by the success, or at least by so much of the success as is dependent merely on the falsehood, and not on his intellectual superiority.

The absolute disdain of all lying belongs rather to Christian chivalry than to mere high breeding; as connected merely with this latter, and with general resolution and courage, the exact relations of truthfulness may be best studied in the well-trained Greek mind. The Greeks believed that mercy and truth were co-relative virtues—cruelty and falsehood, co-relative vices. But they did not call necessary severity, cruelty; nor necessary deception, falsehood. It was

* Among the reckless losses of the right service of intellectual power with which this century must be charged, very few are, to my mind, more to be regretted than that which is involved in its having turned to no higher purpose than the illustration of the career of Jack Sheppard, and of the Irish Rebellion, the great, grave (I use the words deliberately and with large meaning), and singular genius of Cruikshank.

needful sometimes to slay men, and sometimes to deceive them. When this had to be done, it should be done well and thoroughly; so that to direct a spear well to its mark, or a lie well to its end, was equally the accomplishment of a perfect gentleman. Hence, in the pretty diamond-cut-diamond scene between Pallas and Ulysses, when she receives him on the coast of Ithaca, the goddess laughs delightedly at her hero's good lying, and gives him her hand upon it; she feels herself then in her woman's form, as just a little more than his match. "Subtle would he be, and stealthy, who should go beyond thee in deceit, even were he a god, thou many-witted! What! here in thine own land, too, wilt thou not cease from cheating? Knowest thou not me, Pallas Athena, maid of Jove, who am with thee in all thy labours, and gave thee favour with the Phæacians, and keep thee, and have come now to weave cunning with thee?" But how completely this kind of cunning was looked upon as a part of a man's power, and not as a diminution of faithfulness, is perhaps best shown by the single line of praise in which the high qualities of his servant are summed up by Chremulus in the Plutus—"Of all my house servants, I hold you to be the faithfullest, and the greatest cheat (or thief)."

Thus, the primal difference between honourable and base lying in the Greek mind lay in honourable purpose. A man who used his strength wantonly to hurt others was a monster; so, also, a man who used his cunning wantonly to hurt others. Strength and cunning were to be used only in self-defence, or to save the weak, and then were alike admirable. This was their first idea. Then the second, and perhaps the more essential difference between noble and ignoble lying in the Greek mind, was that the honourable lie—or, if we may use the strange, yet just, expression, the true lie—knew and confessed itself for such—was ready to take the full responsi bility of what it did. As the sword answered for its blow so the lie for its snare. But what the Greeks hated with all their heart was the false lie; the lie that did not know itself, feared to confess itself, which slunk to its aim under a cloak of truth, and sought to do liars' work, and yet not take liars' pay, excusing itself to the conscience by quibble and quirk. Hence the great expression of Jesuit principle by Euripides, "The tongue has sworn, but not the heart," was a subject of execration throughout Greece, and the satirists exhausted their arrows on it—no audience was ever tired hearing (τὸ Εὐριπίδειον ἐκεῖνο) "that Euripidian thing" brought to shame.

And this is especially to be insisted on in the early education of young people. It should be pointed out to them with continual earnestness that the essence of lying is in deception, not in words; a lie may be told by silence, by equivocation, by the accent on a syllable, by a glance of the eye attaching a peculiar significance to a sentence; and all these kinds of lies are worse and baser by many degrees than a lie plainly worded; so that no form of blinded conscience is so far sunk as that which comforts itself for having deceived, because the deception was by gesture or silence, instead of utterance, and, finally, according to Tennyson's deep and trenchant line, "A lie which is half a truth is ever the worst of lies."

Although, however, ungenerous cunning is usually so distinct an outward manifestation of vulgarity, that I name it separately from insensibility, it is in truth only an effect of insensibility, producing want of affection to others, and blindness to the beauty of truth. The degree in which political subtlety in men such as Richelieu, Machiavel, or Metternich, will efface the gentleman, depends on the selfishness of political purpose to which the cunning is directed, and on the base delight taken in its use. The command, "Be ye wise as serpents, harmless as doves," is the ultimate expression of this principle, misunderstood usually because the word "wise" is referred to the intellectual power instead of the subtlety of the serpent. The serpent has very little intellectual power but according to that which it has, it is yet, as of old, the subtlest of the beasts of the field.

Another great sign of vulgarity is also, when traced to its root, another phase of insensibility, namely, the undue regard to appearances and manners, as in the households of vulgar persons, of all stations, and the assumption of behaviour, language, or dress unsuited to them, by persons in inferior stations of life. I say "undue" regard to appearances, because in the undueness consists, of course, the vulgarity. It is due and wise in some sort to care for appearances, in another sort undue and unwise. Wherein lies the difference?

At first one is apt to answer quickly: the vulgarity is simply in pretending to be what you are not. But that answer will not stand. A queen may dress like a waiting-maid,—perhaps succeed, if she chooses, in passing for one; but she will not, therefore, be vulgar; nay, a waiting-maid may dress like a queen, and pretend to be one, and yet need not be vulgar, unless there is inherent vulgarity in her. In Scribe's very absurd but very amusing *Reine d'un jour*, a milliner's girl sustains the part of a queen for a day. She several times amazes and disgusts her courtiers by her straightforwardness; and once or twice very nearly betrays herself to her maids of honour by an unqueenly knowledge of sewing; but she is not in the least vulgar, for she is sensitive, simple, and generous, and a queen could be no more.

Is the vulgarity, then, only in trying to play a part you cannot play, so as to be continually detected? No; a bad amateur actor may be continually detected in his part, but yet continually detected to be a gentleman: a vulgar regard to appearances has nothing in it necessarily of hypocrisy. You shall know a man not to be a gentleman by the perfect and neat pronunciation of his words: but he does not pretend to pronounce accurately; he *does* pronounce accurately, the vulgarity is in the real (not assumed) scrupulousness.

It will be found on farther thought, that a vulgar regard for appearances is, primarily, a selfish one, resulting, not out of a wish to give pleasure (as a wife's wish to make herself beautiful for her husband), but out of an endeavour to mortify others, or attract for pride's sake;—the common "keeping up appearances" of society, being a mere selfish struggle of the vain with the vain. But the deepest stain of the vulgarity depends on this being done, not selfishly only, but stupidly, without understanding the impression which is really produced, nor the relations of importance between oneself and others, so as to suppose that their attention is fixed upon us, when we are in reality cyphers in their eyes—all which comes of insensibility. Hence pride simple is not vulgar (the looking down on others because of their true inferiority to us), nor vanity simple (the desire of praise), but conceit simple (the attribution to ourselves of qualities we have not), is always so. In cases of over-studied pronunciation, &c., there is insensibility, first, in the person's thinking more of himself than of what he is saying; and, secondly, in his not having musical fineness of ear enough to feel that his talking is uneasy and strained.

Finally, vulgarity is indicated by coarseness of language or manners, only so far as this coarseness has been contracted under circumstances not necessarily producing it. The illiterateness of a Spanish or Calabrian peasant is not vulgar, because they had never an opportunity of acquiring letters: but the illiterateness of an English school-boy is. So again, provincial dialect is not vulgar; but cockney dialect, the corruption, by blunted sense, of a finer language continually heard, is so in a deep degree; and again, of this corrupted dialect, that is the worst which consists, not in the direct or expressive alteration of the form of a word, but in an unmusical destruction of it by dead utterance and bad or swollen formation of lip. There is no vulgarity in—

> "Blythe, blythe, blythe was she,
> Blythe was she, but and ben,
> And weel she liked a Hawick gill,
> And leugh to see a tappit hen;"

but much in Mrs. Gamp's inarticulate "bottle on the chumley-piece, and let me put my lips to it when I am so disposed."

So also of personal defects, those only are vulgar which imply insensibility or dissipation.

There is no vulgarity in the emaciation of Don Quixote, the deformity of the Black Dwarf, or the corpulence of Falstaff; but much in the same personal characters as they are seen in Uriah Heep, Quilp, and Chadband.

Disorder in a drawing-room is vulgar; in an antiquary's study, not; the black battle-stain on a soldier's face is not vulgar, but the dirty face of a housemaid is.

And lastly, courage, so far as it is a sign of race, is peculiarly the mark of a gentleman or a lady: but it becomes vulgar if rude or insensitive, while timidity is not vulgar, if it be a characteristic of race or fineness of make. A fawn is not vulgar in being timid, nor a crocodile "gentle" because courageous.

———o———

VIRTUES SQUARED AND COUNTED.

It was not possible to measure the waves of the water of life, but it was perfectly possible to measure the bricks of the Tower of Babel; and gradually, as the thoughts of men were withdrawn from their Redeemer, and fixed upon themselves, the virtues began to be squared, and counted, and classified, and put into separate heaps of firsts and seconds; some things being virtuous cardinally, and other things virtuous only north-north-west. It is very curious to put in close juxtaposition the words of the Apostles and of some of the writers of the fifteenth century touching sanctification. For instance, hear first St. Paul to the Thessalonians: "The very God of peace sanctify you wholly: and I pray God your whole spirit and soul and body be preserved blameless unto the coming of our Lord Jesus Christ. Faithful is he that calleth you, who also will do it." And then the following part of a prayer which I translate from a MS. of the fifteenth century: "May He (the Holy Spirit) govern the five Senses of my body; may He cause me to embrace the Seven Works of Mercy, and firmly to believe and observe the Twelve Articles of the Faith and the Ten Commandments of the Law, and defend me from the Seven Mortal Sins, even to the end."

This tendency, as it affected Christian ethics, was confirmed by the Renaissance enthusiasm for the works of Aristotle and Cicero, from whom the code of the fifteenth century virtues was borrowed, and whose authority was then infinitely more revered by all the Doctors of the Church than that either of St. Paul or St. Peter.

Although, however, this change in the tone of the Christian mind was most distinctly manifested when the revival of literature rendered the works of the heathen philosophers the leading study of all the greatest scholars of the period, it had been, as I said before, taking place gradually from the earliest ages. It is, as far as I know, that root of the Renaissance poison-tree, which, of all others, is deepest struck; showing itself in various measures through the writings of all the Fathers, of course exactly in proportion to the respect which they paid to classical authors, especially to Plato, Aristotle, and Cicero. The mode in which the pestilent study of that literature affected them may be well illustrated by the examination of a single passage from the works of one of the best of them, St. Ambrose, and of the mode in which that passage was then amplified and formulized by later writers.

Plato, indeed, studied alone, would have done no one any harm. He is profoundly spiritual and capacious in all his views, and embraces the small systems of Aristotle and Cicero, as the solar system does the Earth. He seems to me especially remarkable for the sense of the great Christian virtue of Holiness, or sanctification; and for the sense of the presence of the Deity in all things, great or small, which always runs in a solemn undercurrent beneath his exquisite playfulness and irony; while all the merely moral virtues may be found in his writings defined in the most noble manner, as a great painter defines his figures, *without outlines.* But the imperfect scholarship of later ages seems to have gone to Plato, only to find in him the system of Cicero; which indeed was very definitely expressed by him. For it having been quickly felt by all men who strove, unhelped by Christian faith, to enter at the strait gate into the paths of virtue, that there were four characters of mind which were protective or preservative of all that was best in man, namely, Prudence, Justice, Courage, and Temperance,* these were afterwards

* This arrangement of the cardinal virtues is said to have been first made

with most illogical inaccuracy, called cardinal *virtues*, Prudence being evidently no virtue, but an intellectual gift: but this inaccuracy arose partly from the ambiguous sense of the Latin word "virtutes," which sometimes, in mediæval language, signifies virtues, sometimes powers (being occasionally used in the Vulgate for the word "hosts," as in Psalm ciii. 21, cxlviii. 2, etc., while "fortitudines" and "exercitus" are used for the same word in other places), so that Prudence might properly be styled a power, though not properly a virtue; and partly from the confusion of Prudence with Heavenly Wisdom. The real rank of these four virtues, if so they are to be called, is however properly expressed by the term "cardinal." They are virtues of the compass, those by which all others are directed and strengthened; they are not the greatest virtues, but the restraining or modifying virtues, thus Prudence restrains zeal, Justice restrains mercy, Fortitude and Temperance guide the entire system of the passions; and, thus understood, these virtues properly assumed their peculiar leading or guiding position in the system of Christian ethics. But in Pagan ethics, they were not only guiding, but comprehensive. They meant a great deal more on the lips of the ancients, than they now express to the Christian mind. Cicero's Justice includes charity, beneficence, and benignity, truth, and faith in the sense of trustworthiness. His Fortitude includes courage, self-command, the scorn of fortune and of all temporary felicities. His Temperance includes courtesy and modesty. So also, in Plato, these four virtues constitute the sum of education. I do not remember any more simple or perfect expression of the idea, than in the account given by Socrates, in the "Alcibiades I.," of the education of the

by Archytas. See D'Ancarville's illustration of the three figures of Prudence, Fortitude, and Charity, in Selvatico's "Cappellina degli Scrovegni," Padua, 1836.

Persian kings, for whom, in their youth, there are chosen, he says, four tutors from among the Persian nobles; namely, the Wisest, the most Just, the most Temperate, and the most Brave of them. Then each has a distinct duty: "the Wisest teaches the young king the worship of the gods, and the duties of a king (something more here, observe, than our 'Prudence!'); the most Just teaches him to speak all truth, and to act out all truth, through the whole course of his life; the most Temperate teaches him to allow no pleasure to have the mastery of him, so that he may be truly free, and indeed a king; and the most Brave makes him fearless of all things, showing him that the moment he fears anything, he becomes a slave."

All this is exceedingly beautiful, so far as it reaches; but the Christian divines were grievously led astray by their endeavours to reconcile this system with the nobler law of love. At first, as in the passage I am just going to quote from St. Ambrose, they tried to graft the Christian system on the four branches of the Pagan one; but finding that the tree would not grow, they planted the Pagan and Christian branches side by side; adding, to the four cardinal virtues, the three called by the schoolmen theological, namely, Faith, Hope, and Charity: the one series considered as attainable by the Heathen, but the other by the Christian only. Thus Virgil to Sordello:

"Loco e laggiù, non tristo da martiri
Ma di tenebre solo, ove i lamenti
Non suonan come guai, ma son sospiri:

. . . . .

Quivi sto io, con quei che le tre sante
Virtù non si vestiro, e senza vizio
Conobber l' altre, e seguir, tutte quante."

. . . . . "There I with those abide
Who the Three Holy Virtues put not on,
But understood the rest, and without blame
Followed them all."

CARY.

This arrangement of the virtues was, however, productive of infinite confusion and error: in the first place, because Faith is classed with its own fruits,—the gift of God, which is the root of the virtues, classed simply as one of them; in the second, because the words used by the ancients to express the several virtues had always a different meaning from the same expressions in the Bible, sometimes a more extended, sometimes a more limited one. Imagine, for instance, the confusion which must have been introduced into the ideas of a student who read St. Paul and Aristotle alternately; considering that the word which the Greek writer uses for Justice, means, with St. Paul, Righteousness. And lastly, it is impossible to overrate the mischief produced in former days, as well as in our own, by the mere habit of reading Aristotle, whose system is so false, so forced, and so confused, that the study of it at our universities is quite enough to occasion the utter want of accurate habits of thought which so often disgraces men otherwise well-educated. In a word, Aristotle mistakes the Prudence or Temperance which must regulate the operation of the virtues, for the essence of the virtues themselves; and, striving to show that all virtues are means between two opposite vices, torments his wit to discover and distinguish as many pairs of vices as are necessary to the completion of his system, not disdaining to employ sophistry where invention fails him.

And, indeed, the study of classical literature, in general, not only fostered in the Christian writers the unfortunate love of systematizing, which gradually degenerated into every spe cies of contemptible formulism, but it accustomed them to work out their systems by the help of any logical quibble, or verbal subtlety, which could be made available for their purpose, and this not with any dishonest intention, but in a sincere desire to arrange their ideas in systematical groups, while yet their powers of thought were not accurate enough, nor their common sense stern enough, to detect the fallacy, or disdain the finesse, by which these arrangements were frequently accomplished.

Thus St. Ambrose, in his commentary on Luke vi. 20, is resolved to transform the four Beatitudes there described into rewards of the four cardinal Virtues, and sets himself thus ingeniously to the task:

"'Blessed be ye poor.' Here you have Temperance. 'Blessed are ye that hunger now.' He who hungers, pities those who are an-hungered; in pitying, he gives to them, and in giving he becomes just (largiendo fit justus). 'Blessed are ye that weep now, for ye shall laugh.' Here you have Prudence, whose part it is to weep, so far as present things are concerned, and to seek things which are eternal. 'Blessed are ye when men shall hate you.' Here you have Fortitude."

As a preparation for this profitable exercise of wit, we have also a reconciliation of the Beatitudes as stated by St. Matthew, with those of St. Luke, on the ground that "in those eight are these four, and in these four are those eight;" with sundry remarks on the mystical value of the number eight, with which I need not trouble the reader. With St. Ambrose, however, this puerile systematization is quite subordinate to a very forcible and truthful exposition of the real nature of the Christian life. But the classification he employs furnishes ground for farther subtleties to future divines; and in a MS. of the thirteenth century I find some expressions in this commentary on St. Luke, and in the treatise on the duties of bishops, amplified into a treatise on the "Steps of the Virtues: by which every one who perseveres may, by a straight path, attain to the heavenly country of the Angels." ("Liber de Gradibus Virtutum: quibus ad patriam angelorum supernam itinere recto ascenditur ab omni perseverante.") These Steps are thirty in number (one expressly for each day of the month), and the curious mode of their association renders the list well worth quoting:—

Primus gradus est		Fides Recta.	Unerring faith.
Secundus	"	Spes firma.	Firm hope.
Tertius	"	Caritas perfecta.	Perfect charity.
4.	"	Patientia vera.	True patience.
5.	"	Humilitas sancta.	Holy humility.
6.	"	Mansuetudo.	Meekness.
7.	"	Intelligentia.	Understanding.
8.	"	Compunctio cordis.	Contrition of heart.
9.	"	Oratio.	Prayer.
10.	"	Confessio pura.	Pure confession.
11.	"	Penitentia digna.	Fitting penance.*
12.	"	Abstinentia.	Abstinence (fasting).
13.	"	Timor Dei.	Fear of God.
14.	"	Virginitas.	Virginity.
15.	"	Justicia.	Justice.
16.	"	Misericordia.	Mercy.
17.	"	Elemosina.	Almsgiving.
18.	"	Hospitalitas.	Hospitality.
19.	"	Honor parentum.	Honouring of parents.
20.	"	Silencium.	Silence.
21.	"	Consilium bonum.	Good counsel.
22.	"	Judicium rectum.	Right judgment.
23.	"	Exemplum bonum.	Good example.

* Or Penitence: but I rather think this is understood only in Compunctio cordis.

24.	gradus est	Visitatio infirmorum.	Visitation of the sick.
25.	"	Frequentatio sanctorum.	Companying with saints.
26.	"	Oblatio justa.	Just oblations.
27.	"	Decimas Deo solvere.	Paying tithes to God.
28.	"	Sap.entia.	Wisdom.
29.	"	Voluntas bona.	Goodwill.
30.	"	Perseverantia.	Perseverance.

The reader will note that the general idea of Christian virtue embodied in this list is true, exalted, and beautiful; the points of weakness being the confusion of duties with virtues, and the vain endeavour to enumerate the various offices of charity as so many separate virtues; more frequently arranged as seven distinct works of mercy. This general tendency to a morbid accuracy of classification was associated, in later times, with another very important element of the Renaissance mind, the love of personification; which appears to have reached its greatest vigour in the course of the sixteenth century, and is expressed to all future ages, in a consummate manner, in the poem of Spenser. It is to be noted that personification is, in some sort, the reverse of symbolism, and is far less noble. Symbolism is the setting forth of a great truth by an imperfect and inferior sign (as, for instance, of the hope of the resurrection by the form of the phœnix); and it is almost always employed by men in their most serious moods of faith, rarely in recreation. Men who use symbolism forcibly are almost always true believers in what they symbolize. But Personification is the bestowing of a human or living form upon an abstract idea: it is, in most cases, a mere recreation of the fancy, and is apt to disturb the belief in the reality of the thing personified. Thus symbolism constituted the entire system of the Mosaic dispensation: it occurs in every word of Christ's teaching; it attaches perpetual mystery to the last and most solemn act of His life. But I do not recollect a single instance of personification in any of his words. And as we watch, thenceforward, the history of the Church, we shall find the declension of its faith exactly marked by the abandonment of symbolism,* and the profuse employment of personification,—even to such an extent that the virtues came, at last, to be confused with the saints; and we find in the later Litanies, St. Faith, St. Hope, St. Charity, and St. Chastity, invoked immediately after St. Clara and St. Bridget.

Nevertheless, in the hands of its early and earnest masters, in whom fancy could not overthrow the foundations of faith, personification is often thoroughly noble and lovely; the earlier conditions of it being just as much more spiritual and vital than the later ones, as the still earlier symbolism was more spiritual than they.

———o———

THE CHRISTIAN THEORY OF BEAUTY.

As it is necessary to the existence of an idea of beauty, that the sensual pleasure which may be its basis, should be accompanied first with joy, then with love of the object, then with the perception of kindness in a superior Intelligence, finally with thankfulness and veneration towards that Intelligence itself, and as no idea can be at all considered as in any way an idea of beauty, until it be made up of these emotions, any more than we can be said to have an idea of a letter of

* The transformation of a symbol into a reality, observe, as in transubstantiation, is as much an abandonment of symbolism as the forgetfulness of symbolic meaning altogether.

which we perceive the perfume and the fair writing, without understanding the contents of it, or intent of it; and as these emotions are in no way resultant from, nor obtainable by, any operation of the intellect, it is evident that the sensation of beauty is not sensual on the one hand, nor is it intellectual on the other, but is dependent on a pure, right, and open state of the heart, both for its truth and for its intensity, insomuch that even the right after action of the intellect upon facts of beauty so apprehended, is dependent on the acuteness of the heart feeling about them; and thus the Apostolic words come true, in this minor respect as in all others, that men are alienated from the life of God, through the ignorance that is in them, having the understanding darkened because of the hardness of their hearts, and so being past feeling, give themselves up to lasciviousness; for we do indeed see constantly that men having naturally acute perceptions of the beautiful, yet not receiving it with a pure heart nor into their hearts at all, never comprehend it, nor receive good from it, but make it a mere minister to their desires, and accompaniment and seasoning of lower sensual pleasures, until all their emotions take the same earthly stamp, and the sense of beauty sinks into the servant of lust.

Nor is what the world commonly understands by the cultivation of taste, anything more or better than this, at least in times of corrupt and over-pampered civilization, when men build palaces and plant groves and gather luxuries, that they and their devices may hang in the corners of the world like fine-spun cobwebs, with greedy, puffed-up, spider-like lusts in the middle. And this, which in Christian times is the abuse and corruption of the sense of beauty, was in that Pagan life of which St. Paul speaks, little less than the essence of it, and the best they had; for I know not that of the expressions of affection towards external nature to be found among Heathen writers, there are any of which the balance and leading thought cleaves not towards the sensual parts of her. Her beneficence they sought, and her power they shunned, her teaching through both, they understood never. The pleasant influences of soft winds and ringing streamlets; and shady coverts; of the violet couch, and plane-tree shade,* they received, perhaps, in a more noble way than we, but they found not anything except fear, upon the bare mountain, or in the ghostly glen. The Hybla heather they loved more for its sweet hives than its purple hues. But the Christian theoria seeks not, though it accepts, and touches with its own purity, what the Epicurean sought, but finds its food and the objects of its love everywhere, in what is harsh and fearful, as well as what is kind, nay, even in all that seems coarse and commonplace; seizing that which is good, and delighting more sometimes at finding its table spread in strange places, and in the presence of its enemies, and its honey coming out of the rock, than if all were harmonized into a less wondrous pleasure; hating only what is self-sighted and insolent of men's work, despising all that is not of God, unless reminding it of God, yet able to find evidence of him still, where all seems forgetful of him, and to turn that into a witness of his working which was meant to obscure it, and so with clear and unoffended sight beholding him for ever, according to the written promise,—Blessed are the pure in heart, for they shall see God.

* Plato, Phædrus, § 9.

———o———

THE BEST KIND OF LIBERTY.

Men may be beaten, chained, tormented, yoked like cattle, slaughtered like summer flies, and yet remain in one sense, and that the best sense, free. But to smother their souls within them, to make the flesh and skin, which, after the worms work on it, is to see God, into leathern thongs to yoke machinery with—this is to be slave-masters indeed; and there might be more freedom in England, though her feudal lords' lightest words were worth men's lives, and though the blood of the vexed husbandman dropped in the furrows of her fields, than there is while the animation of her multitudes is sent like fuel to feed the factory smoke, and the strength of them is given daily to be wasted in the fineness of a web, or racked in the exactness of a line.

I know not if a day is ever to come when the nature of right freedom will be understood, and when men will see, that to obey another man, to labour for him, yield reverence to him or to his place, is not slavery. It is often the best kind of liberty,—liberty from care.

———o———

INFLUENCE OF ART ON RELIGION.

Much attention has lately been directed to the subject of religious art, and we are now in possession of all kinds of interpretations and classifications of it, and of the leading facts of its history. But the greatest question of all connected with it remains entirely unanswered, What good did it do to real religion? There is no subject into which I should so much rejoice to see a serious and conscientious inquiry instituted as this; an inquiry, neither undertaken in artistical enthusiasm nor in monkish sympathy, but dogged, merciless, and fearless. I love the religious art of Italy as well as most men, but there is a wide difference between loving it as a manifestation of individual feeling, and looking to it as an instrument of popular benefit. I have not knowledge enough to form even the shadow of an opinion on this latter point, and I should be most grateful to any one who would put it in my power to do so. There are, as it seems to me, three distinct questions to be considered: the first, What has been the effect of external splendour on the genuineness and earnestness of Christian worship? the second, What the use of pictorial or sculptural representation in the communication of Christian historical knowledge, or excitement of affectionate imagination? the third, What the influence of the practice of religious art on the life of the artist?

In answering these inquiries, we should have to consider separately every collateral influence and circumstance; and, by a most subtle analysis, to eliminate the real effect of art from the effects of the abuses with which it was associated. This could be done only by a Christian; not a man who would fall in love with a sweet colour or sweet expression, but who would look for true faith and consistent life as the object of all. It never has been done yet, and the question remains a subject of vain and endless contention between parties of opposite prejudices and temperaments.

———o———

LOSS.

There is no subject of thought more melancholy, more wonderful, than the way in which God permits so often His best gifts to be trodden under foot of men, His richest treasures to be wasted by the moth, and the mightiest influences of His Spirit, given but once in the world's history, to be quenched and shortened by miseries of chance and guilt. I do not wonder at what men Suffer, but I wonder often at what they Lose. We may see how good rises out of pain and evil; but the dead, naked, eyeless loss, what good comes of that? The fruit struck to the earth before its ripeness; the glowing life and goodly purpose dissolved away in sudden death; the words, half spoken, choked upon the lips with clay for ever; or, stranger than all, the whole majesty of humanity raised to its fulness, and every gift and power necessary for a given purpose, at a given moment, centred in one man, and all this perfected blessing permitted to be refused, perverted, crushed, cast aside by those who need it most,—the city which is Not set on a hill, the candle that giveth light to None that are in the house:—these are the heaviest mysteries of this strange world, and, it seems to me, those which mark its curse the most.

———o———

MRS. BROWNING'S APPEAL FOR ITALY.

I have seen, when the thunderclouds came down on those Italian hills, and all their crags were dipped in the dark, terrible purple, as if the winepress of the wrath of God had stained their mountain-raiment—I have seen the hail fall in Italy till the forest branches stood stripped and bare as if blasted by the locust; but the white hail never fell from those clouds of heaven as the black hail will fall from the clouds of hell, if ever one breath of Italian life stirs again in the streets of Verona.

Sad as you will feel this to be, I do not say that you can

directly prevent it; you cannot drive the Austrians out of Italy, nor prevent them from building forts where they choose.*

* The reader can hardly but remember Mrs. Browning's beautiful appeal for Italy made on the occasion of the first great Exhibition of Art in England —

O Magi of the east and of the west,
Your incense, gold, and myrrh are excellent!—
What gifts for Christ, then, bring ye with the rest?
Your hands have worked well. Is your courage spent
In handwork only? Have you nothing best,
Which generous souls may perfect and present,
And He shall thank the givers for? no light
Of teaching, liberal nations, for the poor,
Who sit in darkness when it is not night?
No cure for wicked children? Christ,—no cure,
No help for women, sobbing out of sight
Because men made the laws?—no brothel-lure
Burnt out by popular lightnings? Hast thou found
No remedy, my England, for such woes?
No outlet, Austria, for the scourged and bound,
No call back for the exiled? no repose,
Russia, for knouted Poles worked under ground,
And gentle ladies bleached among the snows?
No mercy for the slave, America?
No hope for Rome, free France, chivalric France?
Alas, great nations have great shames, I say.
No pity, O world! no tender utterance
Of benediction, and prayers stretched this way
For poor Italia, baffled by mischance?
O gracious nations, give some ear to me!
You all go to your Fair, and I am one
Who at the roadside of humanity
Beseech your alms,—God's justice to be done,
So prosper!

DANTE AND SPENSER.

By the form or name of opposed vice, we may often ascertain, with much greater accuracy than would otherwise be possible, the particular idea of the contrary virtue in the mind of the writer or painter. Thus, when opposed to Prudence, or Prudentia, on the one side, we find Folly, or Stultitia, on the other, it shows that the virtue understood by Prudence, is not the mere guiding or cardinal virtue, but the Heavenly Wisdom,* opposed to that folly which "hath said in its heart, there is no God;" and of which it is said, "the thought of foolishness is sin;" and again, "Such as be foolish shall not stand in thy sight." This folly is personified, in early painting and illumination, by a half-naked man, greedily eating an apple or other fruit, and brandishing a club; showing that sensuality and violence are the two principal characteristics of Foolishness, and lead into atheism. The figure, in early Psalters, always forms the letter D, which commences the fifty-third Psalm, "*Dixit insipiens.*"

In reading Dante, this mode of reasoning from contraries is a great help, for his philosophy of the vices is the only one which admits of classification; his descriptions of virtue, while they include the ordinary formal divisions, are far too profound and extended to be brought under definition. Every line of the "Paradise" is full of the most exquisite and spiritual expressions of Christian truth; and that poem is only less read than the "Inferno" because it requires far greater attention, and, perhaps, for its full enjoyment, a holier heart.

His system in the "Inferno" is briefly this. The whole nether world is divided into seven circles, deep within deep, in each of which, according to its depth, severer punishment

* Uniting the three ideas expressed by the Greek philosophers under the terms φρονησις σοφία, and ἐπιστήμη; and part of the idea of σωφροσύνη.

is inflicted. These seven circles, reckoning them downwards, are thus allotted:

1. To those who have lived virtuously, but knew not Christ.
2. To Lust.
3. To Gluttony.
4. To Avarice and Extravagance.
5. To Anger and *Sorrow.*
6. To Heresy.
7. To Violence and Fraud.

This seventh circle is divided into two parts; of which the first, reserved for those who have been guilty of Violence, is again divided into three, apportioned severally to those who have committed, or desire to commit, violence against their neighbours, against themselves, or against God.

The lowest hell, reserved for the punishment of Fraud, is itself divided into ten circles, wherein are severally punished the sins of,—

1. Betraying women.
2. Flattery.
3. Simony.
4. False prophecy.
5. Peculation.
6. Hypocrisy.
7. Theft.
8. False counsel.
9. Schism and Imposture.
10. Treachery to those who repose entire trust in the traitor.

There is, perhaps, nothing more notable in this most interesting system than the profound truth couched under the attachment of so terrible a penalty to sadness or sorrow. It is true that Idleness does not elsewhere appear in the scheme, and is evidently intended to be included in the guilt of sadness by the word "accidioso;" but the main meaning of the poet is to mark the duty of rejoicing in God, according both to St. Paul's command, and Isaiah's promise, "Thou meetest him that rejoiceth and worketh righteousness."* I do not know words that might with more benefit be borne with us, and set in our hearts momentarily against the minor regrets and rebelliousnesses of life, than these simple ones:

"Tristi fummo
Nel aer dolce, che del sol s' allegra,
Or ci attristiam, nella belletta negra."

"We once were sad,
In the sweet air, made gladsome by the sun,
Now in these murky settlings are we sad."† CARY.

The virtue usually opposed to this vice of sullenness is Alacritas, uniting the sense of activity and cheerfulness. Spenser has cheerfulness simply, in his description, never enough to be loved or praised, of the virtues of Womanhood, first, feminineness or womanhood in specialty; then,—

"Next to her sate goodly Shamefastnesse,
Ne ever durst her eyes from ground upreare,
Ne ever once did looke up from her desse,‡

* Isa. lxiv. 5.

† I hardly think it necessary to point out to the reader the association between sacred cheerfulness and solemn thought, or to explain any appearance of contradiction between passages in which I have had to oppose sacred pensiveness to unholy mirth, and those in which I have to oppose sacred cheerfulness to unholy sorrow.

‡ "Desse," seat.

As if some blame of evill she did feare
That in her cheekes made roses oft appeare:
And her against sweet Cherefulnesse was placed,
Whose eyes, like twinkling stars in evening cleare,
Were deckt with smyles that all sad humours chace l.

"And next to her sate sober Modestie,
Holding her hand upon her gentle hart;
And her against, sate comely Curtesie,
That unto every person knew her part;
And her before was seated overthwart
Soft Silence, and Submisse Obedience,
Both linckt together never to dispart."

Another notable point in Dante's system is the intensity of uttermost punishment given to treason, the peculiar sin of Italy, and that to which, at this day, she attributes her own misery with her own lips. An Italian, questioned as to the causes of the failure of the campaign of 1848, always makes one answer, "We were betrayed;" and the most melancholy feature of the present state of Italy is principally this, that she does not see that, of all causes to which failure might be attributed, this is at once the most disgraceful, and the most hopeless. In fact, Dante seems to me to have written almost prophetically, for the instruction of modern Italy, and chiefly so in the sixth canto of the "Purgatorio."

The system of Spenser is unfinished, and exceedingly complicated, the same vices and virtues occurring under different forms in different places, in order to show their different relations to each other. I shall not therefore give any general sketch of it, but only refer to the particular personification of each virtue.* The peculiar superiority of his system is in

* The "Faerie Queen," like Dante's "Paradise," is only half estimated, because few persons take the pains to think out its meaning. No time

its exquisite setting forth of Chastity under the figure of Britomart; not monkish chastity, but that of the purest Love. In completeness of personification no one can approach him; not even in Dante do I remember anything quite so great as the description of the Captain of the Lusts of the Flesh:

> "As pale and wan as ashes was his looke;
> His body lean and meagre as a rake;
> And skin all withered like a dryed rooke;
> Thereto as cold and drery as a snake;
> That seemd to tremble evermore, and quake:
> *All in a canvas thin he was bedight,*
> *And girded with a belt of twisted brake:*
> Upon his head he wore an helmet light,
> Made of a dead mans skull."

He rides upon a tiger, and in his hand is a bow, bent;

> "And many arrows under his right side,
> Headed with flint, and fethers bloody dide."

The horror and the truth of this are beyond everything that I know, out of the pages of Inspiration. Note the heading of the arrows with flint, because sharper and more subtle in the edge than steel, and because steel might consume away with rust, but flint not; and consider in the whole description how the wasting away of body and soul together, and the *coldness* of the heart, which unholy fire has consumed into ashes, and the loss of all power, and the kindling of all terrible impatience, and the implanting of thorny and inextricable griefs, are set forth by the various images, the belt of brake, the tiger steed, and the *light* helmet, girding the head with death.

devoted to profane literature will be better rewarded than that spent *earnestly* on Spenser.

Spenser's Faith (Fidelia) is spiritual and noble:

"She was araied all in lilly white,
And in her right hand bore a cup of gold,
With wine and water fild up to the hight,
In which a serpent did himselfe enfold,
That horrour made to all that did behold;
But she no whitt did chaunge her constant mood:
And in her other hand she fast did hold
A booke, that was both signd and seald with blood;
Wherein darke things were writt, hard to be understood."

Spenser's Gluttony is more than usually fine:

"His belly was upblowne with luxury,
And eke with fatnesse swollen were his eyne,
And like a crane his necke was long and fyne,
Wherewith he swallowed up excessive feast,
For want whereof poore people oft did pyne."

The Envy of Spenser is fine; joining the idea of fury, in the wolf on which he rides, with that of corruption on his lips, and of discoloration or distortion in the whole mind:

"Malicious Envy rode
Upon a ravenous wolfe, and still did chaw
Between his cankred teeth a venemous tode,
That all the poison ran about his jaw.
All in a kirtle of discolourd say
He clothed was, ypaynted full of eies,
And in his bosome secretly there lay
An hatefull snake, the which his taile uptyes
In many folds, and mortall sting implyes."

Spenser has analysed this vice (Pride) with great care. He first represents it as the Pride of life; that is to say, the pride which runs in a deep under current through all the thoughts and acts of men. As such, it is a feminine vice, directly opposed to Holiness, and mistress of a castle called the House of Pryde, and her chariot is driven by Satan, with a team of beasts, ridden by the mortal sins. In the throne chamber of her palace she is thus described:

"So proud she shyned in her princely state,
Looking to Heaven, for Earth she did disdayne;
And sitting high, for lowly she did hate:
Lo, underneath her scornefull feete was layne
A dreadfull dragon with an hideous trayne;
And in her hand she held a mirrhour bright,
Wherein her face she often vewed fayne."

———o———

KNOWING AND DOING.

Some years ago, in conversation with an artist whose works, perhaps, alone, in the present day, unite perfection of drawing with resplendence of colour, the writer made some inquiry respecting the general means by which this latter quality was most easily to be attained. The reply was as concise as it was comprehensive—"Know what you have to do, and do it"—comprehensive, not only as regarded the branch of art to which it temporarily applied, but as expressing the great principle of success in every direction of human effort; for I believe that failure is less frequently attributable to either insufficiency of means or impatience of labour, than to a confused understanding of the thing actually to be done; and therefore, while it is properly a subject of ridicule, and sometimes of blame, that men propose to themselves a perfection of any kind, which reason, temperately consulted, might have shown to be impossible with the means at their command, it is a more dangerous error to permit the consideration of means to interfere with our conception, or, as is not impossible, even hinder our acknowledgment of goodness and perfection in themselves. And this is the more cautiously to be remembered; because, while a man's sense and conscience, aided by Revelation, are always enough, if earnestly directed, to enable him to discover what is right, neither his sense, nor conscience, nor feeling, are ever enough, because they are not intended, to determine for him what is possible. He knows neither his own strength, nor that of his fellows, neither the exact dependence to be placed on his allies nor resistance to be expected from his opponents. These are questions respecting which passion may warp his conclusions, and ignorance must limit them; but it is his own fault if either interfere with the apprehension of duty, or the acknowledgment of right. And, as far as I have taken cognizance of the causes of the many failures to which the efforts of intelligent men are liable, more especially in matters political, they seem to me more largely to spring from this single error than from all others, that the inquiry into the doubtful, and in some sort inexplicable, relations of capability, chance, resistance, and inconvenience, invariably precedes, even if it do not altogether supersede, the determination of what is absolutely desirable and just. Nor is it any wonder that sometimes the too cold calculation of our powers should reconcile us too easily to our shortcomings, and even lead us into the fatal error of supposing that our conjectural utmost is in itself well, or, in other words, that the necessity of offences renders them inoffensive.

———o———

THE POWER OF INTELLECT.

The temperament which admits the pathetic fallacy is that of a mind and body in some sort too weak to deal fully with what is before them or upon them; borne away, or over-clouded, or over-dazzled by emotion; and it is a more or less noble state, according to the force of the emotion which has induced it. For it is no credit to a man that he is not morbid or inaccurate in his perceptions, when he has no strength of feeling to warp them; and it is in general a sign of higher capacity and stand in the ranks of being, that the emotions should be strong enough to vanquish, partly, the intellect, and make it believe what they choose. But it is still a grander condition when the intellect also rises, till it is strong enough to assert its rule against, or together with, the utmost efforts of the passions; and the whole man stands in an iron glow, white hot, perhaps, but still strong, and in no wise evaporating; even if he melts, losing none of his weight.

So, then, we have the three ranks: the man who perceives rightly, because he does not feel, and to whom the primrose is very accurately the primrose, because he does not love it. Then, secondly, the man who perceives wrongly, because he feels, and to whom the primrose is anything else than a primrose: a star, or a sun, or a fairy's shield, or a forsaken maiden.

———o———

VOLUNTARILY ADMITTED RESTRAINTS.

The highest greatness and the highest wisdom are shown, the first by a noble submission to, the second by a thoughtful providence for, certain voluntarily admitted restraints. Nothing is more evident than this, in that supreme government which is the example, as it is the centre of all others. The Divine Wisdom is, and can be, shown to us only in its meeting and contending with the difficulties which are voluntarily, and *for the sake of that contest*, admitted by the Divine Omnipotence: and these difficulties, observe, occur in the form of natural laws or ordinances which might, at many times and in countless ways, be infringed with apparent advantage, but which are never infringed, whatever costly arrangements or adaptations their observance may necessitate for the accomplishment of given purposes. The example most apposite to our present subject is the structure of the bones of animals. No reason can be given, I believe, why the system of the higher animals should not have been made capable, as that of the *Infusoria* is, of secreting flint, instead of phosphate of lime, or more naturally still, carbon; so framing the bones of adamant at once. The elephant or rhinoceros, had the earthy part of their bones been made of diamond, might have been as agile and light as grasshoppers, and other animals might have been framed far more magnificently colossal than any that walk the earth. In other worlds we may, perhaps, see such creations; a creation for every element, and elements infinite. But the architecture of animals *here*, is appointed by God to be a marble architecture, not a flint nor adamant architecture; and all manner of expedients are adopted to attain the utmost degree of strength and size possible under that great limitation. The jaw of the ichthyosaurus is pieced and riveted, the leg of the megatherium is a foot thick, and the head of the myodon has a double skull; we, in our wisdom, should, doubtless, have given the lizard a steel jaw, and the myodon a cast-iron head-piece, and forgotten the great principle to which all creation bears witness, that order and system are nobler things than power. But God shows us in Himself, strange as it may seem, not only authoritative perfection, but even the perfection of Obedience—an obedience to His own laws: and in the cumbrous movement of those unwieldiest of His creatures we are reminded, even in His divine essence, of that attribute of uprightness in the human creature "that sweareth to his own hurt and changeth not."

———o———

PROGRESS IN KNOWLEDGE.

If we consider that, till within the last fifty years, the nature of the ground we tread on, of the air we breathe, and of the light by which we see, were not so much as conjecturally conceived by us; that the duration of the globe, and the races of animal life by which it was inhabited, are just beginning to be apprehended; and that the scope of the magnificent science which has revealed them, is as yet so little received by the public mind, that presumption and ignorance are still permitted to raise their voices against it unrebuked; that perfect veracity in the representation of general nature by art has never been attempted until the present day, and has in the present day been resisted with all the energy of the popular voice; * that the simplest problems of social science are yet so little understood, as that doctrines of liberty and equality can be openly preached, and so successfully as to affect the whole body of the civilized world with apparently incurable disease; that the first principles of commerce were acknowledged by the English Parliament only a few months ago, in its free trade measures, and are still so

* In the works of Turner and the Pre-Raphaelites.

little understood by the million, that no nation dares to abolish its custom-houses; * that the simplest principles of policy are still not so much as stated, far less received, and that civilized nations persist in the belief that the subtlety and dishonesty which they know to be ruinous in dealings between man and man, are serviceable in dealings between multitude and multitude; finally, that the scope of the Christian religion, which we have been taught for two thousand years, is still so little conceived by us, that we suppose the laws of charity and of self-sacrifice bear upon individuals in all their social relations, and yet do not bear upon nations in any of their political relations;—when, I say, we thus review the depth of simplicity in which the human race are still plunged with respect to all that it most profoundly concerns them to know, and which might, by them, with most ease have been ascertained, we can hardly determine how far back on the narrow path of human progress we ought to place the generation to which we belong, how far the swaddling clothes are unwound from us, and childish things beginning to be put away.

On the other hand, a power of obtaining veracity in the representation of material and tangible things, which, within certain limits and conditions, is unimpeachable, has now been

* Observe, I speak of these various principles as self-evident, only under the present circumstances of the world, not as if they had always been so; and I call them now self-evident, not merely because they seem so to myself, but because they are felt to be so likewise by all the men in whom I place most trust. But granting that they are not so, then their very disputability proves the state of infancy above alleged, as characteristic of the world. For I do not suppose that any Christian reader will doubt the first great truth, that whatever facts or laws are important to mankind, God has made ascertainable by mankind; and that as the decision of all these questions is of vital importance to the race, that decision must have been long ago arrived at, unless they were still in a state of childhood.

placed in the hands of all men,* almost without labour. The foundation of every natural science is now at last firmly laid, not a day passing without some addition of buttress and pinnacle to their already magnificent fabric. Social theorems, if fiercely agitated, are therefore the more likely to be at last determined, so that they never can be matters of question more. Human life has been in some sense prolonged by the increased powers of locomotion, and an almost limitless power of converse. Finally, there is hardly any serious mind in Europe but is occupied, more or less, in the investigation of the questions which have so long paralyzed the strength of religious feeling, and shortened the dominion of religious faith. And we may therefore at least look upon ourselves as so far in a definite state of progress, as to justify our caution in guarding against the dangers incident to every period of change, and especially to that from childhood into youth.

Those dangers appear, in the main, to be twofold; consisting partly in the pride of vain knowledge, partly in the pursuit of vain pleasure.

———o———

IGNOBLE EMOTION.

A Turk declares that "God is great," when he means only that he himself is lazy. The "heaven is bright" of many

* I intended to have given a sketch in this place (above referred to) of the probable results of the daguerreotype and calotype within the next few years, in modifying the application of the engraver's art, but I have not had time to complete the experiments necessary to enable me to speak with certainty. Of one thing, however, I have little doubt, that an infinite service will soon be done to a large body of our engravers; namely, the making them draughtsmen.

vulgar painters, has precisely the same amount of signification; it means that they know nothing—will do nothing—are without thought—without care—without passion. They will not walk the earth, nor watch the ways of it, nor gather the flowers of it. They will sit in the shade, and only assert that very perceptible, long-ascertained fact, "heaven is bright." And as it may be *asserted* basely, so it may be *accepted* basely. Many of our capacities for receiving noblest emotion are abused, in mere idleness, for pleasure's sake, and people take the excitement of a solemn sensation as they do that of a strong drink. Thus the abandoned court of Louis XIV. had on fast days its sacred concerts, doubtless entering in some degree into the religious expression of the music, and thus idle and frivolous women at the present day will weep at an oratorio.

———o———

SACRED ASSOCIATIONS WITH OLIVE-TREES.

I do not want painters to tell me any scientific facts about olive-trees. But it had been well for them to have felt and seen the olive-tree; to have loved it for Christ's sake, partly also for the helmed Wisdom's sake which was to the heathen in some sort as that nobler Wisdom which stood at God's right hand, when He founded the earth and established the heavens. To have loved it, even to the hoary dimness of its delicate foliage, subdued and faint of hue, as if the ashes of the Gethsemane agony had been cast upon it for ever; and to have traced, line by line, the gnarled writhing of its intricate branches, and the pointed fretwork of its light and narrow leaves, inlaid on the blue field of the sky, and the small, rosy-white stars of its spring blossoming, and the beads of sable fruit scattered by autumn along its topmost boughs—the right, in Israel, of the stranger, the fatherless, and the widow,—and, more than all, the softness of the mantle, silver grey, and tender like the down on a bird's breast, with which, far away, it veils the undulation of the mountains.

———o———

SIMPLICITY.

It is far more difficult to be simple than to be complicated; far more difficult to sacrifice skill and cease exertion in the proper place, than to expend both indiscriminately. We shall find, in the course of our investigation, that beauty and difficulty go together; and that they are only mean and paltry difficulties which it is wrong or contemptible to wrestle with. Be it remembered then—Power is never wasted. Whatever power has been employed, produces excellence in proportion to its own dignity and exertion; and the faculty of perceiving this exertion, and appreciating this dignity, is the faculty of perceiving excellence.

———o———

LOVE OF CHANGE.

We must note carefully what distinction there is between a healthy and a diseased love of change; for as it was in healthy love of change that the Gothic architecture rose, it was partly in consequence of diseased love of change that it was destroyed. In order to understand this clearly, it will be necessary to consider the different ways in which change and monotony are presented to us in nature; both having their use, like darkness and light, and the one incapable of being enjoyed without the other: change being most delightful after some prolongation of monotony, as light appears most brilliant after the eyes have been for some time closed.

I believe that the true relations of monotony and change may be most simply understood by observing them in music We may therein notice, first, that there is a sublimity and majesty in monotony which there is not in rapid or frequent variation. This is true throughout all nature. The greater part of the sublimity of the sea depends on its monotony; so also that of desolate moor and mountain scenery; and especially the sublimity of motion, as in the quiet, unchanged fall and rise of an engine beam. So also there is sublimity in darkness which there is not in light.

Again, monotony after a certain time, or beyond a certain degree, becomes either uninteresting or intolerable, and the musician is obliged to break it in one or two ways: either while the air or passage is perpetually repeated, its notes are variously enriched and harmonized; or else, after a certain number of repeated passages, an entirely new passage is introduced, which is more or less delightful according to the length of the previous monotony. Nature, of course, uses both these kinds of variation perpetually. The sea-waves, resembling each other in general mass, but none like its brother in minor divisions and curves, are a monotony of the first kind; the great plain, broken by an emergent rock or clump of trees, is a monotony of the second.

Farther: in order to the enjoyment of the change in either case, a certain degree of patience is required from the hearer or observer. In the first case, he must be satisfied to endure with patience the recurrence of the great masses of sound or form, and to seek for entertainment in a careful watchfulness of the minor details. In the second case, he must bear patiently the infliction of the monotony for some moments, in order to feel the full refreshment of the change. This is true even of the shortest musical passage in which the element of monotony is employed. In cases of more majestic monotony, the patience required is so considerable that it becomes a kind of pain,—a price paid for the future pleasure.

Again: the talent of the composer is not in the monotony, but in the changes: he may show feeling and taste by his use of monotony in certain places or degrees; that is to say, by his *various* employment of it; but it is always in the new arrangement or invention that his intellect is shown, and not in the monotony which relieves it.

Lastly: if the pleasure of change be too often repeated, it ceases to be delightful, for then change itself becomes monotonous, and we are driven to seek delight in extreme and fantastic degrees of it. This is the diseased love of change of which we have above spoken.

From these facts we may gather generally that monotony is, and ought to be, in itself painful to us, just as darkness is; that an architecture which is altogether monotonous is a dark or dead architecture; and, of those who love it, it may be truly said, "they love darkness rather than light." But monotony in certain measure, used in order to give value to change, and, above all, that *transparent* monotony which, like the shadows of a great painter, suffers all manner of dimly suggested form to be seen through the body of it, is an essential in architectural as in all other composition; and the endurance of monotony has about the same place in a healthy mind that the endurance of darkness has: that is to say, as a strong intellect will have pleasure in the solemnities of storm and twilight, and in the broken and mysterious lights that gleam among them, rather than in mere brilliancy and glare, while a frivolous mind will dread the shadow and the storm;

and as a great man will be ready to endure much darkness of fortune in order to reach greater eminence of power or felicity, while an inferior man will not pay the price; exactly in like manner a great mind will accept, or even delight in, monotony which would be wearisome to an inferior intellect, because it has more patience and power of expectation, and is ready to pay the full price for the great future pleasure of change. But in all cases it is not that the noble nature loves monotony, any more than it loves darkness or pain. But it can bear with it, and receives a high pleasure in the endurance or patience, a pleasure necessary to the well-being of this world; while those who will not submit to the temporary sameness, but rush from one change to another, gradually dull the edge of change itself, and bring a shadow and weariness over the whole world from which there is no more escape.

———o———

THE MAN OF GENIUS.

His science is inexpressibly subtle, directly taught him by his Maker, not in anywise communicable or imitable. Neither can any written or definitely observable laws enable us to do any great thing. It is possible, by measuring and administering quantities of colour, to paint a room wall so that it shall not hurt the eye; but there are no laws by observing which we can become Titians. It is possible so to measure and administer syllables, as to construct harmonious verse; but there are no laws by which we can write Iliads. Out of the poem or the picture, once produced, men may elicit laws by the volume, and study them with advantage, to the better understanding of the existing poem or picture; but no more write or paint another, than by discovering laws of vegetation they can make a tree to grow. And therefore, wheresoever we find the system and formality of rules much dwelt upon, and spoken of as anything else than a help for children, there we may be sure that noble art is not even understood, far less reached. And thus it was with all the common and public mind in the fifteenth and sixteenth centuries. The greater men, indeed, broke through the thorn hedges; and, though much time was lost by the learned among them in writing Latin verses and anagrams, and arranging the framework of quaint sonnets and dexterous syllogisms, still they tore their way through the sapless thicket by force of intellect or of piety; for it was not possible that, either in literature or in painting, rules could be received by any strong mind, so as materially to interfere with its originality; and the crabbed discipline and exact scholarship became an advantage to the men who could pass through and despise them; so that in spite of the rules of the drama we had Shakspeare, and in spite of the rules of art we had Tintoret,—both of them, to this day, doing perpetual violence to the vulgar scholarship and dim-eyed proprieties of the multitude.

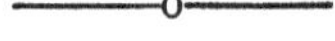

THE CLASSICAL.

On the absence of belief in a good supreme Being, follows, necessarily, the habit of looking to ourselves for supreme judgment in all matters, and for supreme government. Hence, first, the irreverent habit of judgment instead of admiration. It is generally expressed under the justly degrading term "good taste."

Hence, in the second place, the habit of restraint or self

government (instead of impulsive and limitless obedience), based upon pride, and involving, for the most part, scorn of the helpless and weak, and respect only for the orders of men who have been trained to this habit of self-government. Whence the title classical, from the Latin *classicus.*

The school is, therefore, generally to be characterized as that of taste and restraint. As the school of taste, everything is, in its estimation, beneath it, so as to be tasted or tested; not above it, to be thankfully received. Nothing was to be fed upon as bread; but only palated as a dainty. This spirit has destroyed art since the close of the sixteenth century, and nearly destroyed French literature, our English literature being at the same time severely depressed, and our education (except in bodily strength) rendered nearly nugatory by it, so far as it affects common-place minds. It is not possible that the classical spirit should ever take possession of a mind of the highest order. Pope is, as far as I know, the greatest man who ever fell strongly under its influence; and though it spoiled half his work, he broke through it continually into true enthusiasm and tender thought.* Again, as the school of reserve, it refuses to allow itself in any violent or "spasmodic" passion; the schools of literature which have been in modern times called "spasmodic," being reactionary against it. The word, though an ugly one, is quite accurate, the most spasmodic books in the world being Solomon's Song, Job, and Isaiah.

* Cold-hearted, I have called him. He was so in writing the Pastorals, of which I then spoke, but in after life his errors were those of his time, his wisdom was his own; it would be well if we also made it ours.

———o———

THE MOTHER-NATION.

I believe that no Christian nation has any business to see one of its members in distress without helping him, though, perhaps, at the same time punishing him: help, of course—in nine cases out of ten—meaning guidance, much more than gift, and, therefore, interference with liberty. When a peasant mother sees one of her careless children fall into a ditch, her first proceeding is to pull him out; her second, to box his ears; her third, ordinarily, to lead him carefully a little way by the hand, or send him home for the rest of the day. The child usually cries, and very often would clearly prefer remaining in the ditch; and if he understood any of the terms of politics, would certainly express resentment at the interference with his individual liberty: but the mother has done her duty. Whereas the usual call of the mother-nation to any of her children, under such circumstances, has lately been nothing more than the foxhunter's,—"Stay still there; I shall clear you." And if we always *could* clear them, their requests to be left in muddy independence might be sometimes allowed by kind people, or their cries for help disdained by unkind ones. But we can't clear them. The whole nation is, in fact, bound together, as men are by ropes on a glacier—if one falls, the rest must either lift him or drag him along with them as dead weight, not without much increase of danger to themselves. And the law of right being manifestly in this, as, whether manifestly or not, it is always, the law of prudence, the only question is, how this wholesome help and interference are to be administered.

———o———

JUSTICE, MERCY, AND TRUTH.

Every person who tries to buy an article for less than its proper value, or who tries to sell it at more than its proper value—every consumer who keeps a tradesman waiting for his money, and every tradesman who bribes a consumer to extravagance by credit, is helping forward, according to his own measure of power, a system of baseless and dishonourable commerce, and forcing his country down into poverty and shame. And people of moderate means and average powers of mind would do far more real good by merely carrying out stern principles of justice and honesty in common matters of trade, than by the most ingenious schemes of extended philanthropy, or vociferous declarations of theological doctrine. There are three weighty matters of the law—justice, mercy, and truth; and of these the Teacher puts truth last, because that cannot be known but by a course of acts of justice and love. But men put, in all their efforts, truth first, because they mean by it their own opinions; and thus, while the world has many people who would suffer martyrdom in the cause of what they call truth, it has few who will suffer even a little inconvenience in that of justice and mercy.

———o———

PROPHETIC DESIGNERS.

The nations whose chief support was in the chase, whose chief interest was in the battle, whose chief pleasure was in the banquet, would take small care respecting the shapes of leaves and flowers; and notice little in the forms of the forest trees which sheltered them, except the signs indicative of the wood which would make the toughest lance, the closest roof, or the clearest fire. The affectionate observation of the grace and outward character of vegetation is the sure sign of a more tranquil and gentle existence, sustained by the gifts, and gladdened by the splendour, of the earth. In that careful distinction of species, and richness of delicate and undisturbed organization, which characterize the Gothic design, there is the history of rural and thoughtful life, influenced by habitual tenderness, and devoted to subtle inquiry; and every discriminating and delicate touch of the chisel, as it rounds the petal or guides the branch, is a prophecy of the development of the entire body of the natural sciences, beginning with that of medicine, of the recovery of literature, and the establishment of the most necessary principles of domestic wisdom and national peace.

———o———

THE FOOD OF THE SOUL.

That sentence of Genesis, "I have given thee every green herb for meat," like all the rest of the book, has a profound symbolical as well as a literal meaning. It is not merely the nourishment of the body, but the food of the soul, that is intended. The green herb is, of all nature, that which is most essential to the healthy spiritual life of man. Most of us do not need fine scenery; the precipice and the mountain peak are not intended to be seen by all men,—perhaps their power is greatest over those who are unaccustomed to them. But trees, and fields, and flowers were made for all, and are necessary for all. God has connected the labour which is essential to the bodily sustenance, with the pleasures which are healthiest for the heart; and while He made the ground stubborn, He made its herbage fragrant, and its blossoms fair.

The proudest architecture that man can build has no higher honour than to bear the image and recall the memory of that grass of the field which is, at once, the type and the support of its existence; the goodly building is then most glorious when it is sculptured into the likeness of the leaves of Paradise; and the great Gothic spirit, as we showed it to be noble in its disquietude, is also noble in its hold of nature; it is, indeed, like the dove of Noah, in that she found no rest upon the face of the waters,—but like her in this also, "Lo, IN HER MOUTH WAS AN OLIVE BRANCH, PLUCKED OFF."

———o———

DIVISION OF LABOUR.

Let me not be thought to speak wildly or extravagantly. It is verily this degradation of the operative into a machine, which, more than any other evil of the times, is leading the mass of the nations everywhere into vain, incoherent, destructive struggling for a freedom of which they cannot explain the nature to themselves. Their universal outcry against wealth, and against nobility, is not forced from them either by the pressure of famine, or the sting of mortified pride. These do much, and have done much in all ages; but the foundations of society were never yet shaken as they are at this day. It is not that men are ill fed, but that they have no pleasure in the work by which they make their bread, and therefore look to wealth as the only means of pleasure. It is not that men are pained by the scorn of the upper classes, but they cannot endure their own; for they feel that the kind of labour to which they are condemned is verily a degrading one, and makes them less than men. Never had the upper classes so much sympathy with the lower, or charity for them, as they have at this day, and yet never were they so much hated by them: for, of old, the separation between the noble and the poor was merely a wall built by law; now it is a veritable difference in level of standing, a precipice between upper and lower grounds in the field of humanity, and there is pestilential air at the bottom of it. I know not if a day is ever to come when the nature of right freedom will be understood, and when men will see that to obey another man, to labour for him, yield reverence to him or to his place, is not slavery. It is often the best kind of liberty,—liberty from care. The man who says to one, Go, and he goeth, and to another, Come, and he cometh, has, in most cases, more sense of restraint and difficulty than the man who obeys him. The movements of the one are hindered by the burden on his shoulder; of the other, by the bridle on his lips: there is no way by which the burden may be lightened; but we need not suffer from the bridle if we do not champ at it. To yield reverence to another, to hold ourselves and our lives at his disposal, is not slavery; often, it is the noblest state in which a man can live in this world. There is, indeed, a reverence which is servile, that is to say, irrational or selfish: but there is also noble reverence, that is to say, reasonable and loving; and a man is never so noble as when he is reverent in this kind; nay, even if the feeling pass the bounds of mere reason, so that it be loving, a man is raised by it. Which had, in reality, most of the serf nature in him,—the Irish peasant who was lying in wait yesterday for his landlord, with his musket muzzle thrust through the ragged hedge; or that old mountain servant who, 200 years ago, at Inverkeithing, gave up his own life and the lives of his seven sons for his chief?*—and as each fell, calling forth his brother to the death,

* Vide Preface to "Fair Maid of Perth."

"Another for Hector!" And therefore, in all ages and all countries, reverence has been paid and sacrifice made by men to each other, not only without complaint, but rejoicingly; and famine, and peril, and sword, and all evil, and all shame, have been borne willingly in the causes of masters and kings; for all these gifts of the heart ennobled the men who gave, not less than the men who received them, and nature prompted, and God rewarded the sacrifice. But to feel their souls withering within them, unthanked, to find their whole being sunk into an unrecognized abyss, to be counted off into a heap of mechanism, numbered with its wheels, and weighed with its hammer strokes;—this nature bade not,—this God blesses not,—this humanity for no long time is able to endure.

We have much studied and much perfected, of late, the great civilized invention of the division of labour; only we give it a false name. It is not, truly speaking, the labour that is divided; but the men:—Divided into mere segments of men—broken into small fragments and crumbs of life; so that all the little piece of intelligence that is left in a man is not enough to make a pin, or a nail, but exhausts itself in making the point of a pin, or the head of a nail. Now it is a good and desirable thing, truly, to make many pins in a day; but if we could only see with what crystal sand their points were polished,—sand of human soul, much to be magnified before it can be discerned for what it is,—we should think there might be some loss in it also. And the great cry that rises from all our manufacturing cities, louder than their furnace blast, is all in very deed for this,—that we manufacture everything there except men; we blanch cotton, and strengthen steel, and refine sugar, and shape pottery; but to brighten, to strengthen, to refine, or to form a single living spirit, never enters into our estimate of advantages. And all the evil to which that cry is urging our myriads can be met only in one way: not by teaching nor preaching, for to teach them is but to show them their misery, and to preach to them, if we do nothing more than preach, is to mock at it. It can be met only by a right understanding, on the part of all classes, of what kinds of labour are good for men, raising them and making them happy; by a determined sacrifice of such convenience, or beauty, or cheapness as is to be got only by the degradation of the workman; and by equally determined demand for the products and results of healthy and ennobling labour.

And how, it will be asked, are these products to be recognized, and this demand to be regulated? Easily: by the observance of three broad and simple rules:

1. Never encourage the manufacture of any article not absolutely necessary, in the production of which *Invention* has no share.

2. Never demand an exact finish for its own sake, but only for some practical or noble end.

3. Never encourage imitation or copying of any kind, except for the sake of preserving record of great works.

The second of these principles is the only one which directly rises out of the consideration of our immediate subject; but I shall briefly explain the meaning and extent of the first also, reserving the enforcement of the third for another place.

1. Never encourage the manufacture of anything not necessary, in the production of which invention has no share.

For instance. Glass beads are utterly unnecessary, and there is no design or thought employed in their manufacture. They are formed by first drawing out the glass into rods; these rods are chopped up into fragments of the size of beads by the human hand, and the fragments are then rounded in the furnace. The men who chop up the rods sit at their work all day, their hands vibrating with a perpetual and exquisitely timed palsy, and the beads dropping beneath their vibration like hail. Neither they, nor the men who draw out the rods or fuse the fragments, have the smallest occasion for the use of any single human faculty; and every young lady, therefore, who buys glass beads is engaged in the slave-trade, and in a much more cruel one than that which we have so long been endeavouring to put down.

But glass cups and vessels may become the subject of exquisite invention; and if in buying these we pay for the invention, that is to say, for the beautiful form, or colour, or engraving, and not for mere finish of execution, we are doing good to humanity.

———o———

THE MODERN INFIDEL CREED.

Co-relative with the assertion, "There is a foolish God," is the assertion, "There is a brutish man." "As no laws but those of the Devil are practicable in the world, so no impulses but those of the brute" (says the modern political economist) "are appealable to in the world. Faith, generosity, honesty, zeal, and self-sacrifice are poetical phrases. None of these things can, in reality, be counted upon; there is no truth in man which can be used as a moving or productive power. All motive force in him is essentially brutish, covetous, or contentious. His power is only power of prey: otherwise than the spider, he cannot design; otherwise than the tiger, he cannot feed." This is the modern interpretation of that embarrassing article of the Creed, "the communion of saints."

It has always seemed very strange to me, not indeed that this creed should have been adopted, it being the entirely necessary consequence of the previous fundamental article ;—but that no one should ever seem to have any misgivings about it ;—that, practically, no one had *seen* how strong work *was* done by man; how either for hire, or for hatred, it never had been done; and that no amount of pay had ever made a good soldier, a good teacher, a good artist, or a good workman. You pay your soldiers and sailors so many pence a day, at which rated sum, one will do good fighting for you; another, bad fighting. Pay as you will, the entire goodness of the fighting depends, always, on its being done for nothing; or rather, less than nothing, in the expectation of no pay but death. Examine the work of your spiritual teachers, and you will find the statistical law respecting them is, "The less pay, the better work." Examine also your writers and artists: for ten pounds you shall have a Paradise Lost, and for a plate of figs, a Durer drawing; but for a million of money sterling, neither. Examine your men of science: paid by starvation, Kepler will discover the laws of the orbs of heaven for you; —and, driven out to die in the street, Swammerdam shall discover the laws of life for you—such hard terms do they make with you, these brutish men, who can only be had for hire.

Neither is good work ever done for hatred, any more than hire—but for love only.

———o———

CONCESSION AND COMPANIONSHIP.

The leaves, as we shall see immediately, are the feeders of the plant. Their own orderly habits of succession must not interfere with their main business of finding food. Where the sun and air are the leaf must go, whether it be out of order or not. So, therefore, in any group, the first consideration with the young leaves is much like that of young bees, how to keep out of each other's way, that every one may at once leave its neighbours as much free-air pasture as possible, and obtain a relative freedom for itself. This would be a quite simple matter, and produce other simply balanced forms, if each branch, with open air all round it, had nothing to think of but reconcilement of interests among its own leaves. But every branch has others to meet or to cross, sharing with them, in various advantage, what shade or sun or rain is to be had. Hence every single leaf-cluster presents the general aspect of a little family, entirely at unity among themselves, but obliged to get their living by various shifts, concessions, and infringements of the family rules, in order not to invade the privileges of other people in their neighbourhood.

And in the arrangement of these concessions there is an exquisite sensibility among the leaves. They do not grow each to his own liking, till they run against one another, and then turn back sulkily; but by a watchful instinct, far apart, they anticipate their companions' courses, as ships at sea, and in every new unfolding of their edged tissue, guide themselves by the sense of each other's remote presence, and by a watchful penetration of leafy purpose in the far future. So that every shadow which one casts on the next, and every glint of sun which each reflects to the next, and every touch which in toss of storm each receives from the next, aid or arrest the development of their advancing form, and direct, as will be safest and best, the curve of every fold and the current of every vein.

And this peculiar character exists in all the structures thus developed, that they are always visibly the result of a volition on the part of the leaf, meeting an external force or fate, to which it is never passively subjected. Upon it, as on a mineral in the course of formation, the great merciless influences of the universe, and the oppressive powers of minor things immediately near it, act continually. Heat and cold gravity and the other attractions, windy pressure, or local and unhealthy restraint, must, in certain inevitable degrees, affect the whole of its life. But it is *life* which they affect;—a life of progress and will,—not a merely passive accumulation of substance. This may be seen by a single glance. The mineral,—suppose an agate in the course of formation—shows in every line nothing but a dead submission to surrounding force. Flowing, or congealing, its substance is here repelled, there attracted, unresisting to its place, and its languid sinuosities follow the clefts of the rock that contains them, in servile deflexion and compulsory cohesion, impotently calculable, and cold. But the leaf, full of fears and affections, shrinks and seeks, as it obeys. Not thrust, but awed into its retiring; not dragged, but won to its advance; not bent aside, as by a bridle, into new courses of growth: but persuaded and converted through tender continuance of voluntary change.

The mineral and it differing thus widely in separate being, they differ no less in modes of companionship. The mineral crystals group themselves neither in succession, nor in sympathy; but great and small recklessly strive for place, and deface or distort each other as they gather into opponent asperities. The confused crowd fills the rock cavity, hanging together in a glittering, yet sordid heap, in which nearly every crystal, owing to their vain contention, is imperfect, or impure. Here and there one, at the cost and in defiance of the rest, rises into unwarped shape or unstained clearness. But the order of the leaves is one of soft and subdued concession. Patiently each awaits its appointed time, accepts its prepared place, yields its required observance. Under every oppression of external accident, the group yet follows a law laid down in its own heart; and all the members of it, whether in sickness or health, in strength or languor, combine to carry out this first and last heart law; receiving, and seeming to desire for themselves and for each other, only life which they may communicate, and loveliness which they may reflect.

———o———

MOUNTAIN INFLUENCE.

We have found mountains, invariably, calculated for the delight, the advantage, or the teaching of men; prepared, it seems, so as to contain, alike in fortitude or feebleness, in kindliness or in terror, some beneficence of gift, or profoundness of counsel. We have found that where at first all seemed disturbed and accidental, the most tender laws were appointed to produce forms of perpetual beauty; and that where to the careless or cold observer it seemed severe or purposeless, the well-being of man has been chiefly consulted, and his rightly directed powers, and sincerely awakened intelligence, may find wealth in every falling rock, and wisdom in every talking wave.

It remains for us to consider what actual effect upon the human race has been produced by the generosity, or the instruction of the hills; how far, in past ages, they have been thanked, or listened to; how far, in coming ages, it may be well for us to accept them for tutors, or acknowledge them for friends.

What they have already taught us may, one would think, be best discerned in the midst of them,—in some place where they have had their own way with the human soul; where no veil has been drawn between it and them, no contradicting voice has confused their ministries of sound, or broken their pathos of silence: where war has never streaked their streams with bloody foam, nor ambition sought for other throne than their cloud-courtiered pinnacles, nor avarice for other treasure than, year by year, is given to their unlaborious rocks, in budded jewels, and mossy gold.

I do not know any district possessing a more pure or uninterrupted fulness of mountain character (and that of the highest order), or which appears to have been less disturbed by foreign agencies, than that which borders the course of the Trient between Valorsine and Martigny. The paths which lead to it out of the valley of the Rhone, rising at first in steep circles among the walnut trees, like winding stairs among the pillars of a Gothic tower, retire over the shoulders of the hills into a valley almost unknown, but thickly inhabited by an industrious and patient population. Along the ridges of the rocks, smoothed by old glaciers into long, dark, billowy swellings, like the backs of plunging dolphins, the peasant watches the slow colouring of the tufts of moss and roots of herb which, little by little, gather a feeble soil over the iron substance; then, supporting the narrow strip of clinging ground with a few stones, he subdues it to the spade; and in a year or two a little crest of corn is seen waving upon the rocky casque. The irregular meadows run in and out like inlets of lake among these harvested rocks, sweet with perpetual streamlets, that seem always to have chosen the steepest places to come down, for the sake of the leaps, scattering their handfuls of crystal this way and that, as the wind takes them, with all the grace, but with none of the formalism, of fountains; dividing into fanciful change of dash and spring, yet with the seal of their granite channels upon them, as the lightest play of human speech may bear the seal of past toil, and closing back out of their spray to lave the rigid angles, and brighten with silver fringes and glassy films each lower and lower step of sable stone; until at last, gathered altogether again,—except, perhaps, some chance drops caught on the apple-blossom, where it has budded a little nearer the cascade than it did last spring,—they find their way down to the turf, and lose themselves in that silently; with quiet depth of clear water furrowing among the grass blades, and looking only like their shadow, but presently emerging again in little startled gushes and laughing hurries, as if they had remembered suddenly that the day was too short for them to get down the hill.

Green field, and glowing rock, and glancing streamlet, all slope together in the sunshine towards the brows of the ravines, where the pines take up their own dominion of saddened shade; and with everlasting roar in the twilight, the stronger torrents thunder down pale from the glaciers, filling all their chasms with enchanted cold, beating themselves to pieces against the great rocks that they have themselves cast down, and forcing fierce way beneath their ghastly poise.

The mountain paths stoop to these glens in forky zigzags, leading to some grey and narrow arch, all fringed under its shuddering curve with the ferns that fear the light; a cross of rough-hewn pine, iron-bound to its parapet, standing dark against the lurid fury of the foam. Far up the glen, as we pause beside the cross, the sky is seen through the openings in the pines, thin with excess of light; and, in its clear, consuming flame of white space, the summits of the rocky mountains are gathered into solemn crowns and circlets, all flushed in that strange, faint silence of possession by the sunshine which has in it so deep a melancholy; full of power, yet as frail as shadows; lifeless, like the walls of a sepulchre, yet beautiful in tender fall of crimson folds, like the veil of some sea spirit, that lives and dies as the foam flashes; fixed on a perpetual throne, stern against all strength, lifted above all sorrow, and yet effaced and melted utterly into the air by that last sunbeam that has crossed to them from between the two golden clouds.

High above all sorrow: yes; but not unwitnessing to it. The traveller on his happy journey, as his foot springs from the deep turf and strikes the pebbles gaily over the edge of the mountain road, sees with a glance of delight the clusters of nut-brown cottages that nestle among those sloping orchards, and glow beneath the boughs of the pines. Here, it may well seem to him, if there be sometimes hardship, there must be at least innocence and peace, and fellowship of the human soul with nature. It is not so. The wild goats that leap along those rocks have as much passion of joy in all that fair work of God as the men that toil among them. Perhaps more. Enter the street of one of those villages, and you will find it foul with that gloomy foulness that is suffered only by torpor, or by anguish of soul. Here, it is torpor—not absolute suffering,—not starvation or disease, but darkness of calm enduring; the spring known only as the time of the scythe, and the autumn as the time of the sickle, and the sun only as a warmth, the wind as a chill, and the mountains as a danger. They do not understand so much as the name of beauty, or of knowledge. They understand dimly that of virtue. Love, patience, hospitality, faith,—these things they know. To glean their meadows side by side, so happier; to bear the burden up the breathless mountain flank, unmurmuringly; to bid the stranger drink from their vessel of milk; to see at the foot of their low deathbeds a pale figure upon a cross, dying also, patiently;—in this they are different from the cattle and from the stones, but in all this unrewarded as far as concerns the present life. For them, there is neither hope nor passion of spirit; for them neither advance nor exultation. Black bread, rude roof, dark night, laborious day, weary arm at sunset; and life ebbs away. No books, no thoughts, no attainments, no rest; except only sometimes a little sitting in the sun under the church wall, as the bell tolls thin and far in the mountain air; a pattering of a few prayers, not understood, by the altar rails of the dimly gilded chapel, and so back to the sombre home, with the cloud upon them still unbroken—that cloud of rocky gloom, born out of the wild torrents and ruinous stones, and unlightened, even in their religion, except by the vague promise of some better thing unknown, mingled with threatening, and obscured by an unspeakable horror,—a smoke, as it were, of martyrdom, coiling up with the incense, and, amidst the images of tortured bodies and lamenting spirits in hurtling flames, the very cross, for them, dashed more deeply than for others, with gouts of blood.

Do not let this be thought a darkened picture of the life of these mountaineers. It is literal fact. No contrast can be more painful than that between the dwelling of any well conducted English cottager, and that of the equally honest Savoyard. The one, set in the midst of its dull flat fields and uninteresting hedgerows, shows in itself the love of brightness and beauty; its daisy-studded garden beds, its smoothly swept brick path to the threshold, its freshly sanded floor and orderly shelves of household furniture, all testify to energy of heart, and happiness in the simple course and simple possessions of daily life. The other cottage, in the midst of an inconceivable, inexpressible beauty, set on some sloping bank of golden sward, with clear fountains flowing beside it, and wild flowers, and noble trees, and goodly rocks gathered round into a perfection as of Paradise, is itself a dark and plague-like stain in the midst of the gentle landscape. Within a certain distance of its threshold the ground is foul and cattle-trampled; its timbers are black with smoke, its garden choked with weeds and nameless refuse, its chambers empty and joyless, the light and wind gleaming and filtering through the crannies of their stones. All testifies that to its inhabitant the world is labour and vanity; that for him neither flowers bloom, nor birds sing, nor fountains glisten; and that his soul hardly differs from the grey cloud that coils and dies upon his hills; except in having no fold of it touched by the sunbeams.

Is it not strange to reflect, that hardly an evening passes in London or Paris but one of those cottages is painted for the better amusement of the fair and idle, and shaded with pasteboard pines by the scene-shifter; and that good and kind people,—poetically minded,—delight themselves in imagining the happy life led by peasants who dwell by Alpine fountains, and kneel to crosses upon peaks of rock? that nightly we lay down our gold to fashion forth simulacra of peasants, in gay ribands and white bodices, singing sweet songs, and bowing gracefully to the picturesque crosses; and all the while the veritable peasants are kneeling, songlessly, to veritable crosses, in another temper than the kind and fair audiences dream of, and assuredly with another kind of answer than is got out of the opera catastrophe; an answer having reference, it may be, in dim futurity, to those very audiences themselves? If all the gold that has gone to paint the simulacra of the cottages, and to put new songs in the mouths of the simulacra of the peasants, had gone to brighten the existent cottages, and to put new songs into the mouths of the existent peasants, it might in the end, perhaps, have turned out better so, not only for the peasants, but for even the audience. For that form of the False Ideal has also its correspondent True Ideal,

—consisting not in the naked beauty of statues, nor in the gauze flowers and crackling tinsel of theatres, but in the clothed and fed beauty of living men, and in the lights and laughs of happy homes. Night after night, the desire of such an ideal springs up in every idle human heart; and night after night, as far as idleness can, we work out this desire in costly lies. We paint the faded actress, build the lath landscape, feed our benevolence with fallacies of felicity, and satisfy our righteousness with poetry of justice. The time will come when, as the heavy-folded curtain falls upon our own stage of life, we shall begin to comprehend that the justice we loved was intended to have been done in fact, and not in poetry, and the felicity we sympathized in, to have been bestowed and not feigned. We talk much of money's worth, yet perhaps may one day be surprised to find that what the wise and charitable European public gave to one night's rehearsal of hypocrisy,—to one hour's pleasant warbling of Linda or Lucia,—would have filled a whole Alpine Valley with happiness, and poured the waves of harvest over the famine of many a Lammermoor.

———o———

MAN'S ISOLATION.

Let man stand in his due relation to other creatures, and to inanimate things—know them all and love them, as made for him, and he for them;—and he becomes himself the greatest and holiest of them. But let him cast off this relation, despise and forget the less creation around him, and instead of being the light of the world, he is as a sun in space—a fiery ball, spotted with storm.

All the diseases of mind leading to fatalest ruin consist primarily in this isolation. They are the concentration of man upon himself, whether his heavenly interests or his worldly interests, matters not; it is the being *his own* interests which makes the regard of them so mortal. Every form of asceticism on one side, of sensualism on the other, is an isolation of his soul or of his body; the fixing his thoughts upon them alone: while every healthy state of nations and of individual minds consists in the unselfish presence of the human spirit everywhere, energizing over all things; speaking and living through all things.

It is a matter of the simplest demonstration, that no man can be really appreciated but by his equal or superior. His inferior may over-estimate him in enthusiasm; or, as is more commonly the case, degrade him, in ignorance; but he cannot form a grounded and just estimate. Without proving this, however—which it would take more space to do than I can spare—it is sufficiently evident that there is no process of amalgamation by which opinions, wrong individually, can become right merely by their multitude.

———o———

SHAMEFACEDNESS.

If it were at this moment proposed to any of us, by our architects, to remove the grinning head of a satyr, or other classical or Palladian ornament, from the keystone of the door, and to substitute for it a cross, and an inscription testifying our faith, I believe that most persons would shrink from the proposal with an obscure and yet overwhelming sense that things would be sometimes done, and thought, within the house which would make the inscription on its gate a base hypocrisy. And if so, let us look to it, whether that strong reluctance to utter a definite religious profession, which so many of us feel, and which, not very carefully examining into its dim nature, we conclude to be modesty, or fear of hypocrisy, or other such form of amiableness, be not, in very deed, neither less nor more than Infidelity; whether Peter's "I know not the man" be not the sum and substance of all these misgivings and hesitations; and whether the shamefacedness which we attribute to sincerity and reverence, be not such shamefacedness as may at last put us among those of whom the Son of Man shall be ashamed.

———o———

MAN THE IMAGE OF GOD.

The directest manifestation of Deity to man is in His own image, that is, in man.

"In his own image. After His likeness." *Ad imaginem et similitudinem Suam.* I do not know what people in general understand by those words. I suppose they ought to be understood. The truth they contain seems to lie at the foundation of our knowledge both of God and man; yet do we not usually pass the sentence by, in dull reverence, attaching no definite sense to it at all? For all practical purpose, might it not as well be out of the text?

I have no time, nor much desire, to examine the vague expressions of belief with which the verse has been encumbered. Let us try to find its only possible plain significance.

It cannot be supposed that the bodily shape of man resembles or resembled any bodily shape in Deity. The likeness must therefore be, or have been, in the soul. Had it wholly passed away, and the Divine soul been altered into a soul brutal or diabolic, I suppose we should have been told of the change. But we are told of nothing of the kind. The verse still stands as if for our use and trust. It was only death which was to be our punishment. Not *change.* So far as we live, the image is still there; defiled, if you will; broken, if you will; all but effaced, if you will, by death and the shadow of it. But not changed. We are not made now in any other image than God's. There are, indeed, the two states of this image—the earthly and the heavenly, but both Adamite, both human, both the same likeness; only one defiled, and one pure. So that the soul of man is still a mirror, wherein may be seen, darkly, the image of the mind of God. These may seem daring words. I am sorry that they do; but I am helpless to soften them. Discover any other meaning of the text if you are able;—but be sure that it *is* a meaning—a meaning in your head and heart,—not a subtle gloss, nor a shifting of one verbal expressionin to another, both idealess. I repeat, that, to me, the verse has, and can have, no other signification than this—that the soul of man is a mirror of the mind of God. A mirror dark, distorted, broken, use what blameful words you please of its state; yet in the main, a true mirror, out of which alone, and by which alone, we can know anything of God at all. "How?" the reader, perhaps, answers indignantly. "I know the nature of God by revelation, not by looking into myself."

Revelation to what? To a nature incapable of receiving truth? That cannot be; for only to a nature capable of truth, desirous of it, distinguishing it, feeding upon it, revelation is possible. To a being undesirous of it, and hating it, revelation is impossible. There can be none to a brute, or fiend. In so far, therefore, as you love truth, and live therein, in so far revelation can exist for you;—and in so far your mind is the image of God's.

But consider farther, not only *to* what, but *by* what is the revelation. By sight? or word? If by sight, then to eyes which see justly. Otherwise, no sight would be revelation. So far, then, as your sight is just, it is the image of God's sight.

If by words,—how do you know their meanings? Here is a short piece of precious word-revelation, for instance. "God is love."

Love! yes. But what is *that?* The revelation does not tell you that, I think. Look into the mirror, and you will see. Out of your own heart you may know what love is. In no other possible way,—by no other help or sign. All the words and sounds ever uttered, all the revelations of cloud, or flame, or crystal, are utterly powerless. They cannot tell you, in the smallest point, what love means. Only the broken mirror can.

Here is more revelation. "God is just!" Just! What is that? The revelation cannot help you to discover. You say it is dealing equitably or equally. But how do you discern the equality? Not by inequality of mind; not by a mind incapable of weighing, judging, or distributing. If the lengths seem unequal in the broken mirror, for you they are unequal; but if they seem equal, then the mirror is true. So far as you recognize equality, and your conscience tells you what is just, so far your mind is the image of God's: and so far as you do *not* discern this nature of justice or equality, the words "God is just" bring no revelation to you.

"But His thoughts are not as our thoughts." No; the sea is not as the standing pool by the wayside. Yet when the breeze crisps the pool, you may see the image of the breakers, and a likeness of the foam. Nay, in some sort, the same foam. If the sea is for ever invisible to you, something you may learn of it from the pool. Nothing, assuredly, any otherwise.

"But this poor miserable Me! Is *this*, then, all the book I have got to read about God in?" Yes, truly so. No other book, nor fragment of book, than that, will you ever find;—no velvet-bound missal, nor frankincensed manuscript;—nothing hieroglyphic nor cuneiform; papyrus and pyramid are alike silent on this matter;—nothing in the clouds above, nor in the earth beneath. That flesh-bound volume is the only revelation that is, that was, or that can be. In that is the image of God painted; in that is the law of God written; in that is the promise of God revealed. Know thyself; for through thyself only thou canst know God.

Through the glass, darkly. But, except through the glass, in nowise.

A tremulous crystal, waved as water, poured out upon the ground;—you may defile it, despise it, pollute it at your pleasure, and at your peril; for on the peace of those weak waves must all the heaven you shall ever gain be first seen; and through such purity as you can win for those dark waves, must all the light of the risen Sun of righteousness be bent down, by faint refraction. Cleanse them, and calm them, as you love your life.

Therefore it is that all the power of nature depends on subjection to the human soul. Man is the sun of the world; more than the real sun. The fire of his wonderful heart is the only light and heat worth gauge or measure. Where he is, are the tropics; where he is not, the ice-world.

———o———

THE DREAMERS.

Newton, probably, did not perceive whether the apple which suggested his meditations on gravity was withered or rosy;

nor could Howard be affected by the picturesqueness of the architecture which held the sufferers it was his occupation to relieve.

This wandering away in thought from the thing seen to the business of life is not, however, peculiar to men of the highest reasoning powers or the most active benevolence. It takes place, more or less, in nearly all persons of average mental endowment. They see and love what is beautiful, but forget their admiration of it in following some train of thought which it suggested, and which is of more personal interest to them.

Suppose that three or four persons come in sight of a group of pine-trees, not having seen pines for some time. One, perhaps an engineer, is struck by the manner in which their roots hold the ground, and sets himself to examine their fibres, in a few minutes retaining little more consciousness of the beauty of the trees than if he were a ropemaker untwisting the strands of a cable; to another, the sight of the trees calls up some happy association, and presently he forgets them, and pursues the memories they summoned; a third is struck by certain groupings of their colours, useful to him as an artist, which he proceeds to note mechanically for future use with as little feeling as a cook setting down the constituents of a newly-discovered dish; and a fourth, impressed by the wild wailing of boughs and roots, will begin to change them in his fancy into dragons and monsters, and lose his grasp of the scene in fantastic metamorphosis; while in the mind of the man who has most the power of contemplating the thing itself, all these perceptions and ideas are partially present, not distinctly, but in a mingled and perfect harmony. He will not see the colours of the tree so well as the artist, nor its fibres so well as the engineer; he will not altogether share the emotion of the sentimentalist, nor the trance of the idealist; but fancy, and feeling, and perception, and imagination, will all obscurely meet and balance themselves in him, and he will see the pine-trees somewhat in this manner:

> "Worthier still of note
> Are those fraternal Four of Borrowdale,
> Joined in one solemn and capacious grove;
> Huge trunks! and each particular trunk a growth
> Of intertwisted fibres serpentine
> Up-coiling, and inveterately convolved;
> Nor uniformed with Phantasy, and looks
> That threaten the profane; a pillared shade,
> Upon whose grassless floor of red-brown hue,
> By sheddings from the pining umbrage tinged
> Perennially,—beneath whose sable roof
> Of boughs, as if for festal purpose, decked
> With unrejoicing berries, ghostly Shapes
> May meet at noontide; Fear and trembling Hope,
> Silence and Foresight; Death the Skeleton,
> And Time the Shadow; there to celebrate,
> As in a natural temple scattered o'er
> With altars undisturbed of mossy stone,
> United worship."

The power, therefore, of thus fully *perceiving* any natural object depends on our being able to group and fasten all our fancies about it as a centre, making a garland of thoughts for it, in which each separate thought is subdued and shortened of its own strength, in order to fit it for harmony with others; the intensity of our enjoyment of the object depending, first, on its own beauty, and then on the richness of the garland. And men who have this habit of clustering and harmonizing their thoughts are a little too apt to look scornfully upon the harder workers who tear the bouquet to pieces to examine the stems. This was the chief narrowness of Wordsworth's mind; he could not understand that to break a rock with a hammer in search of crystal may sometimes be an act not disgraceful to human nature, and that to dissect a flower may sometimes be as proper as to dream over it; whereas, all experience goes to teach us that among men of average intellect, the most useful members of society are the dissectors, not the dreamers. It is not that they love nature or beauty less, but that they love result, effect, and progress more.

———o———

THE OLD CATHEDRALS.

Men say their pinnacles point to heaven. Why, so does every tree that buds, and every bird that rises as it sings. Men say their aisles are good for worship. Why, so is every mountain glen, and rough sea-shore. But this they have of distinct and indisputable glory,—that their mighty walls were never raised, and never shall be, but by men who love and aid each other in their weakness;—that all their interlacing strength of vaulted stone has its foundation upon the stronger arches of manly fellowship, and all their changing grace of depressed or lifted pinnacle owes its cadence and completeness to sweeter symmetries of human soul.

———o———

PLAGIARISM.

Touching plagiarism in general, it is to be remembered that all men who have sense and feeling are being continually helped: they are taught by every person whom they meet and enriched by everything that falls in their way The greatest is he who has been oftenest aided; and, if the attainments of all human minds could be traced to their real sources, it would be found that the world had been laid most under contribution by the men of most original power, and that every day of their existence deepened their debt to their race, while it enlarged their gifts to it. The labour devoted to trace the origin of any thought, or any invention, will usually issue in the blank conclusion that there is nothing new under the sun; yet nothing that is truly great can ever be altogether borrowed; and he is commonly the wisest, and is always the happiest, who receives simply, and without envious question, whatever good is offered him, with thanks to its immediate giver.

———o———

THE "LET ALONE" PRINCIPLE.

A nation's labour, well applied, is amply sufficient to provide its whole population with good food, comfortable clothing, and pleasant luxury. But the good, instant, and constant application is everything. We must not, when our strong hands are thrown out of work, look wildly about for want of something to do with them. If ever we feel that want, it is a sign that all our household is out of order. Fancy a farmer's wife, to whom one or two of her servants should come at twelve o'clock at noon, crying that they had got nothing to do; that they did not know what to do next: and fancy still farther, the said farmer's wife looking hopelessly about her rooms and yard, they being all the while considerably in disorder, not knowing where to set the spare hand-maidens to work, and at last complaining bitterly that she had been obliged to give them their dinner for nothing. Would you not at once assert of such a mistress that she knew nothing of her duties? and would you not be certain, if the household were rightly managed, the mistress would be only too glad at any moment to have the help of any number of spare hands; that she would know in an instant what to set them to;—in an instant what part of to-morrow's work might be most serviceably forwarded, what part of next month's work most wisely provided for, or what new task of some profitable kind undertaken? and when the evening came, and she dismissed her servants to their recreation or their rest, or gathered them to the reading round the work-table, under the eaves in the sunset, would you not be sure to find that none of them had been overtasked by her, just because none had been left idle; that everything had been accomplished because all had been employed; that the kindness of the mistress had aided her presence of mind, and the slight labour had been entrusted to the weak, and the formidable to the strong; and that as none had been dishonoured by inactivity, so none had been broken by toil? Now the precise counterpart of such a household would be seen in a nation in which political economy was rightly understood.

---o---

DISCIPLINE AND INTERFERENCE.

For half an hour every Sunday we expect a man in a black gown, supposed to be telling us truth, to address us as brethren, though we should be shocked at the notion of any brotherhood existing among us out of church. And we can hardly read a few sentences on any political subject without running a chance of crossing the phrase "paternal government," though we should be utterly horror-struck at the idea of governments claiming anything like a father's authority over us. Now, I believe those two formal phrases are in both instances perfectly binding and accurate, and that the image of the farm and its servants which I have hitherto used, as expressing a wholesome national organization, fails only of doing so, not because it is too domestic, but because it is not domestic enough; because the real type of a well-organized nation must be presented, not by a farm cultivated by servants who wrought for hire, and might be turned away if they refused to labour, but by a farm in which the master was a father, and in which all the servants were sons; which implied, therefore, in all its regulations, not merely the order of expediency, but the bonds of affection and responsibilities of relationship; and in which all acts and services were not only to be sweetened by brotherly concord, but to be enforced by fatherly authority.

Observe, I do not mean in the least that we ought to place such an authority in the hands of any one person, or of any class, or body of persons. But I do mean to say that as an individual who conducts himself wisely must make laws for himself which at some time or other may appear irksome or injurious, but which, precisely at the time they appear most irksome, it is most necessary he should obey, so a nation which means to conduct itself wisely, must establish authority over itself, vested either in kings, councils, or laws, which it must resolve to obey, even at times when the law or authority appears irksome to the body of the people, or injurious to certain masses of it. And this kind of national law has hitherto been only judicial; contented, that is, with an endeavour to prevent and punish violence and crime; but, as we advance in our social knowledge, we shall endeavour to make our government paternal as well as judicial; that is, to establish such laws and authorities as may at once direct us in our occupations, protect us against our follies, and visit us in our distresses: a government which shall repress dishonesty, as now it punishes theft; which shall show how the discipline of the masses may be brought to aid the toils of peace, as discipline of the masses has hitherto knit the sinews of battle; a government which shall have its soldiers of the ploughshare as well as its soldiers of the sword, and which shall distribute more proudly its golden crosses of industry—golden as the glow of the harvest, than now it grants its bronze crosses of honour—bronzed with the crimson of blood.

I have not, of course, time to insist on the nature or details of government of this kind; only I wish to plead for your several and future consideration of this one truth, that the notion of Discipline and Interference lies at the very root of all human progress or power; that the "Let alone" principle is, in all things which man has to do with, the principle of death; that it is ruin to him, certain and total, if he lets his land alone—if he lets his fellow-men alone—if he lets his own soul alone. That his whole life, on the contrary, must, if it is healthy life, be continually one of ploughing and pruning, rebuking and helping, governing and punishing; and that therefore it is only in the concession of some great principle of restraint and interference in national action that he can ever hope to find the secret of protection against national degradation.

LESSONS FROM ROCKS.

There is one lesson evidently intended to be taught by the different characters of these rocks, which we must not allow to escape us. We have to observe, first, the state of perfect powerlessness, and loss of all beauty, exhibited in those beds of earth in which the separated pieces or particles are entirely independent of each other, more especially in the gravel whose pebbles have all been *rolled into one shape:* secondly, the greater degree of permanence, power, and beauty possessed by the rocks whose component atoms have some affection and attraction for each other, though all of one kind; and, lastly, the utmost form and highest beauty of the rocks in which the several atoms have all *different shapes, characters*, and *offices;* but are inseparably united by some fiery process which has purified them all.

It can hardly be necessary to point out how these natural ordinances seem intended to teach us the great truths which are the basis of all political science; how the polishing friction which separates, the affection which binds, and the affliction that fuses and confirms, are accurately symbolized by the processes to which the several ranks of hills appear to owe their present aspect; and how, even if the knowledge of those processes be denied to us, that present aspect may in itself seem no imperfect image of the various states of mankind; first, that which is powerless through total disorganization; secondly, that which, though united, and in some degree powerful, is yet incapable of great effort or result, owing to the too great similarity and confusion of offices, both in ranks and individuals; and finally, the perfect state of brotherhood and strength in which each character is clearly distinguished, separately perfected, and employed in its proper place and office.

———o———

REVERENCE.

When the flowers and grass were regarded as means of life, and therefore (as the thoughtful labourer of the soil must always regard them) with the reverence due to those gifts of God which were most necessary to his existence, although their own beauty was less felt, their proceeding from the Divine hand was more seriously acknowledged, and the herb yielding seed, and fruit-tree yielding fruit, though in themselves less admired, were yet solemnly connected in the heart with the reverence of Ceres, Pomona, or Pan. But when the sense of these necessary uses was more or less lost, among the upper classes, by the delegation of the art of husbandry to the hands of the peasant, the flower and fruit, whose bloom or richness thus became a mere source of pleasure, were regarded with less solemn sense of the Divine gift in them; and were converted rather into toys than treasures, chance gifts for gaiety, rather than promised rewards of labour; so that while the Greek could hardly have trodden the formal furrow, or plucked the clusters from the trellised vine, without reverent thoughts of the deities of field and leaf, who gave the seed to fructify, and the bloom to darken, the mediæval knight plucked the violet to wreathe in his lady's hair, or strewed the idle rose on the turf at her feet, with little sense of anything in the nature that gave them, but a frail, accidental, involuntary exuberance; while also the Jewish sacrificial system being now done away, as well as the Pagan mythology, and, with it, the whole conception of meat offering or firstfruits offering, the chiefest seriousness of all the thoughts connected with the gifts of nature faded from the minds of the classes of men concerned with art and literature; while the peasant, reduced to serf level, was incapable of imaginative thought, owing to his want of general cultivation.

———o———

MYSTERY IN LANGUAGE.

All noble language-mystery is reached only by intense labour. Striving to speak with uttermost truth of expression, weighing word against word, and wasting none, the great speaker, or writer, toils first into perfect intelligibleness, then, as he reaches to higher subject, and still more concentrated and wonderful utterance, he becomes ambiguous—as Dante is ambiguous,—half a dozen different meanings lightening out in separate rays from every word, and, here and there, giving rise to much contention of critics as to what the intended meaning actually was. But it is no drunkard's babble for all that, and the men who think it so, at the third hour of the day, do not highly honour *themselves* in the thought.

---o---

ALL THINGS HAVE THEIR PLACE.

Many plants are found alone on a certain soil or subsoil in a wild state, not because such soil is favourable to them, but because they alone are capable of existing on it, and because all dangerous rivals are by its inhospitality removed. Now if we withdraw the plant from this position, which it hardly endures, and supply it with the earth, and maintain about it the temperature that it delights in; withdrawing from it at the same time all rivals which, in such conditions, nature would have thrust upon it; we shall indeed obtain a magnificently developed example of the plant, colossal in size, and splendid in organization, but we shall utterly lose in it that moral ideal which is dependent on its right fulfilment of its appointed functions. It was intended and created by the

Deity for the covering of those lonely spots where no other plant could live; it has been thereto endowed with courage, and strength, and capacities of endurance unequalled; its character and glory are not therefore in the gluttonous and idle feeling of its own over luxuriance, at the expense of other creatures utterly destroyed and rooted out for its good alone, but in its right doing of its hard duty, and forward climbing into those spots of forlorn hope where it alone can bear witness to the kindness and presence of the Spirit that cutteth out rivers among the rocks, as it covers the valleys with corn.

———o———

PERFECT AND PARTIAL TRUTH.

At least, in the midst of its malice, misery, and baseness, it is often a relief to glance at the graceful shadows, and take, for momentary companionship, creatures full only of love, gladness, and honour. But the perfect truth will at last vindicate itself against the partial truth; the help which we can gain from the unsubstantial vision will be only like that which we may sometimes receive, in weariness, from the scent of a flower or the passing of a breeze.

———o———

THE REALITY.

Whatever delight we may have been in the habit of taking in pictures, if it were but truly offered to us, to remove at our will the canvass from the frame, and in lieu of it to behold, fixed for ever, the image of some of those mighty scenes which it has been our way to make mere themes for the artist's fancy; if, for instance, we could again behold the Magdalene receiving her pardon at Christ's feet, or the disciples sitting with Him at the table of Emmaus; and this not feebly nor fancifully, but as if some silver mirror, that had leaned against the wall of the chamber, had been miraculously commanded to retain for ever the colours that had flashed upon it for an instant,—would we not part with our picture —Titian's or Veronese's though it might be?

———o———

RESPECT FOR THE DEAD.

Our respect for the dead, when they are *just* dead, is something wonderful, and the way we show it more wonderful still. We show it with black feathers and black horses; we show it with black dresses and bright heraldries; we show it with costly obelisks and sculptures of sorrow, which spoil half of our most beautiful cathedrals. We show it with frightful gratings and vaults, and lids of dismal stone, in the midst of the quiet grass; and last, not least, we show it by permitting ourselves to tell any number of lies we think amiable or credible, in the epitaph. This feeling is common to the poor as well as the rich; and we all know how many a poor family will nearly ruin themselves, to testify their respect for some member of it in his coffin, whom they never much cared for when he was out of it; and how often it happens that a poor old woman will starve herself to death, in order that she may be respectably buried.

Now, this being one of the most complete and special ways of wasting money;—no money being less productive of good, or of any percentage whatever, than that which we shake away from the ends of undertakers' plumes—it is of course the duty of all good economists, and kind persons, to prove and proclaim continually, to the poor as well as the rich, that respect for the dead is not really shown by laying great stones on them to tell us where they are laid; but by remembering where they are laid without a stone to help us; trusting them to the sacred grass and saddened flowers; and still more, that respect and love are shown to them, not by great monuments to them which we build with *our* hands, but by letting the monuments stand, which they built with *their own.* And this is the point now in question.

Observe, there are two great reciprocal duties concerning industry, constantly to be exchanged between the living and the dead. We, as we live and work, are to be always thinking of those who are to come after us; that what we do may be serviceable, as far as we can make it so, to them, as well as to us. Then, when we die, it is the duty of those who come after us to accept this work of ours with thanks and remembrance, not thrusting it aside or tearing it down the moment they think they have no use for it. And each generation will only be happy or powerful to the pitch that it ought to be, in fulfilling these two duties to the Past and the Future. Its own work will never be rightly done, even for itself—never good, or noble, or pleasurable to its own eyes—if it does not also prepare it for the eyes of generations yet to come. And its own possessions will never be enough for it, unless it avails itself gratefully and tenderly of the treasures and wisdom bequeathed to it by its ancestors. For, be assured, that all the best things and treasures of this world are not to be produced by each generation for itself; but we are all intended, not to carve our work in snow that will melt, but each and all of us to be rolling a great white gathering snowball,—higher and higher, larger and larger,—along the Alps of human power. Thus the science of nations is to be accumulative from father to son; the history and poetry of nations is to be accumulative; each generation treasuring the history and the songs of its ancestors, adding its own history and its own songs; and the art of nations is to be accumulative,—the work of living men not superseding, but building itself upon the work of the past. Nearly every great and intellectual race of the world has produced, at every period of its career, with some peculiar and precious character about it wholly unattainable by any other race, and at any other time, and the intention of Providence concerning that art is evidently that it should all grow together into one mighty temple; the rough and the smooth all finding their place, and rising, day by day, in richer and higher pinnacles to heaven.

Now just fancy what a position the world would have been in by this time, if it had in the least understood this duty or been capable of it. Fancy what we should have had around us now if, instead of quarrelling and fighting over their work, the nations had aided each other in their work, or if even in their conquests, instead of effacing the memorials of those they succeeded and subdued, they had guarded the spoils of their victories. Fancy what Europe would be now, if the delicate statues and temples of the Greeks,—if the broad roads and massy walls of the Romans,—if the noble and pathetic architecture of the middle ages, had not been ground to dust by mere human rage. You talk of the scythe of Time, and the tooth of Time: I tell you, Time is scytheless and toothless; it is we who gnaw like the worm—we who smite like the scythe. It is ourselves who abolish—ourselves who consume: we are the mildew, and the flame, and the soul of man is to its own work as the moth, that frets when it cannot fly, and as the hidden flame that blasts where it cannot illumine. All these lost treasures of human intellect have been wholly destroyed by human industry of destruction; the marble would have stood its two thousand years as well in the polished statue as in the Parian cliff; but we men have ground it to powder, and mixed it with our own ashes. The walls and the ways would have stood—it is we who have left not one stone upon another, and restored its pathlessness to the desert; the great cathedrals of old religion would have stood —it is we who have dashed down the carved work with axes and hammers, and bid the mountain-grass bloom upon the pavement, and the sea-winds chaunt in the galleries.

———o———

IDOLATRY.

I do not intend, in thus applying the word "Idolatry" to certain ceremonies of Romanist worship, to admit the propriety of the ordinary Protestant manner of regarding those ceremonies as distinctively idolatrous, and as separating the Romanist from the Protestant Church by a gulf across which we must not look to our fellow-Christians but with utter reprobation and disdain. The Church of Rome does indeed distinctively violate the *second* commandment; but the true force and weight of the sin of idolatry are in the violation of the first, of which we are all of us guilty, in probably a very equal degree, considered only as members of this or that communion, and not as Christians or unbelievers. Idolatry is, both literally and verily, not the mere bowing down before scuptures, but the serving or becoming the slave of any images or imaginations which stand between us and God, and it is otherwise expressed in Scripture as "walking after the *Imagination*" of our own hearts. And observe also that while, at least on one occasion, we find in the Bible an indulgence granted to the mere eternal and literal violation of the second commandment, "When I bow myself in the house of Rimmon, the Lord pardon thy servant in this thing," we find no indulgence in any instance, or in the slightest degree, granted to "covetousness, which is idolatry" (Col. iii. 5; no casual association of terms, observe, but again energetically repeated in Ephesians, v. 5, "No covetous man, who is an idolater, hath any inheritance in the kingdom of Christ"); nor any to that denial of God, idolatry in one of its most subtle forms, following so often on the possession of that wealth against which Agur prayed so earnestly, "Give me neither poverty nor riches, lest I be full and deny thee, and say, 'Who is the Lord?'"

And in this sense, which of us is not an idolater? Which of us has the right, in the fulness of that better knowledge, in spite of which he nevertheless is not yet separated from the service of this world, to speak scornfully of any of his brethren, because, in a guiltless ignorance, they have been accustomed to bow their knees before a statue? Which of us shall say that there may not be a spiritual worship in their apparent idolatry, or that there is not a spiritual idolatry in our own apparent worship?

For indeed it is utterly impossible for one man to judge of the feeling with which another bows down before an image. From that pure reverence in which Sir Thomas Brown wrote, "I can dispense with my hat at the sight of a cross, but not with a thought of my Redeemer," to the worst superstition of the most ignorant Romanist, there is an infinite series of subtle transitions; and the point where simple reverence and the use of the image merely to render conception more vivid, and feeling more intense, change into definite idolatry by the attribution of Power to the image itself, is so difficultly determinable that we cannot be too cautious in asserting that such a change has actually taken place in the case of any individual.

OBEDIENCE TO LAW, OR LOYALTY.

In one of the noblest poems,* for its imagery and its music,

* "Ye Clouds! that far above me float and pause,
Whose pathless march no mortal may control!
Ye Ocean-Waves! that wheresoe'er ye roll,
Yield homage only to eternal laws!
Ye Woods! that listen to the night-birds singing,
Midway the smooth and perilous slope reclined,
Save when your own imperious branches swinging,
Have made a solemn music of the wind!
Where, like a man beloved of God,
Through glooms, which never woodman trod,
How oft, pursuing fancies holy,
My moonlight way o'er flowering weeds I wound,
Inspired, beyond the guess of folly,
By each rude shape and wild unconquerable sound!
O ye loud Waves! and O ye Forests high!
And O ye Clouds that far above me soared!
Thou rising Sun! thou blue rejoicing Sky!
Yea, everything that is and will be free!
Bear witness for me, wheresoe'er ye be,
With what deep worship I have still adored
The spirit of divinest Liberty."—COLERIDGE.

Noble verse, but erring thought: contrast George Herbert:—

"Slight those who say amidst their sickly healths,
Thou livest by rule. What doth not so but man?
Houses are built by rule and Commonwealths.
Entice the trusty sun, if that you can,
From his ecliptic line; beckon the sky.
Who lives by rule then, keeps good company.

"Who keeps no guard upon himself is slack,
And rots to nothing at the next great thaw;
Man is a shop of rules: a well-truss'd pack
Whose every parcel underwrites a law.
Lose not thyself, nor give thy humours way;
God gave them to thee under lock and key."

belonging to the recent school of our literature, the writer has sought in the aspect of inanimate nature the expression of that liberty which, having once wooed, he had seen among men in its true dyes of darkness. But with what strange fallacy of interpretation! since in one noble line of his invocation he has contradicted the assumptions of the rest, and acknowledged the presence of a subjection, surely not less severe than eternal. How could he otherwise? since if there be any one principle more widely than another confessed by every utterance, or more sternly than another imprinted on every atom of the visible creation, that principle is not Liberty, but Law.

Obedience is, indeed, founded on a kind of freedom, else it would become mere subjugation, but that freedom is only granted that obedience may be more perfect; and thus, while a measure of license is necessary to exhibit the individual energies of things, the fairness and pleasantness and perfection of them all consist in their Restraint. Compare a river that has burst its banks with one that is bound by them, and the clouds that are scattered over the face of the whole heaven with those that are marshalled into ranks and orders by its winds. So that though restraint, utter and unrelaxing, can never be comely, this is not because it is in itself an evil, but only because, when too great, it overpowers the nature of the thing restrained, and so counteracts the other laws of which that nature is itself composed. And the balance wherein consists the fairness of creation is between the laws of life and being in the things governed and the laws of general sway to which they are subjected; and the suspension or infringement of either kind of law, or, literally, disorder, is equivalent to, and synonymous with, disease; while the increase of both honour and beauty is habitually on the side of restraint (or the action of superior law) rather than of character (or the action of inherent law). The noblest word in the catalogue of social virtue is "Loyalty," and the sweetest which men have learned in the pastures of the wilderness is "Fold."

Nor is this all; but we may observe, that exactly in proportion to the majesty of things in the scale of being, is the completeness of their obedience to the laws that are set over them. Gravitation is less quietly, less instantly obeyed by a grain of dust than it is by the sun and moon; and the ocean falls and flows under influences which the lake and river do not recognise. So also in estimating the dignity of any action or occupation of men, there is perhaps no better test than the question "are its laws strait?" For their severity will probably be commensurate with the greatness of the numbers whose labour it concentrates or whose interest it concerns.

---o---

THE GOODNESS OF GOD IN CREATION.

There is this difference between the positions held in creation by animals and plants, and thence in the dispositions with which we regard them; that the animals, being for the most part locomotive, are capable both of living where they choose, and of obtaining what food they want, and of fulfilling all the conditions necessary to their health and perfection. For which reason they are answerable for such health and perfection, and we should be displeased and hurt if we did not find it in one individual as well as another.

But the case is evidently different with plants. They are intended fixedly to occupy many places comparatively unfit for them, and to fill up all the spaces where greenness, and coolness, and ornament, and oxygen are wanted, and that with very little reference to their comfort or convenience.

Now it would be hard upon the plant if, after being tied to a particular spot, where it is indeed much wanted, and is a great blessing, but where it has enough to do to live, whence it cannot move to obtain what it wants or likes, but must stretch its unfortunate arms here and there for bare breath and light, and split its way among rocks, and grope for sustenance in unkindly soil; it would be hard upon the plant, I say, if under all these disadvantages, it were made answerable for its appearance, and found fault with because it was not a fine plant of the kind. And so we find it ordained that in order that no unkind comparisons may be drawn between one and another, there are not appointed to plants the fixed number, position, and proportion of members which are ordained in animals, (and any variation from which in these is unpardonable,) but a continually varying number and position, even among the more freely growing examples, admitting therefore all kinds of license to those which have enemies to contend with, and that without in any way detracting from their dignity and perfection.

So then there is in trees no perfect form which can be fixed upon or reasoned out as ideal; but that is always an ideal oak which, however poverty-stricken, or hunger-pinched, or tempest-tortured, is yet seen to have done, under its appointed circumstances, all that could be expected of oak.

And herein, then, we at last find the cause of that fact, that the exalted or seemingly improved condition, whether of plant or animal, induced by human interference, is not the true but artistical ideal of it.* It has been well shown by Dr.

* I speak not here of those conditions of vegetation which have especial reference to man, as of seeds and fruits, whose sweetness and farina seem in great measure given, not for the plant's sake but for his, and to which therefore the interruption in the harmony of creation of which he was the cause is extended, and their sweetness and larger measure of good

Herbert, that many plants are found alone on a certain soil or sub-soil in a wild state, not because such soil is favorable to them, but because they alone are capable of existing on it, and because all dangerous rivals are by its inhospitality removed. Now if we withdraw the plant from this position, which it hardly endures, and supply it with the earth, and maintain about it the temperature that it delights in; withdrawing from it at the same time all rivals which, in such conditions, nature would have thrust upon it, we shall indeed obtain a magnificently developed example of the plant, colossal in size, and splendid in organization, but we shall utterly lose in it that moral ideal which is dependent on its right fulfilment of its appointed functions. It was intended and created by the Deity for the covering of those lonely spots where no other plant could live; it has been thereto endowed with courage, and strength, and capacities of endurance unequalled; its character and glory are not therefore in the gluttonous and idle feeling of its own over luxuriance, at the expense of other creatures utterly destroyed and rooted out for its good alone, but in its right doing of its hard duty, and forward climbing into those spots of forlorn hope where it alone can bear witness to the kindness and presence of the Spirit that cutteth out rivers among the rocks, as it covers the valleys with corn: and there, in its vanward place, and only there, where nothing is withdrawn for it, nor hurt by it, and where nothing can take part of its honour, nor usurp its throne, are its strength, and fairness, and price, and goodness in the sight of God, to be truly esteemed.

The first time that I saw the soldanella alpina, it was growing, of magnificent size, on a sunny Alpine pasture, among

to be obtained only by his redeeming labour His curse has fallen on the corn and the vine, and the wild barley misses of its fulness, that he may eat bread by the sweat of his brow bleating of sheep and lowing of cattle, associated with a profusion of geum montanum, and ranunculus pyrenæus. I noticed it only because new to me, nor perceived any peculiar beauty in its cloven flower. Some days after, I found it alone, among the rack of the higher clouds, and howling of glacier winds, and, as I described it, piercing through an edge of avalanche, which in its retiring had left the new ground brown and lifeless, and as if burned by recent fire; the plant was poor and feeble, and seemingly exhausted with its efforts, but it was then that I comprehended its ideal character, and saw its noble function and order of glory among the constellations of the earth.

———o———

THE PRINCIPLES OF GOOD GOVERNMENT.

One of the frescoes by Ambrozio Lorenzetti, in the town-hall of Siena, represents, by means of symbolical figures, the principles of Good Civic Government and of Good Government in general. The figure representing this noble Civic Government is enthroned, and surrounded by figures representing the Virtues, variously supporting or administering its authority. Now, observe what work is given to each of these virtues. Three winged ones—Faith, Hope, and Charity—surrounded the head of the figure, not in mere compliance with the common and heraldic laws of precedence among Virtues, such as we moderns observe habitually, but with peculiar purpose on the part of the painter. Faith, as thus represented, ruling the thoughts of the Good Governor, does not mean merely religious faith, understood in those times to be necessary to all persons—governed no less than governors—but it means the faith which enables work to be carried out steadily, in spite of adverse appearances and expediencies, the faith in great principles, by which a civic ruler looks past all the immediate checks and shadows that would daunt a common man, knowing that what is rightly done will have a right issue, and holding his way in spite of pullings at his cloak and whisperings in his ear, enduring, as having in him a faith which is evidence of things unseen. And Hope, in like manner, is here not the heavenward hope which ought to animate the hearts of all men; but she attends upon Good Government, to show that all such government is *expectant* as well as *conservative;* that if it ceases to be hopeful of better things, it ceases to be a wise guardian of present things: that it ought never, as long as the world lasts, to be wholly content with any existing state of institution or possession, but to be hopeful still of more wisdom and power; not clutching at it restlessly or hastily, but feeling that its real life consists in steady ascent from high to higher: conservative, indeed, and jealously conservative of old things, but conservative of them as pillars not as pinnacles—as aids, but not as Idols; and hopeful chiefly, and active, in times of national trial or distress, according to those first and notable words describing the queenly nation. "She riseth, *while it is yet night.*" And again, the winged Charity which is attendant on Good Government has, in this fresco, a peculiar office. Can you guess what? If you consider the character of contest which so often takes place among kings for their crowns, and the selfish and tyrannous means they commonly take to aggrandize or secure their power, you will, perhaps, be surprised to hear that the office of Charity is to crown the King. And yet, if you think of it a little, you will see the beauty of the thought which sets her in this function: since in the first place, all the authority of a good governor should be desired by him only for the good of his people, so that it is only Love that makes him accept or guard his crown: in the second place, his chief greatness consists in the exercise of this love, and he is truly to be revered only so far as his acts and thoughts are those of kindness; so that Love is the light of his crown, as well as the giver of it: lastly, because his strength depends on the affections of his people, and it is only their love which can securely crown him, and for ever. So that Love is the strength of his crown as well as the light of it.

Then, surrounding the King, or in various obedience to him, appear the dependent virtues, as Fortitude, Temperance, Truth, and other attendant spirits, of all which I cannot now give account, wishing you only to notice the one to whom are entrusted the guidance and administration of the public revenues. Can you guess which it is likely to be? Charity, you would have thought, should have something to do with the business; but not so, for she is too hot to attend carefully to it. Prudence, perhaps, you think of in the next place. No, she is too timid, and loses opportunities in making up her mind. Can it be Liberality then? No: Liberality is entrusted with some small sums; but she is a bad accountant, and is allowed no important place in the exchequer. But the treasures are given in charge to a virtue of which we hear too little in modern times, as distinct from others; Magnanimity: largeness of heart: not softness or weakness of heart, mind you—but capacity of heart—the great *measuring* virtue, which weighs in heavenly balances all that may be given, and all that may be gained; and sees how to do noblest things in noblest ways: which of two goods comprehends and therefore chooses the greatest: which of two personal sacrifices dares and accepts the largest: which, out of the avenues of beneficence, treads always that which opens farthest into the blue fields of futurity: that character, in fine, which, in those words taken by us at first for the description of a Queen among the nations, looks less to the present power than to the distant promise; "Strength and honour are in her clothing,—and she shall rejoice IN TIME TO COME."

———o———

ASSIMILATION AND INDIVIDUALITY.

It is a lamentable and unnatural thing to see a number of men subject to no government, actuated by no ruling principle, and associated by no common affection: but it would be a more lamentable thing still, were it possible, to see a number of men so oppressed into assimilation as to have no more any individual hope or character, no differences in aim, no dissimilarities of passion, no irregularities of judgment; a society in which no man could help another, since none would be feebler than himself; no man admire another, since none would be stronger than himself; no man be grateful to another, since by none he could be relieved; no man reverence another, since by none he could be instructed; a society in which every soul would be as the syllable of a stammerer instead of the word of a speaker, in which every man would walk as in a frightful dream, seeing spectres of himself, in everlasting multiplication, gliding helplessly around him in a speechless darkness. Therefore it is that perpetual difference, play, and change in groups of form are more essential to them even than their being subdued by some great gathering law: the law is needful to them for their perfection and their power, but the difference is needful to them for their *life.*

———o———

A SOLEMN WARNING.

The phases of transition in the moral temper of the falling Venetians, during their fall, were from pride to infidelity, and from infidelity to the unscrupulous *pursuit of pleasure.* During the last years of the existence of the state, the minds both of the nobility and the people seem to have been set simply upon the attainment of the means of self-indulgence. There was not strength enough in them to be proud, nor forethought enough to be ambitious. One by one the possessions of the state were abandoned to its enemies; one by one the channels of its trade were forsaken by its own languor, or occupied and closed against it by its more energetic rivals; and the time, the resources, and the thoughts of the nation were exclusively occupied in the invention of such fantastic and costly pleasures as might best amuse their apathy, lull their remorse, or disguise their ruin.

It is as needless, as it is painful, to trace the steps of her final ruin. That ancient curse was upon her, the curse of the cities of the plain, "Pride, fulness of bread, and abundance of idleness." By the inner burning of her own passions, as fatal as the fiery rain of Gomorrah, she was consumed from her place among the nations; and her ashes are choking the channels of the dead salt sea.

———o———

LIFE.

Among the countless analogies by which the nature and relations of the human soul are illustrated in the material creation, none are more striking than the impressions inseparably connected with the active and dormant states of matter.

I have elsewhere endeavoured to show, that no inconsiderable part of the essential characters of Beauty depended on the expression of vital energy in organic things, or on the subjection to such energy, of things naturally passive and powerless. I need not here repeat, of what was then advanced, more than the statement which I believe will meet with general acceptance, that things in other respects alike, as in their substance, or uses, or outward forms, are noble or ignoble in proportion to the fulness of the life which either they themselves enjoy, or of whose action they bear the evidence, as sea sands are made beautiful by their bearing the seal of the motion of the waters. And this is especially true of all objects which bear upon them the impress of the highest order of creative life, that is to say, of the mind of man: they become noble or ignoble in proportion to the amount of the energy of that mind which has visibly been employed upon them. But most peculiarly and imperatively does the rule hold with respect to the creations of Architecture, which being properly capable of no other life than this, and being not essentially composed of things pleasant in themselves,—as music of sweet sounds, or painting of fair colours, but of inert substance,—depend, for their dignity and pleasurableness in the utmost degree, upon the vivid expression of the intellectual life which has been concerned in their production.

Now in all other kind of energies except that of man's mind, there is no question as to what is life, and what is not. Vital sensibility, whether vegetable or animal, may, indeed, be reduced to so great feebleness, as to render its existence a matter of question, but when it is evident at all, it is evident as such: there is no mistaking any imitation or pretence of it for the life itself; no mechanism nor galvanism can take its place; nor is any resemblance of it so striking as to involve even hesitation in the judgment; although many occur which the human imagination takes pleasure in exalting, without for an instant losing sight of the real nature of the dead things it animates; but rejoicing rather in its own excessive life, which puts gesture into clouds, and joy into waves, and voices into rocks.

But when we begin to be concerned with the energies of man, we find ourselves instantly dealing with a double creature. Most part of his being seems to have a fictitious counterpart, which it is at his peril if he do not cast off and deny. Thus he has a true and false (otherwise called a living and dead, or a feigned or unfeigned) faith. He has a true and a false hope, a true and a false charity, and, finally, a true and a false life. His true life is like that of lower organic beings, the independent force by which he moulds and governs external things; it is a force of assimilation which converts everything around him into food, or into instruments; and which, however humbly or obediently it may listen to or follow the guidance of superior intelligence, never forfeits its own authority as a judging principle, as a will capable either of obeying or rebelling. His false life is, indeed, but one of the conditions of death or stupor, but it acts, even when it cannot be said to animate, and is not always easily known from the true. It is that life of custom and accident in which many of us pass much of our time in the world; that life in which we do what we have not purposed, and speak what we do not mean, and assent to what we do not understand; that life which is overlaid by the weight of things external to it, and is moulded by them, instead of assimilating them; that, which instead of growing and blossoming under any wholesome dew, is crystallised over with it, as with hoar frost, and becomes to the true life what an arborescence is to a tree, a candied agglomeration of thoughts and habits foreign to it, brittle, obstinate, and icy, which can neither bend nor grow but must be crushed and broken to bits, if it stand in our way. All men are liable to be in some degree frost-bitten in this sort; all are partly encumbered and crusted over with idle matter; only, if they have real life in them, they are always breaking this bark away in noble rents, until it becomes, like the black strips upon the birch-tree, only a witness of their own inward strength. But, with all the efforts that the best men make, much of their being passes in a kind of dream, in which they indeed move, and play their parts sufficiently, to the eyes of their fellow-dreamers, but have no clear consciousness of what is around them, or within them; blind to the one, insensible to the other, νωθροι. I would not press the definition into its darker application to the dull heart and heavy ear; I have to do with it only as it refers to the too frequent condition of natural existence, whether of nations or individuals, settling commonly upon them in proportion to their age. The life of a nation is usually, like the flow of a lava stream, first bright and fierce, then languid and covered, at last advancing only by the tumbling over and over of its frozen blocks. And that last condition is a sad one to look upon. All the steps are marked most clearly in the arts, and in Architecture more than in any other; for it, being especially dependent, as we have just said, on the warmth of the true life, is also peculiarly sensible of the hemlock cold of the false, and I do not know anything more oppressive, when the mind is once awakened to its characteristics, than the aspect of a dead architecture. The feebleness of childhood is full of promise and of interest,—the struggle of imperfect knowledge full of energy and continuity,—but to see impotence and rigidity settling upon the form of the developed man; to see the types which once had the die of thought struck fresh upon them, worn flat by overuse; to see the shell of the living creature in its adult form, when its colours are faded, and its inhabitant perished,—this is a sight more humiliating, more melancholy, than the vanishing of all knowledge, and the return to confessed and helpless infancy.

———o———

LOVE AND FEAR.

Two great and principal passions are evidently appointed by the Deity to rule the life of man; namely, the love of God, and the fear of sin, and of its companion—Death. How many motives we have for Love, how much there is in the universe to kindle our admiration and to claim our gratitude, there are, happily, multitudes among us who both feel and teach. But it has not, I think, been sufficiently considered how evident, throughout the system of creation, is the purpose of God that we should often be affected by Fear; not the sudden, selfish, and contemptible fear of immediate danger, but the fear which arises out of the contemplation of great powers in destructive operation, and generally from the perception of the presence of death. Nothing appears to me more remarkable than the array of scenic magnificence by which the imagination is appalled, in myriads of instances, when the actual danger is comparatively small; so that the utmost possible impression of awe shall be produced upon the minds of all, though direct suffering is inflicted upon few. Consider, for instance, the moral effect of a single thunder-storm Perhaps two or three persons may be struck dead within the space of a hundred square miles; and their deaths, unaccompanied by the scenery of the storm, would produce little more than a momentary sadness in the busy hearts of living men. But the preparation for the Judgment, by all that mighty gathering of clouds; by the questioning of the forest leaves, in their terrified stillness, which way the winds shall go forth; by the murmuring to each other, deep in the distance, of the destroying angels before they draw forth their swords of fire; by the march of the funeral darkness in the midst of the noon-day, and the rattling of the dome of heaven beneath the chariot-wheels of death;—on how many minds do not these produce an impression almost as great as the actual witnessing of the fatal issue! and how strangely are the expressions of the threatening elements fitted to the apprehension of the human soul! The lurid colour, the long, irregular, convulsive sound, the ghastly shapes of flaming and heaving cloud, are all as true and faithful in their appeal to our instinct of danger, as the moaning or wailing of the human voice itself is to our instinct of pity. It is not a reasonable calculating terror which they awake in us; it is no matter that we count distance by seconds, and measure probability by averages. That shadow of the thunder-cloud will still do its work upon our hearts, and we shall watch its passing away as if we stood upon the threshing-floor of Araunah.

And this is equally the case with respect to all the other destructive phenomena of the universe. From the mightiest of them to the gentlest, from the earthquake to the summer hower, it will be found that they are attended by certain aspects of threatening, which strike terror into the hearts of multitudes more numerous a thousandfold than those who actually suffer from the ministries of judgment; and that besides the fearfulness of these immediately dangerous phenomena, there is an occult and subtle horror belonging tc many aspects of the creation around us, calculated often tc fill us with serious thought, even in our times of quietness and peace.*

———o———

INVOLUNTARY INSTRUMENTS OF GOOD.

Wherever we see the virtue of ardent labour and self-surrendering to a single purpose, wherever we find constant reference made to the written scripture of natural beauty, this at least we know is great and good, this we know is not granted by the counsel of God, without purpose, nor maintained without result: Their interpretation we may accept, into their labour we may enter, but they themselves must look to it, if what they do has no intent of good, nor any reference to the Giver of all gifts. Selfish in their industry, unchastened in their wills, ungrateful for the Spirit that is upon them, they may yet be helmed by that Spirit whithersoever the Governor listeth; involuntary instruments they may become of others' good; unwillingly they may bless Israel, doubtingly discomfit Amalek, but shortcoming there will be of their glory, and sure, of their punishment.

———o———

THE SPIRIT OF SACRIFICE.

It seems to me, not only that this feeling is in most cases wholly wanting in those who forward the devotional build-

* The Love of God is, however, always shown by the predominance or greater sum of good in the end; but never by the annihilation of evil. The modern doubts of eternal punishment are not so much the consequence of benevolence as of feeble powers of reasoning. Every one admits that God brings finite good out of finite evil. Why not, therefore, infinite good out of infinite evil?

ings of the present day; but that it would even be regarded as an ignorant, dangerous, or perhaps criminal principle by many among us. I have not space to enter into dispute of all the various objections which may be urged against it—they are many and specious; but I may, perhaps, ask the reader's patience while I set down those simple reasons which cause me to believe it a good and just feeling, and as well-pleasing to God and honourable in men, as it is beyond all dispute necessary to the production of any great work in the kind with which we are at present concerned.

Now, first, to define this Spirit of Sacrifice, clearly. I have said that it prompts us to the offering of precious things, merely because they are precious, not because they are useful or necessary. It is a spirit, for instance, which of two marbles, equally beautiful, applicable, and durable, would choose the more costly, because it was so, and of two kinds of decoration, equally effective, would choose the more elaborate because it was so, in order that it might in the same compass present more cost and more thought. It is therefore most unreasoning and enthusiastic, and perhaps best negatively defined, as the opposite of the prevalent feeling of modern time, which desires to produce the largest results at the least cost.

Of this feeling, then, there are two distinct forms: the first, the wish to exercise self-denial for the sake of self-discipline merely, a wish acted upon in the abandonment of things loved or desired, there being no direct call or purpose to be answered by so doing; and the second, the desire to honour or please some one else by the costliness of the sacrifice. The practice is, in the first case, either private or public; but most frequently, and perhaps most properly, private; while, in the latter case, the act is commonly, and with greatest advantage, public. Now, it cannot but at first appear futile to assert the expediency of self-denial for its own sake, when, for so many sakes, it is every day necessary to a far greater degree than any of us practise it. But I believe it is just because we do not enough acknowledge or contemplate it as a good in itself, that we are apt to fail in its duties when they become imperative, and to calculate, with some partiality, whether the good proposed to others measures or warrants the amount of grievance to ourselves, instead of accepting with gladness the opportunity of sacrifice as a personal advantage. Be this as it may, it is not necessary to insist upon the matter here; since there are always higher and more useful channels of self-sacrifice, for those who choose to practise it, than any connected with the arts.

While in its second branch, that which is especially concerned with the arts, the justice of the feeling is still more doubtful; it depends on our answer to the broad question, can the Deity be indeed honoured by the presentation to Him of any material objects of value, or by any direction of zeal or wisdom which is not immediately beneficial to men?

For, observe, it is not now the question whether the fairness and majesty of a building may or may not answer any moral purpose; it is not the *result* of labour in any sort of which we are speaking, but the bare and mere costliness—the substance and labour and time themselves: are these, we ask, independently of their result, acceptable offerings to God, and considered by Him as doing Him honour? So long as we refer this question to the decision of feeling, or of conscience, or of reason merely, it will be contradictorily or imperfectly answered; it admits of entire answer only when we have met another and a far different question, whether the Bible be indeed one book or two, and whether the character of God revealed in the Old Testament be other than His character revealed in the New.

Now, it is a most secure truth, that, although the particular ordinances divinely appointed for special purposes at any given period of man's history, may be by the same divine authority abrogated at another, it is impossible that any character of God, appealed to or described in any ordinance past or present, can ever be changed, or understood as changed, by the abrogation of that ordinance. God is one and the same, and is pleased or displeased by the same thing for ever, although one part of His pleasure may be expressed at one time rather than another, and although the mode in which His pleasure is to be consulted may be by Him graciously modified to the circumstances of men. Thus, for instance, it was necessary that, in order to the understanding by man of the scheme of Redemption, that scheme should be foreshown from the beginning by the type of bloody sacrifice. But God had no more pleasure in such sacrifice in the time of Moses than He has now; He never accepted as a propitiation for sin any sacrifice but the single one in prospective; and that we may not entertain any shadow of doubt on this subject, the worthlessness of all other sacrifice than this is proclaimed at the very time when typical sacrifice was most imperatively demanded. God was a spirit, and could be worshipped only in spirit and in truth, as singly and exclusively when every day brought its claim of typical and material service or offering, as now when He asks for none but that of the heart.

So, therefore, it is a most safe and sure principle that, if in the manner of performing any rite at any time, circumstances can be traced which we are either told, or may legitimately conclude, *pleased* God at that time, those same circumstances will please Him at all times, in the performance of all rites or offices to which they may be attached in like manner; unless it has been afterwards revealed that, for some special purpose, it is now His will that such circumstances should be withdrawn. And this argument will have all the more force if it can be shown that such conditions were not essential to the completeness of the rite in its human uses and bearings, and only were added to it as being in *themselves* pleasing to God

Now, was it necessary to the completeness, as a type, of the Levitical sacrifice, or to its utility as an explanation of divine purposes, that it should cost anything to the person in whose behalf it was offered? On the contrary, the sacrifice which it foreshowed, was to be God's free gift; and the cost of, or difficulty of obtaining, the sacrificial type, could only render that type in a measure obscure, and less expressive of the offering which God would in the end provide for all men. Yet this costliness was *generally* a condition of the acceptableness of the sacrifice. "Neither will I offer unto the Lord my God of that which doth cost me nothing." That costliness, therefore, must be an acceptable condition in all human offerings at all times; for if it was pleasing to God once, it must please Him always, unless directly forbidden by Him afterwards, which it has never been.

Again, was it necessary to the typical perfection of the Levitical offering, that it should be the best of the flock? Doubtless the spotlessness of the sacrifice renders it more expressive to the Christian mind; but was it because so expressive that it was actually, and in so many words, demanded by God? Not at all. It was demanded by Him expressly on the same grounds on which an earthly governor would demand it, as a testimony of respect. "Offer it now unto thy governor." And the less valuable offering was rejected, not because it did not image Christ, nor fulfil the purposes of sacrifice, but because it indicated a feeling that would grudge the best of its possessions to Him who gave them; and because it was a bold dishonouring of God in the sight of man. Whence it may be infallibly concluded, that in whatever offerings we may now see reason to present unto God (I say not what these may be), a condition of their acceptableness will be now, as it was then, that they should be the best of their kind.

But farther, was it necessary to the carrying out of the Mosaical system, that there should be either art or splendour in the form or services of the tabernacle or temple? Was it necessary to the perfection of any one of their typical offices, that there should be that hanging of blue, and purple, and scarlet? those taches of brass and sockets of silver? that working in cedar and overlaying with gold? One thing at least is evident: there was a deep and awful danger in it; a danger that the God whom they so worshipped, might be associated in the minds of the serfs of Egypt with the gods to whom they had seen similar gifts offered and similar honours paid. The probability, in our times, of fellowship with the feelings of the idolatrous Romanist is absolutely as nothing compared with the danger to the Israelite of a sympathy with the idolatrous Egyptian; no speculative, no unproved danger; but proved fatally by their fall during a month's abandonment to their own will; a fall into the most servile idolatry; yet marked by such offerings to their idol as their leader was, in the close sequel, instructed to bid them offer to God. This danger was imminent, perpetual, and of the most awful kind: it was the one against which God made provision, not only by commandments, by threatenings, by promises, the most urgent, repeated, and impressive; but by temporary ordinances of a severity so terrible as almost to dim for a time, in the eyes of His people, His attribute of mercy

———o———

HUMAN LIFE.

At the debate of King Edwin with his courtiers and priests, whether he ought to receive the Gospel preached to him by Paulinus, one of his nobles spoke as follows:—

"The present life, O king! weighed with the time that is unknown, seems to me like this. When you are sitting at a feast with your earls and thanes in winter time, and the fire is lighted, and the hall is warmed, and it rains and snows, and the storm is loud without, there comes a sparrow, and flies through the house. It comes in at one door, and goes out at the other. While it is within, it is not touched by the winter's storm; but it is but for the twinkling of an eye, for from winter it comes and to winter it returns. So also this life of man endureth for a little space; what goes before, or what follows after, we know not. Wherefore, if this new lore bring anything more certain, it is fit that we should follow it."

Hear another story of those early times.

The king of Jerusalem, Godfrey of Bouillon, at the siege of Asshur, or Arsur, gave audience to some emirs from Samaria and Naplous. They found him seated on the ground on a sack of straw. They expressing surprise, Godfrey answered them: "May not the earth, out of which we came, and which is to be our dwelling after death, serve us for a seat during life?"

It is long since such a throne has been set in the reception-chambers of Christendom, or such an answer heard from the lips of a king.

———o———

ASCETICISM.

Three principal forms of asceticism have existed in this weak world. Religious asceticism, being the refusal of pleasure and knowledge for the sake (as supposed) of religion; seen chiefly in the middle ages. Military asceticism, being the refusal of pleasure and knowledge for the sake of power; seen chiefly in the early days of Sparta and Rome. And monetary asceticism, consisting in the refusal of pleasure and knowledge for the sake of money; seen in the present days of London and Manchester.

"We do not come here to look at the mountains," said the Carthusian to me at the Grande Chartreuse. "We do not come here to look at the mountains," the Austrian generals would say, encamping by the shores of Garda. "We do not come here to look at the mountains," so the thriving manufacturers tell me, between Rochdale and Halifax.

All these asceticisms have their bright and their dark sides. I myself like the military asceticism best, because it is not so necessarily a refusal of general knowledge as the two others, but leads to acute and marvellous use of mind, and perfect use of body. Nevertheless, none of the three are a healthy or central state of man. There is much to be respected in each, but they are not what we should wish large numbers of men to become. A monk of La Trappe, a French soldier of the Imperial Guard, and a thriving mill-owner, supposing each a type, and no more than a type, of his class, are all interesting specimens of humanity, but narrow ones,—so narrow that even all the three together would not make a perfect man. Nor does it appear in any way desirable that either of the three classes should extend itself so as to include a majority of the persons in the world.

CHEERFULNESS.

Cheerfulness is just as natural to the heart of a man in strong health as color to his cheek; and wherever there is habitual gloom, there must be either bad air, unwholesome food, improperly severe labour, or erring habits of life.

———o———

FANCY AND REALITY.

Be assured of the great truth—that what is impossible in reality is ridiculous in fancy. If it is not in the nature of things that peasants should be gentle and happy, then the imagination of such peasantry is ridiculous, and to delight in such imagination wrong; as delight in any kind of falsehood is always. But if in the nature of things it be possible that among the wildness of hills the human heart should be refined, and if the comfort of dress, and the gentleness of language, and the joy of progress in knowledge, and of variety in thought, are possible to the mountaineer in his true existence, let us strive to write this true poetry upon the rocks before we indulge it in our visions, and try whether, among all the fine arts, one of the finest be not that of painting cheeks with health rather than rouge.

"But is such refinement possible? Do not the conditions of the mountain peasant's life, in the plurality of instances, necessarily forbid it?"

As bearing sternly on this question, it is necessary to examine one peculiarity of feeling which manifests itself among the European nations, so far as I have noticed, irregularly,—appearing sometimes to be the characteristic of a particular time, sometimes of a particular race, sometimes of a particular locality, and to involve at once much that is to be blamed and much that is praiseworthy. I mean the capability of enduring, or even delighting in, the contemplation of objects of terror—a sentiment which especially influences the temper of some groups of mountaineers, and of which it is necessary to examine the causes, before we can form any conjecture whatever as to the real effect of mountains on human character.

For instance, the unhappy alterations which have lately taken place in the town of Lucerne have still spared two of its ancient bridges; both of which, being long covered walks, appear, in past times, to have been to the population of the town what the Mall was to London, or the Gardens of the Tuileries are to Paris. For the continual contemplation of those who sauntered from pier to pier, pictures were painted on the woodwork of the roof. These pictures, in the one bridge, represent all the important Swiss battles and victories; in the other they are the well-known series of which Longfellow has made so beautiful a use in the Golden Legend, the *Dance of Death.*

Imagine the countenances with which a committee, appointed for the establishment of a new "promenade" in some flourishing modern town, would receive a proposal to adorn such promenade with pictures of the Dance of Death.

Now just so far as the old bridge at Lucerne, with the pure, deep, and blue water of the Reuss eddying down between its piers, and with the sweet darkness of green hills, and far-away gleaming of lake and Alps alternating upon the eye on either side; and the gloomy lesson frowning in the shadow, as if the deep tone of a passing-bell, overhead, were mingling for ever with the plashing of the river as it glides by beneath; just so far, I say, as this differs from the straight and smooth strip of level dust, between two rows of round-topped acacia trees, wherein the inhabitants of an English watering-place or French fortified town take their delight,—so far I believe the life of the old Lucernois, with all its happy waves of light, and mountain strength of will, and solemn expectation of eternity, to have differed from the generality of the lives of those who saunter for their habitual hour up and down the modern promenade. But the gloom is not always of this noble kind. As we penetrate farther among the hills we shall find it becoming very painful. We are walking, perhaps, in a summer afternoon, up the valley of Zermatt (a German valley), the sun shining brightly on grassy knolls and through fringes of pines, the goats leaping happily, and the cattle bells ringing sweetly, and the snowy mountains shining like heavenly castles far above. We see, a little way off, a small white chapel, sheltered behind one of the flowery hillocks of mountain turf; and we approach its little window, thinking to look through it into some quiet home of prayer; but the window is grated with iron, and open to the winds, and when we look through it, behold—a heap of white human bones mouldering into whiter dust!

So also in that same sweet valley, of which I have just been speaking, between Chamouni and the Valais, at every turn of the pleasant pathway, where the scent of the thyme lies richest upon its rocks, we shall see a little cross and shrine set under one of them; and go up to it, hoping to receive some happy thought of the Redeemer, by whom all these lovely things were made, and still consist. But when we come near—behold, beneath the cross, a rude picture of souls tormented in red tongues of hell fire, and pierced by demons.

As we pass towards Italy the appearance of this gloom deepens; and when we descend the southern slope of the Alps we shall find this bringing forward of the image of Death associated with an endurance of the most painful aspects of disease; so that conditions of human suffering, which in any other country would be confined in hospitals, are permitted to be openly exhibited by the wayside; and with this exposure of the degraded human form is farther connected an insensibility to ugliness and imperfection in other things; so that the ruined wall, neglected garden, and uncleansed chamber, seem to unite in expressing a gloom of spirit possessing the inhabitants of the whole land. It does not appear to arise from poverty, nor careless contentment with little: there is here nothing of Irish recklessness or humour; but there seems a settled obscurity in the soul,—a chill and plague, as if risen out of a sepulchre, which partly deadens, partly darkens, the eyes and hearts of men, and breathes a leprosy of decay through every breeze and every stone. "Instead of well-set hair, baldness, and burning instead of beauty."

Nor are definite proofs wanting that the feeling is independent of mere poverty or indolence. In the most gorgeous and costly palace garden the statues will be found green with moss, the terraces defaced or broken; the palace itself, partly coated with marble, is left in other places rough with cementless and jagged brick, its iron balconies bent and rusted, its pavements overgrown with grass. The more energetic the effort has been to recover from this state, and to shake off all appearance of poverty, the more assuredly the curse seems to fasten on the scene, and the unslaked mortar, and unfinished wall, and ghastly desolation of incompleteness, entangled in decay, strike a deeper despondency into the beholder.

The feeling would be also more easily accounted for if it appeared consistent in its regardlessness of beauty,—if what was *done* were altogether as inefficient as what was deserted. But the balcony, though rusty and broken, is delicate in design, and supported on a nobly carved slab of marble; the window, though a mere black rent in ragged plaster, is encircled by a garland of vine and fronted by a thicket of the sharp leaves and aurora-coloured flowers of the oleander; the court-yard, overgrown by mournful grass, is terminated by a bright fresco of gardens and fountains; the corpse, borne with the bare face to heaven, is strewn with flowers; beauty is continually mingled with the shadow of death.

So also is a kind of merriment,—not true cheerfulness, neither careless or idle jesting, but a determined effort at gaiety, a resolute laughter, mixed with much satire, grossness, and practical buffoonery, and, it always seemed to me, void of all comfort or hope,—with this eminent character in it also, that it is capable of touching with its bitterness even the most fearful subjects, so that as the love of beauty retains its tenderness in the presence of death, this love of jest also retains its boldness, and the skeleton becomes one of the standard masques of the Italian comedy. When I was in Venice, in 1850, the most popular piece of the *comic* opera was "Death and the Cobbler," in which the point of the plot was the success of a village cobbler as a physician, in consequence of the appearance of Death to him beside the bed of every patient who was not to recover; and the most applauded scene in it was one in which the physician, insolent in success, and swollen with luxury, was himself taken down into the abode of Death, and thrown into an agony of terror by being shown lives of men, under the form of wasting lamps, and his own ready to expire.

———o———

THE PRESENCE OF GOD.

The reason that preaching is so commonly ineffectual is, that it calls on men oftener to work for God, than to behold God working for them. In every rebuke that we utter of men's vices, we put forth a claim upon their hearts: if for every assertion of God's demands from them, we could substitute a display of his kindness to them; if side by side with every warning of death, we could exhibit proofs and promises of immortality; if, in fine, instead of assuming the being of an awful Deity, which men, though they cannot and dare not deny, are always unwilling, sometimes unable, to conceive, we were to show them a near, visible, inevitable, but all-beneficent Deity, whose presence makes the earth itself a heaven, I think there would be fewer deaf children sitting in the market-place. At all events, whatever may be the inability in this present life to mingle the full enjoyment of the Divine works with the full discharge of every practical duty, and confessedly in many cases this must be, let us not attribute the inconsistency to any indignity of the faculty of contemplation, but to the sin and the suffering of the fallen state, and the change of order from the keeping of the garden to the tilling of the ground. We cannot say how far it is right or agreeable with God's will, while men are perishing round about us, while grief, and pain, and wrath, and impiety, and death, and all the powers of the air, are working wildly and evermore, and the cry of blood going up to heaven, that any of us should take hand from the plough; but this we know, that there will come a time when the service of God shall be the beholding of him; and though in these stormy seas, where we are now driven up and down, his Spirit is dimly seen on the face of the waters, and we are left to cast anchors out of the stern, and wish for the day, that day will come, when, with the evangelists on the crystal and stable sea, all the creatures of God shall be full of eyes within, and there shall be "no more curse, but his servants shall serve him, and shall see his face."

MILTON'S AND DANTE'S SATAN.

It is not possible to express intense wickedness without some condition of degradation. Malice, subtlety, and pride, in their extreme, cannot be written upon noble forms; and I am aware of no effort to represent the Satanic mind in the angelic form, which has succeeded in painting. Milton succeeds only because he separately describes the movements of the mind, and therefore leaves himself at liberty to make the form heroic; but that form is never distinct enough to be painted. Dante, who will not leave even external forms obscure, degrades them before he can feel them to be demoniacal; so also John Bunyan: both of them, I think, having firmer faith than Milton's in their own creations, and deeper insight into the nature of sin. Milton makes his fiends too noble, and misses the foulness, inconstancy, and fury of wickedness. His Satan possesses some virtues, not the less virtues for being applied to evil purpose. Courage, resolution, patience, deliberation in council, this latter being eminently a wise and holy character, as opposed to the "Insania" of excessive sin: and all this, if not a shallow and false, is a smoothed and artistical, conception. On the other hand, I have always felt that there was a peculiar grandeur in the indescribable ungovernable fury of Dante's fiends, ever shortening its own powers, and disappointing its own purposes; the deaf, blind, speechless, unspeakable rage, fierce as the lightning, but erring from its mark or turning senselessly against itself, and still further debased by foulness of form and action. Something is indeed to be allowed for the rude feelings of the time, but I believe all such men as Dante are sent into the world at the time when they can do their work best; and that, it being appointed for him to give to mankind the most vigorous realization possible both of Hell and Heaven, he was born both in the country and at the time which furnished the most stern opposition of Horror and Beauty, and permitted it to be written in the clearest terms.

———o———

MAN'S DELIGHT IN GOD'S WORKS.

Let us once comprehend the holier nature of the art of man, and begin to look for the meaning of the spirit, however syllabled, and the scene is changed; and we are changed also. Those small and dexterous creatures whom once we worshipped, those fur-capped divinities with sceptres of camel's hair, peering and poring in their one-windowed chambers over the minute preciousness of the laboured canvass; how are they swept away and crushed into unnoticeable darkness! And in their stead, as the walls of the dismal rooms that enclosed them, and us, are struck by the four winds of Heaven, and rent away, and as the world opens to our sight, lo! far back into all the depths of time, and forth from all the fields that have been sown with human life, how the harvest of the dragon's teeth is springing! how the companies of the gods are ascending out of the earth! The dark stones that have so long been the sepulchres of the thoughts of nations, and the forgotten ruins wherein their faith lay charnelled, give up the dead that were in them; and beneath the Egyptian ranks of sultry and silent rock, and amidst the dim golden lights of the Byzantine dome, and out of the confused and cold shadows of the Northern cloister, behold, the multitudinous souls come forth with singing, gazing on us with the soft eyes of newly comprehended sympathy, and stretching their white arms to us across the grave, in the solemn gladness of everlasting brotherhood.

The other danger to which, it was above said, we were primarily exposed under our present circumstances of life, is the pursuit of vain pleasure, that is to say, false pleasure; delight, which is not indeed delight; as knowledge vainly accumulated, is not indeed knowledge. And this we are exposed to chiefly in the fact of our ceasing to be children. For the child does not seek false pleasure; its pleasures are true, simple, and instinctive: but the youth is apt to abandon his early and true delight for vanities,—seeking to be like men, and sacrificing his natural and pure enjoyments to his pride. In like manner, it seems to me that modern civilization sacrifices much pure and true pleasure to various forms of ostentation from which it can receive no fruit. Consider, for a moment, what kind of pleasures are open to human nature, undiseased. Passing by the consideration of the pleasures of the higher affections, which lie at the root of everything, and considering the definite and practical pleasures of daily life, there is, first, the pleasure of doing good; the greatest of all, only apt to be despised from not being often enough tasted: and then, I know not in what order to put them, nor does it matter,—the pleasure of gaining knowledge; the pleasure of the excitement of imagination and emotion (or poetry and passion); and, lastly, the gratification of the senses, first of the eye, then of the ear, and then of the others in their order.

All these we are apt to make subservient to the desire of

praise; nor unwisely, when the praise sought is God's and the conscience's: but if the sacrifice is made for man's admiration, and knowledge is only sought for praise, passion repressed or affected for praise, and the arts practised for praise, we are feeding on the bitterest apples of Sodom, suffering always ten mortifications for one delight. And it seems to me, that in the modern civilized world we make such sacrifice doubly: first, by labouring for merely ambitious purposes; and secondly, which is the main point in question, by being ashamed of simple pleasure, more especially of the pleasure in sweet colour and form, a pleasure evidently so necessary to man's perfectness and virtue, that the beauty of colour and form has been given lavishly throughout the whole of creation, so that it may become the food of all, and with such intricacy and subtlety that it may deeply employ the thoughts of all. If we refuse to accept the natural delight which the Deity has thus provided for us, we must either become ascetics, or we must seek for some base and guilty pleasures to replace those of Paradise, which we have denied ourselves.

Some years ago, in passing through some of the cells of the Grand Chartreuse, noticing that the window of each apartment looked across the little garden of its inhabitant to the wall of the cell opposite, and commanded no other view, I asked the monk beside me why the window was not rather made on the side of the cell whence it would open to the solemn fields of the Alpine valley. "We do not come here," he replied, "to look at the mountains."

The same answer is given, practically, by the men of this century, to every such question; only the walls with which they enclose themselves are those of Pride, not of Prayer.

THE HIGHLANDER.

The right faith of man is not intended to give him repose, but to enable him to do his work.

It is not intended that he should look away from the place he lives in now, and cheer himself with thoughts of the place he is to live in next, but that he should look stoutly into this world, in faith that if he does his work thoroughly here, some good to others or himself, with which however he is not at present concerned, will come of it hereafter. And this kind of brave, but not very hopeful or cheerful faith, I perceive to be always rewarded by clear practical success and splendid intellectual power; while the faith which dwells on the future fades away into rosy mist, and emptiness of musical air. That result indeed follows naturally enough on its habit of assuming that things must be right, or must come right, when, probably, the fact is, that so far as we are concerned, they are entirely wrong; and going wrong: and also on its weak and false way of looking on what these religious persons call "the bright side of things," that is to say, on one side of them only, when God has given them two sides, and intended us to see both.

I was reading but the other day in a book by a zealous, useful, and able Scotch clergyman, one of these rhapsodies, in which he described a scene in the Highlands to show (he said) the goodness of God. In this Highland scene there was nothing but sunshine, and fresh breezes, and bleating lambs, and clean tartans, and all manner of pleasantness. Now a Highland scene is, beyond dispute, pleasant enough in its own way; but, looked close at, has its shadows. Here, for instance, is the very fact of one, as pretty as I can remember—having seen many. It is a little valley of soft turf, enclosed in its narrow oval by jutting rocks and broad flakes of nodding fern. From one side of it to the other winds, serpentine, a clear brown stream, drooping into quicker ripple as it reaches the end of the oval field, and then, first islanding a purple and white rock with an amber pool, it dashes away into a narrow fall of foam under a thicket of mountain ash and alder. The autumn sun, low but clear, shines on the scarlet ash-berries and on the golden birch-leaves, which, fallen here and there, when the breeze has not caught them, rest quiet in the crannies of the purple rock. Beside the rock, in the hollow under the thicket, the carcass of a ewe, drowned in the last flood, lies nearly bare to the bone, its white ribs protruding through the skin, raven-torn; and the rags of its wool still flickering from the branches that first stayed it as the stream swept it down. A little lower, the current plunges, roaring, into a circular chasm like a well, surrounded on three sides by a chimney-like hollowness of polished rock, down which the foam slips in detached snow-flakes. Round the edges of the pool beneath, the water circles slowly, like black oil; a little butterfly lies on its back, its wings glued to one of the eddies, its limbs feebly quivering; a fish rises and it is gone. Lower down the stream, I can just see, over a knoll, the green and damp turf roofs of four or five hovels, built at the edge of a morass, which is trodden by the cattle into a black Slough of Despond at their doors, and traversed by a few ill-set stepping-stones, with here and there a flat slab on the tops, where they have sunk out of sight; and at the turn of the brook I see a man fishing, with a boy and a dog—a picturesque and pretty group enough certainly, if they had not been there all day starving. I know them, and I know the dog's ribs also, which are nearly as bare as the dead ewe's; and the child's wasted shoulders, cutting his old tartan jacket through, so sharp are they. We will go down and talk with the man.

Or, that I may not piece pure truth with fancy, for I have none of his words set down, let us hear a word or two from another such, a Scotchman also, and as true-hearted, and in just as fair a scene. I write out the passage, in which I have kept his few sentences, word for word, as it stands in my private diary:—" 22d April (1851). Yesterday I had a long walk up the Via Gellia, at Matlock, coming down upon it from the hills above, all sown with anemones and violets, and murmuring with sweet springs. Above all the mills in the valley, the brook, in its first purity, forms a small shallow pool, with a sandy bottom covered with cresses, and other water plants. A man was wading in it for cresses as I passed up the valley, and bade me good-day. I did not go much farther; he was there when I returned. I passed him again, about one hundred yards, when it struck me I might as well learn all I could about water-cresses; so I turned back. I asked the man, among other questions, what he called the common weed, something like water-cress, but with a serrated leaf, which grows at the edge of nearly all such pools. 'We calls that brooklime, hereabouts,' said a voice behind me. I turned, and saw three men, miners or manufacturers—two evidently Derbyshire men, and respectable-looking in their way; the third, thin, poor, old, and harder-featured, and utterly in rags. 'Brooklime?' I said. 'What do you call it lime for?' The man said he did not know, it was called that. 'You'll find that in the British 'Erba,' said the weak, calm voice of the old man. I turned to him in much surprise; but he went on saying something drily (I hardly understood what) to the cress-gatherer; who contradicting him, the old man said he 'didn't know fresh water,' he 'knew enough of sa't.' 'Have you been a sailor?' I asked. 'I was a sailor for eleven years and ten months of my life,' he said, in the same strangely quiet manner. 'And what are you now?' 'I lived for ten years after my wife's death by picking up rags and bones I hadn't much occasion afore.' 'And now how do you live? 'Why, I lives hard and honest, and haven't got to live long,' or something to that effect. He then went on, in a kind of maundering way about his wife. 'She had rheumatism and fever very bad; and her second rib grow'd over her hench-bone. A' was a clever woman, but a' grow'd to be a very little one' (this with an expression of deep melancholy.) (Then, after a pause:) 'She died. I never cared much what come of me since; but I know that I shall soon reach her; that's a knowledge I would na gie for the king's crown.' 'You are a Scotchman, are not you?' I asked. 'I'm from the Isle of Skye, sir; I'm a McGregor.' I said something about his religious faith. 'Ye'll know I was bred in the Church of Scotland, sir,' he said, 'and I love it as I love my own soul; but I think thae Wesleyan Methodists ha' got salvation among them, too.'"

Truly, this Highland and English hill-scenery is fair enough; but has its shadows; and deeper colouring, here and there, than that of heath and rose.

---o---

TITHES.

And let us not now lose sight of this broad and unabrogated principle—I might say, incapable of being abrogated, so long as men shall receive earthly gifts from God. Of all that they have his tithe must be rendered to Him, or in so far and in so much He is forgotten: of the skill and of the treasure, of the strength and of the mind, of the time and of the toil, offering must be made reverently; and if there be any difference between the Levitical and the Christian offering, it is that the latter may be just so much the wider in its range as it is less typical in its meaning, as it is thankful instead of sacrificial. There can be no excuse accepted because the Deity does not now visibly dwell in His temple; if He is invisible it is only through our failing faith: nor any excuse because other calls are more immediate or more sacred; this ought to be done, and not the other left undone.

———o———

THE HOUSEHOLD ALTAR.

When men do not love their hearths, nor reverence their thresholds, it is a sign that they have dishonoured both, and that they have never acknowledged the true universality of that Christian worship which was indeed to supersede the idolatry, but not the piety, of the pagan. Our God is a household God, as well as a heavenly one; He has an altar in every man's dwelling; let men look to it when they rend it lightly and pour out its ashes. It is not a question of mere ocular delight, it is no question of intellectual pride, or of cultivated and critical fancy, how, and with what aspect of durability and of completeness, the domestic buildings of a nation shall be raised. It is one of those moral duties, not with more impunity to be neglected because the perception of them depends on a finely toned and balanced conscientiousness, to build our dwellings with care, and patience, and fondness, and diligent completion, and with a view to their duration at least for such a period as, in the ordinary course of national revolutions, might be supposed likely to extend to the entire alteration of the direction of local interests. This at the least; but it would be better if, in every possible instance, men built their own houses on a scale commensurate rather with their condition at the commencement, than their attainments at the termination, of their worldly career; and built them to stand as long as human work at its strongest can be hoped to stand; recording to their children what they have been, and from what, if so it had been permitted them, they had risen. And when houses are thus built, we may have that true domestic architecture, the beginning of all other, which does not disdain to treat with respect and thoughtfulness the small habitation as well as the large, and which invests with the dignity of contented manhood the narrowness of worldly circumstance.

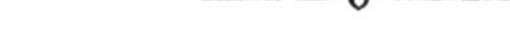

EMOTIONS EXCITED BY THE IMAGINATION.

Examine the nature of your own emotion (if you feel it) at the sight of the Alp, and you find all the brightness of that emotion hanging, like dew on gossamer, on a curious web of subtle fancy and imperfect knowledge. First, you have a vague idea of its size, coupled with wonder at the work of the great Builder of its walls and foundations; then an apprehension of its eternity, a pathetic sense of its perpetualness, and your own transientness, as of the grass upon its sides; then, and in this very sadness, a sense of strange companionship with past generations in seeing what they saw. They did not see the clouds that are floating over your head; nor the cottage wall on the other side of the field; nor the road by which you are travelling. But they saw *that.* The wall of granite in the heavens was the same to them as to you. They have ceased to look upon it; you will soon cease to look also, and the granite wall will be for others. Then, mingled with these more solemn imaginations, come the understandings of the gifts and glories of the Alps, the fan cying forth of all the fountains that well from its rocky walls, and strong rivers that are born out of its ice, and of all the pleasant valleys that wind between its cliffs, and all the châlets that gleam among its clouds, and happy farmsteads couched upon its pastures; while together with the thoughts of these rise strange sympathies with all the unknown of human life, and happiness, and death, signified by that narrow white flame of the everlasting snow, seen so far in the morning sky.

These images, and far more than these, lie at the root of the emotion which you feel at the sight of the Alp. You may not trace them in your heart, for there is a great deal more in your heart, of evil and good, than you ever can trace; but they stir you and quicken you for all that. Assuredly, so far as you feel more at beholding the snowy mountain than any other object of the same sweet silvery grey, these are the kind of images which cause you to do so; and, observe, these are nothing more than a greater apprehension of the *facts* of the thing. We call the power "Imagination," because it imagines or conceives; but it is only noble imagination if it imagines or conceives *the truth.*

LIFE NEVER A JEST.

The playful fancy of a moment may innocently be expressed by the passing word; but he can hardly have learned the preciousness of life, who passes days in the elaboration of a jest. And, as to what regards the delineation of human character, the nature of all noble art is to epitomize and embrace so much at once, that its subject can never be altogether ludicrous; it must possess all the solemnities of the whole, not the brightness of the partial, truth. For all truth that makes us smile is partial. The novelist amuses us by his relation of a particular incident; but the painter cannot set any one of his characters before us without giving some glimpse of its whole career. That of which the historian informs us in successive pages, it is the task of the painter to inform us of at once, writing upon the countenance not merely the expression of the moment, but the history of the life: and the history of a life can never be a jest.

UTILITARIANISM.

The reader will probably remember the sonnets of Wordsworth which were published at the time when the bill for the railroad between Kendal and Bowness was laid before Parliament. His remonstrance was of course in vain; and I have since heard that there are proposals entertained for continuing this line to Whitehaven through *Borrowdale.* I transcribe the note prefixed by Wordsworth to the first sonnet.

"The degree and kind of attachment which many of the yeomanry feel to their small inheritances can scarcely be over-rated. Near the house of one of them stands a magnificent tree, which a neighbour of the owner advised him to fell for profit's sake. 'Fell it!' exclaimed the yeoman; 'I had rather fall on my knees and worship it.' It happens, I believe, that the intended railway would pass through this little property, and I hope that an apology for the answer will not be thought necessary by one who enters into the strength of the feeling."

The men who thus feel will always be few, and overborne by the thoughtless, avaricious crowd; but is it right, because they are a minority, that there should be no respect for them, no concession to them, that their voice should be utterly without regard in the council of the nation, and that any attempt to defend one single district from the offence and foulness of mercenary uses, on the ground of its beauty and power over men's hearts, should be met, as I doubt not it would be, by total and impenetrable scorn?

———o———

THE PRE-EMINENCE OF THE SOUL.

I do not mean to speak of the body and soul as separable. The man is made up of both: they are to be raised and glorified together, and all art is an expression of the one, by and through the other. All that I would insist upon is, the necessity of the whole man being in his work; the body *must* be in it. Hands and habits must be in it, whether we will or not; but the nobler part of the man may often not be in it. And that nobler part acts principally in love, reverence, and admiration, together with those conditions of thought which arise out of them. For we usually fall into much error by considering the intellectual powers as having dignity in themselves, and separable from the heart; whereas the truth is, that the intellect becomes noble and ignoble according to the food we give it, and the kind of subjects with which it is conversant. It is not the reasoning power which, of itself, is noble, but the reasoning power occupied with its proper objects. Half of the mistakes of metaphysicians have arisen from their not observing this; namely, that the intellect, going through the same processes, is yet mean or noble according to the matter it deals with, and wastes itself away in mere rotatory motion, if it be set to grind straws and dust.

If we reason only respecting words, or lines, or any trifling and finite things, the reason becomes a contemptible faculty; but reason employed on holy and infinite things, becomes herself holy and infinite. So that, by work of the soul, I mean the reader always to understand the work of the entire mmortal creature, proceeding from a quick, perceptive, and eager heart, perfected by the intellect, and finally dealt with by the hands, under the direct guidance of these higher powers.

And now observe, the first important consequence of our fully understanding this pre-eminence of the soul, will be the due understanding of that subordination of knowledge respecting which so much has already been said. For it must be felt at once, that the increase of knowledge, merely as such, does not make the soul larger or smaller; that, in the sight of God, all the knowledge man can gain is as nothing: but that the soul, for which the great scheme of redemption was laid, be it ignorant or be it wise, is all in all; and in the activity, strength, health, and well-being of this soul, lies the main difference, in His sight, between one man and another. And that which is all in all in God's estimate is also, be assured, all in all in man's labour; and to have the heart open, and the eyes clear, and the emotions and thoughts warm and quick, and not the knowing of this or the other fact, is the state needed for all mighty doing in this world. And therefore finally, for this, the weightiest of all reasons, let us take no pride in our knowledge. We may, in a certain sense, be proud of being immortal; we may be proud of being God's children; we may be proud of loving, thinking, seeing, and of all that we are by no human teaching: but not of what we have been taught by rote; not of the ballast and freight of the ship of the spirit, but only of its pilotage, without which all the freight will only sink it faster, and strew the sea more richly with its ruin. There is not at this moment a youth of twenty, having received what we moderns ridiculously call education, but he knows more of everything, except the soul, than Plato or St. Paul did ; but he is not for that reason a greater man, or fitter for his work, or more fit to be heard by others, than Plato or St. Paul.

———o———

THIS WORLD A HOSTELRY.

All that in this world enlarges the sphere of affection or imagination is to be reverenced, and all those circumstances enlarge it which strengthen our memory or quicken our conception of the dead ; hence it is no light sin to destroy anything that is old, more especially because, even with the aid of all obtainable records of the past, we, the living, occupy a space of too large importance and interest in our own eyes ; we look upon the world too much as our own, too much as if we had possessed it and should possess it for ever, and forget that it is a mere hostelry, of which we occupy the apartments for a time, which others better than we have sojourned in before, who are now where we should desire to be with them.

———o———

CLOUDS AS GOD'S DWELLING-PLACE.

If we try the interpretation in the theological sense of the word *Heaven*, and examine whether the clouds are spoken of as God's dwelling-place, we find God going before the Israelites in a pillar of cloud ; revealing Himself in a cloud on

Sinai; appearing in a cloud on the mercy-seat, filling the Temple of Solomon with the cloud when its dedication is accepted; appearing in a great cloud to Ezekiel; ascending into a cloud before the eyes of the disciples on Mount Olivet; and in like manner returning to Judgment. "Behold, he cometh with clouds, and every eye shall see him." "Then shall they see the son of man coming in the clouds of heaven, with power and great glory."

———o———

THE NOBLE ENDS OF KNOWLEDGE.

Men are merely on a lower or higher stage of an eminence, whose summit is God's throne, infinitely above all; and there is just as much reason for the wisest as for the simplest man being discontented with his position, as respects the real quantity of knowledge he possesses. And, for both of them, the only true reasons for contentment with the sum of knowledge they possess are these: that it is the kind of knowledge they need for their duty and happiness in life; that all they have is tested and certain, so far as it is in their power; that all they have is well in order, and within reach when they need it; that it has not cost too much time in the getting; that none of it, once got, has been lost; and that there is not too much to be easily taken care of.

Consider these requirements a little, and the evils that result in our education and polity from neglecting them. Knowledge is mental food, and is exactly to the spirit what food is to the body (except that the spirit needs several sorts of food, of which knowledge is only one), and it is liable to the same kind of misuses. It may be mixed and disguised by art, till it becomes unwholesome; it may be refined, sweetened, and made palatable, until it has lost all its power of nourishment; and, even of its best kind, it may be eaten to surfeiting, and minister to disease and death.

Therefore, with respect to knowledge, we are to reason and act exactly as with respect to food. We no more live to know, than we live to eat. We live to contemplate, enjoy, act, adore; and we may know all that is to be known in this world, and what Satan knows in the other, without being able to do any of these. We are to ask, therefore, first, is the knowledge we would have fit food for us, good and simple, not artificial and decorated? and secondly, how much of it will enable us best for our work; and will leave our hearts light, and our eyes clear? For no more than that is to be eaten without the old Eve-sin.

Observe, also, the difference between tasting knowledge, and hoarding it. In this respect it is also like food; since, in some measure, the knowledge of all men is laid up in granaries, for future use; much of it is at any given moment dormant, not fed upon or enjoyed, but in store. And by all it is to be remembered, that knowledge in this form may be kept without air till it rots, or in such unthreshed disorder that it is of no use; and that, however good or orderly, it is still only in being tasted that it becomes of use; and that men may easily starve in their own granaries, men of science, perhaps, most of all, for they are likely to seek accumulation of their store, rather than nourishment from it. Yet let it not be thought that I would undervalue them. The good and great among them are like Joseph, to whom all nations sought to buy corn; or like the sower going forth to sow beside all waters, sending forth thither the feet of the ox and the ass: only let us remember that this is not all men's work. We are not intended to be all keepers of granaries, nor all to be measured by the filling of a storehouse; but many, nay, most of us, are to receive day by day our daily bread, and shall be as well nourished and as fit for our labour, and often, also, fit for nobler and more divine labour, in feeding from the barrel of meal that does not waste, and from the cruse of oil that does not fail, than if our barns were filled with plenty, and our presses bursting out with new wine.

It is for each man to find his own measure in this matter; in great part, also, for others to find it for him, while he is yet a youth. And the desperate evil of the whole Renaissance system is, that all idea of measure is therein forgotten, that knowledge is thought the one and the only good, and it is never inquired whether men are vivified by it or paralyzed. Let us leave figures. The reader may not believe the analogy to have been pressing so far; but let him consider the subject himself, let him examine the effect of knowledge in his own heart, and see whether the trees of knowledge and of life are one now, any more than in Paradise. He must feel that the real animating power of knowledge is only in the moment of its being first received, when it fills us with wonder and joy; a joy for which, observe, the previous ignorance is just as necessary as the present knowledge. That man is always happy who is in the presence of something which he cannot know to the full, which he is always going on to know. This is the necessary condition of a finite creature with divinely rooted and divinely directed intelligence; this, therefore, its happy state,—but observe, a state, not of triumph or joy in what it knows, but of joy rather in the continual discovery of new ignorance, continual self-abasement, continual astonishment. Once thoroughly our own, the knowledge ceases to give us pleasure. It may be practically useful to us, it may be good for others, or good for usury to obtain more; but, in itself, once let it be thoroughly familiar, and it is dead. The wonder is gone from it, and all the fine colour which it had when first we drew it up out of the infinite sea. And what does it matter how much or how little of it we have laid aside, when our only enjoyment is still in the casting of that deep sea line? What does it matter? Nay, in one respect, it matters much, and not to our advantage. For one effect of knowledge is to deaden the force of the imagination and the original energy of the whole man: under the weight of his knowledge he cannot move so lightly as in the days of his simplicity. The pack-horse is furnished for the journey, the war-horse is armed for war; but the freedom of the field and the lightness of the limb are lost for both. Knowledge is, at best, the pilgrim's burden or the soldier's panoply, often a weariness to them both: and the Renaissance knowledge is like the Renaissance armour of plate, binding and cramping the human form; while all good knowledge is like the crusader's chain mail, which throws itself into folds with the body, yet it is rarely so forged as that the clasps and rivets do not gall us. All men feel this, though they do not think of it, nor reason out its consequences. They look back to the days of childhood as of greatest happiness, because those were the days of greatest wonder, greatest simplicity, aud most vigorous imagination. And the whole difference between a man of genius and other men, it has been said a thousand times, and most truly, is that the first remains in great part a child, seeing with the large eyes of children, in perpetual wonder, not conscious of much knowledge,—conscious, rather, of infinite ignorance, and yet infinite power; a fountain of eternal admiration, delight, and creative force within him meeting the ocean of visible and governable things around him.

That is what we have to make men, so far as we may. All are to be men of genius in their degree,—rivulets or rivers, it does not matter, so that the souls be clear and pure; not dead walls encompassing dead heaps of things known and numbered, but running waters in the sweet wilderness of things unnumbered and unknown, conscious only of the living banks, on which they partly refresh and partly reflect the flowers, and so pass on.

Let each man answer for himself how far his knowledge has made him this, or how far it is loaded upon him as the pyramid is upon the tomb. Let him consider, also, how much of it has cost him labour and time that might have been spent in healthy, happy action, beneficial to all mankind; how many living souls may have been left uncomforted and unhelped by him, while his own eyes were failing by the midnight lamp; how many warm sympathies have died within him as he measured lines or counted letters; how many draughts of ocean air, and steps on mountain-turf, and openings of the highest heaven he has lost for his knowledge; how much of that knowledge, so dearly bought, is now forgotten or despised, leaving only the capacity of wonder less within him, and, as it happens in a thousand instances, perhaps even also the capacity of devotion. And let him,—if, after thus dealing with his own heart, he can say that his knowledge has indeed been fruitful to him,—yet consider how many there are who have been forced by the inevitable laws of modern education into toil utterly repugnant to their natures, and that in the extreme, until the whole strength of the young soul was sapped away; and then pronounce with fearfulness how far, and in how many senses, it may indeed be true that the wisdom of this world is foolishness with God.

Now all this possibility of evil, observe, attaches to knowledge pursued for the noblest ends, if it be pursued imprudently. I have assumed, in speaking of its effect both on men generally and on the artist especially, that it was sought in the true love of it, and with all honesty and directness of purpose. But this is granting far too much in its favour. Of knowledge in general, and without qualification, it is said by the Apostle that "it puffeth up;" and the father of all modern science, writing directly in its praise, yet asserts this danger even in more absolute terms, calling it a "venomousness" in the very nature of knowledge itself.

There is, indeed, much difference in this respect between the tendencies of different branches of knowledge; it being a sure rule that exactly in proportion as they are inferior, nugatory, or limited in scope, their power of feeding pride is greater. Thus philology, logic, rhetoric, and the other sciences of the schools, being for the most part ridiculous and trifling, have so pestilent an effect upon those who are devoted to them, that their students cannot conceive of any higher sciences than these, but fancy that all education ends in the knowledge of words: but the true and great sciences, more especially natural history, make men gentle and modest in proportion to the largeness of their apprehension, and just perception of the infiniteness of the things they can never know. And this, it seems to me, is the principal lesson we are intended to be taught by the book of Job; for there God has thrown open to us the heart of a man most just and holy, and apparently perfect in all things possible to human nature except humility. For this he is tried: and we are shown that no suffering, no self-examination, however honest, however stern, no searching out of the heart by its own bitterness, is enough to convince man of his nothingness before God; but that the sight of God's creation will do it. For, when the Deity himself has willed to end the temptation, and to accomplish in Job that for which it was sent, He does not vouchsafe to reason with him, still less does He overwhelm him with terror, or confound him by laying open before his eyes the book of his iniquities. He opens before him only the arch of the dayspring, and the fountains of the deep; and amidst the covert of the reeds, and on the heaving waves, He bids him watch the kings of the children of pride,—"Behold now Behemoth, which I made with thee:" And the work is done.

Thus, if, I repeat, there is any one lesson in the whole book which stands forth more definitely than another, it is this of the holy and humbling influence of natural science on the human heart. And yet, even here, it is not the science, but the perception, to which the good is owing; and the natural sciences may become as harmful as any others, when they lose themselves in classification and catalogue-making. Still, the principal danger is with the sciences of words and methods; and it was exactly into those sciences that the whole energy of men during the Renaissance period was thrown. They discovered suddenly that the world for ten centuries had been living in an ungrammatical manner, and they made it forthwith the end of human existence to be grammatical. And it mattered thenceforth nothing what was said or what was done, so only that it was said with scholarship, and done with system. Falsehood in a Ciceronian dialect had no opposers; truth in patois no listeners. A Roman phrase was thought worth any number of Gothic facts. The sciences ceased at once to be anything more than different kinds of grammars,—grammar of language, grammar of logic, grammar of ethics, grammar of art; and the tongue, wit, and invention of the human race were supposed to have found their utmost and most divine mission in syntax and syllogism, perspective and five orders.

Of such knowledge as this, nothing but pride could come; and, therefore, I have called the first mental characteristic of the Renaissance schools, the "pride" of science. If they had reached any science worth the name, they might have loved it; but of the paltry knowledge they possessed, they could only be proud. There was not anything in it capable of being loved. Anatomy, indeed, then first made the subject of accurate study, is a true science, but not so attractive as to enlist the affections strongly on its side: and therefore, like its meaner sisters, it became merely a ground for pride; and the one main purpose of the Renaissance artists, in all their work, was to show how much they knew.

There were, of course, noble exceptions; but chiefly belonging to the earliest periods of the Renaissance, when its teaching had not yet produced its full effect. Raphael, Leonardo, and Michael Angelo were all trained in the old school; they all had masters who knew the true ends of art, and had reached them; masters nearly as great as they were themselves, but imbued with the old religious and earnest spirit, which their disciples receiving from them, and drinking at the same time deeply from all the fountains of knowledge opened in their day, became the world's wonders. Then the dull wondering world believed that their greatness rose out of their new knowledge, instead of out of that ancient religious root, in which to abide was life, from which to be severed was annihilation. And from that day to this, they have tried to produce Michael Angelos and Leonardos by teaching the barren sciences, and still have mourned and marvelled that no more Michael Angelos came; not perceiving that those great Fathers were only able to receive such nourishment because they were rooted on the rock of all ages, and that our scientific teaching, nowadays, is nothing more nor less than the assiduous watering of trees whose stems are cut through. Nay, I have even granted too much in saying that those great men were able to receive pure nourishment from the sciences; for my own conviction is, and I know it to be shared by most of those who love Raphael truly,—that he painted best when he knew least. Michael Angelo was betrayed again and again, into such vain and offensive exhibition of his anatomical knowledge as, to this day, renders his higher powers indiscernible by the greater part of men; and Leonardo fretted his life away in engineering, so that there is hardly a picture left to bear his name. But, with respect to all who followed, there can be no question that the science they possessed was utterly harmful; serving merely to draw away their hearts at once from the purposes of art and the power of nature, and to make, out of the canvass and marble, nothing more than materials for the exhibition of petty dexterity and useless knowledge.

It is sometimes amusing to watch the naïve and childish way in which this vanity is shown. For instance, when perspective was first invented, the world thought it a mighty discovery, and the greatest men it had in it were as proud of knowing that retiring lines converge, as if all the wisdom of Solomon had been compressed into a vanishing point. And, accordingly, it became nearly impossible for any one to paint a Nativity, but he must turn the stable and manger into a Corinthian arcade, in order to show his knowledge of perspective; and half the best architecture of the time, instead of being adorned with historical sculpture, as of old, was set forth with bas-relief of minor corridors and galleries, thrown into perspective.

Now that perspective can be taught to any schoolboy in a week, we can smile at this vanity. But the fact is, that all pride in knowledge is precisely as ridiculous, whatever its kind, or whatever its degree. There is, indeed, nothing of which man has any right to be proud; but the very last thing of which, with any show of reason, he can make his boast is his knowledge, except only that infinitely small portion of it which he has discovered for himself. For what is there to be more proud of in receiving a piece of knowledge from another person than in receiving a piece of money? Beggars should not be proud, whatever kind of alms they receive. Knowledge is like current coin. A man may have some right to be proud of possessing it, if he has worked for the gold of it, and assayed it, and stamped it, so that it may be received of all men as true; or earned it fairly, being already assayed: but if he has done none of these things, but only had it thrown in his face by a passer-by, what cause has he to be proud? And though, in this mendicant fashion, he had heaped together the wealth of Crœsus, would pride any more, for this, become him, as, in some sort, it becomes the man who has laboured for his fortune, however small? So, if a man tells me the sun is larger than the earth, have I any cause for pride in knowing it? or, if any multitude of men tell me any number of things, heaping all their wealth of knowledge upon me, have I any reason to be proud under the heap? And is not nearly all the knowledge of which we boast in these days cast upon us in this dishonourable way; worked for by other men, proved by them, and then forced upon us, even against our wills, and beaten into us in our youth, before we have the wit even to know if it be good or not? (Mark the distinction between knowledge and thought.) Truly a noble possession to be proud of! Be assured, there is no part of the furniture of a man's mind which he has a right to exult in, but that which he has hewn and fashioned for himself. He who has built himself a hut on a desert heath and carved his bed, and table, and chair out of the nearest forest, may have some right to take pride in the appliances of his narrow chamber, as assuredly he will have joy in them. But the man who has had a palace built, and adorned, and furnished for him, may, indeed, have many advantages above the other, but he has no reason to be proud of his upholsterer's skill; and it is ten to one if he has half the joy in his couches of ivory that the other will have in his pallet of pine.

And observe how we feel this, in the kind of respect we pay to such knowledge as we are indeed capable of estimating the value of. When it is our own, and new to us, we cannot judge of it; but let it be another's also, and long familiar to us, and see what value we set on it. Consider how we regard a schoolboy, fresh from his term's labour. If he begin to display his newly acquired small knowledge to us, and plume himself thereupon, how soon do we silence him with contempt! But it is not so if the schoolboy begins to feel or see anything. In the strivings of his soul within him he is our equal; in his power of sight and thought he stands separate from us, and may be a greater than we. We are ready to hear him forthwith. "You saw that? you felt that? No matter for your being a child; let us hear."

Consider that every generation of men stands in this relation to its successors. It is as the schoolboy: the knowledge of which it is proudest will be as the alphabet to those who follow. It had better make no noise about its knowledge; a time will come when its utmost, in that kind, will be food for scorn. Poor fools! was that all they knew? and behold how proud they were! But what we see and feel will never be mocked at. All men will be thankful to us for telling them that. "Indeed!" they will say, "they felt that in their day? saw that? Would God we may be like them, before we go to the home where sight and thought are not!"

———o———

WHAT USE?

Of what use was that dearly bought water of the well of Bethlehem with which the King of Israel slaked the dust of Adullum? yet was not thus better than if he had drunk it? Of what use was that passionate act of Christian sacrifice, against which, first uttered by the false tongue, the very objection we would now conquer took a sullen tone for ever? So also let us not ask of what use our offering is to the church: it is at least better for *us* than if it had been retained for ourselves. It may be better for others also: there is, at any rate, a chance of this; though we must always fearfully and widely shun the thought that the magnificence of the temple can materially add to the efficiency of the worship or to the power of the ministry. Whatever we do, or whatever we offer, let it not interfere with the simplicity of the one, or abate, as if replacing, the zeal of the other.

———o———

PAGAN DOUBTS.

The Greeks never shrink from horror; down to its uttermost depth, to its most appalling physical detail, they strive to sound the secrets of sorrow. For them there is no passing by on the other side, no turning away the eyes to vanity from pain. Literally, they have not "lifted up their souls unto vanity." Whether there be consolation for them or not, neither apathy nor blindness shall be their saviours; if, for them, thus knowing the facts of the grief of earth, any hope, relief, or triumph may hereafter seem possible,—well; but if not, still hopeless, reliefless, eternal, the sorrow shall be met face to face. This Hector, so righteous, so merciful, so brave, has, nevertheless, to look upon his dearest brother in miserablest death. His own soul passes away in hopeless sobs through the throat-wound of the Grecian spear. That is one aspect of things in this world, a fair world truly, but having, among its other aspects, this one, highly ambiguous.

Meeting it boldly as they may, gazing right into the skeleton face of it, the ambiguity remains; nay, in some sort gains upon them. We trusted in the gods;—we thought that wisdom and courage would save us. Our wisdom and courage themselves deceive us to our death. Athena had the aspect of Deiphobus—terror of the enemy. She has not terrified him, but left us, in our mortal need.

And, beyond that mortality, what hope have we? Nothing is clear to us on that horizon, nor comforting. Funeral honours; perhaps also rest; perhaps a shadowy life—artless, joyless, loveless. No devices in that darkness of the grave, nor daring, nor delight. Neither marrying nor giving in marriage, nor casting of spears, nor rolling of chariots, nor voice of fame. Lapped in pale Elysian mist, chilling the forgetful heart and feeble frame, shall we waste on for ever? Can the dust of earth claim more of immortality than this? Or shall we have even so much as rest? May we, indeed, lie down again in the dust, or have our sins not hidden from us even the things that belong to that peace? May not chance and the whirl of passion govern us there; when there shall be no thought, nor work, nor wisdom, nor breathing of the soul?

———o———

PROPHETIC DREAMS.

Now, so far as the truth is seen by the imagination in its wholeness and quietness, the vision is sublime; but so far as it is narrowed and broken by the inconsistencies of the human capacity, it becomes grotesque: and it would seem to be rare that any very exalted truth should be impressed on the imagination without some grotesqueness in its aspect, proportioned to the degree of *diminution of breadth* in the grasp which is given of it. Nearly all the dreams recorded in the Bible,—Jacob's, Joseph's, Pharaoh's, Nebuchadnezzar's,—are grotesques; and nearly the whole of the accessary scenery in the books of Ezekiel and the Apocalypse. Thus Jacob's dream revealed to him the ministry of angels; but because this ministry could not be seen or understood by him in its fulness, it was narrowed to him into a ladder between heaven and earth, which was a grotesque. Joseph's two dreams were evidently intended to be signs of the steadfastness of the Divine purpose towards him, by possessing the clearness of special prophecy; yet were couched in such imagery, as not to inform him prematurely of his destiny, and only to be understood after their fulfilment. The sun, and moon, and stars were at the period, and are indeed throughout the Bible, the symbols of high authority. It was not revealed to Joseph that he should be lord over all Egypt; but the representation of his family by symbols of the most magnificent dominion, and yet as subject to him, must have been afterwards felt by him as a distinctly prophetic indication of his own supreme power. It was not revealed to him that the occasion of his brethren's special humiliation before him should be their coming to buy corn; but when the event took place, must he not have felt that there was prophetic purpose in the form of the sheaves of wheat which first imaged forth their subjection to him? And these two images of the sun doing obeisance, and the sheaves bowing down,—narrowed and imperfect intimations of great truth which yet could not be otherwise conveyed,—are both grotesques. The kine of Pharaoh eating each other, the gold and clay of Nebuchadnezzar's image, the four beasts full of eyes, and other imagery of Ezekiel and the Apocalypse, are grotesques of the same kind, on which I need not further insist.

---o---

CHRISTIAN SYMBOLISM.

As the heathen, in their alienation from God, changed His glory into an image made like unto corruptible man, and to birds, and four-footed beasts, the Christian, in his approach to God, is to undo this work, and to change the corruptible things into the image of His glory; believing that there is nothing so base in creation, but that our faith may give it wings which shall raise us into companionship with heaven; and that, on the other hand, there is nothing so great or so goodly in creation, but that it is a mean symbol of the Gospel of Christ, and of the things He has prepared for them that love Him.

---o---

THANKFULNESS.

No man can indeed be a lover of what is best in the higher walks of art, who has not feeling and charity enough to rejoice with the rude sportiveness of hearts that have escaped out of prison, and to be thankful for the flowers which men have laid their burdens down to sow by the wayside.

"STAND FAST, CRAIG ELLACHIE."

All the highest points of the Scottish character are connected with impressions derived straight from the natural scenery of their country. No nation has ever before shown, in the general tone of its language—in the general current of its literature—so constant a habit of hallowing its passions and confirming its principles by direct association with the charm, or power, of nature. The writings of Scott and Burns—and yet more, of the far greater poets than Burns who gave Scotland her traditional ballads,—furnish you in every stanza—almost in every line—with examples of this association of natural scenery with the passions; but an instance of its farther connection with moral principle struck me forcibly just at the time when I was most lamenting the absence of art among the people. In one of the loneliest districts of Scotland, where the peat cottages are darkest, just at the western foot of that great mass of the Grampians which encircles the sources of the Spey and the Dee, the main road which traverses the chain winds round the foot of a broken rock called Crag, or Craig Ellachie. There is nothing remarkable in either its height or form; it is darkened with a few scattered pines, and touched along its summit with a flush of heather; but it constitutes a kind of headland, or leading promontory, in the group of hills to which it belongs —a sort of initial letter of the mountains; and thus stands in the mind of the inhabitants of the district, the Clan GRANT, for a type of their country, and of the influence of that country upon themselves. Their sense of this is beautifully indicated in the war-cry of the clan, "Stand fast, Craig Ellachie." You may think long over those few words without exhausting the deep wells of feeling and thought contained in them —the love of the native land, the assurance of their faithful ness to it; the subdued and gentle assertion of indomitable courage—I *may* need to be told to stand, but, if I do, Craig Ellachie does. You could not but have felt, had you passed beneath it at the time when so many of England's dearest children were being defended by the strength of heart of men born at its foot, how often among the delicate Indian palaces, whose marble was pallid with horror, and whose vermilion was darkened with blood, the remembrance of its rough grey rocks and purple heaths must have risen before the sight of the Highland soldier; how often the hailing of the shot and the shriek of battle would pass away from his hearing, and leave only the whisper of the old pine branches, —"Stand fast, Craig Ellachie!"*

———o———

CARE FOR TRIFLES.

In mortals, there is a care for trifles which proceeds from love and conscience, and is most holy; and a care for trifles which comes of idleness and frivolity, and is most base. And so, also, there is a gravity proceeding from thought, which is most noble; and a gravity proceeding from dulness and mere incapability of enjoyment, which is most base.

———o———

DURER AND SALVATOR.

The reader might see at a glance the elements of the Nuremberg country, as they still exist. Wooden cottages, thickly grouped, enormously high in the roofs; the sharp

* Is not this the "war-cry" of our own GRANT?—L. C. T.

church spire, small and slightly grotesque, surmounting them beyond, a richly cultivated, healthy plain bounded by woody hills. By a strange coïncidence the very plant which constitutes the staple produce of those fields, is in almost ludicrous harmony with the grotesqueness and neatness of the architecture around; and one may almost fancy that the builders of the little knotted spires and turrets of the town, and workers of its dark iron flowers, are in spiritual presence, watching and guiding the produce of the field,—when one finds the footpaths bordered everywhere, by the bossy spires and lustrous jetty flowers of the black hollyhock.

Lastly, when Durer penetrated among those hills of Franconia he would find himself in a pastoral country, much resembling the Gruyère districts of Switzerland, but less thickly inhabited, and giving in its steep, though not lofty, rocks,—its scattered pines,—and its fortresses and chapels, the motives of all the wilder landscape introduced by the painter in such pieces as his St. Jerome, or St. Hubert. His continual and forced introduction of sea in almost every scene, much as it seems to me to be regretted, is possibly owing to his happy recollections of the sea-city where he received the rarest of all rewards granted to a good workman; and for once in his life was understood.

Among this pastoral simplicity and formal sweetness of domestic peace, Durer had to work out his question concerning the grave. It haunted him long; he learned to engrave death's heads well before he had done with it; looked deeper than any other man into those strange rings, their jewels lost; and gave answer at last conclusively in his great Knight and Death—of which more presently. But while the Nuremberg landscape is still fresh in our minds, we had better turn south quickly and compare the elements of education which formed, and of creation which companioned, Salvator.

Born with a wild and coarse nature (how coarse I will show you soon), but nevertheless an honest one, he set himself in youth hotly to the war, and cast himself carelessly on the current, of life. No rectitude of ledger-lines stood in his way; no tender precision of household customs; no calm successions of rural labour. But past his half-starved lips rolled profusion of pitiless wealth; before him glared and swept the troops of shameless pleasure. Above him muttered Vesuvius; beneath his feet shook the Solfatara.

In heart disdainful, in temper adventurous; conscious of power, impatient of labour, and yet more of the pride of the patrons of his youth, he fled to the Calabrian hills, seeking not knowledge, but freedom. If he was to be surrounded by cruelty and deceit, let them at least be those of brave men or savage beasts, not of the timorous and the contemptible. Better the wrath of the robber, than the enmity of the priest; and the cunning of the wolf than of the hypocrite.

We are accustomed to hear the south of Italy spoken of as a beautiful country. Its mountain forms are graceful above others, its sea bays exquisite in outline and hue; but it is only beautiful in superficial aspect. In closer detail it is wild and melancholy. Its forests are sombre-leafed, labyrinth-stemmed; the carubbe, the olive, laurel, and ilex, are alike in that strange feverish twisting of their branches, as if in spasms of half human pain:—Avernus forests: one fears to break their boughs, lest they should cry to us from their rents; the rocks they shade are of ashes, or thrice-molten lava; iron sponge, whose every pore has been filled with fire. Silent villages, earthquake-shaken, without commerce, without industry, without knowledge, without hope, gleam in white ruin from hillside to hillside; far-winding wrecks of immemorial walls surround the dust of cities long forsaken: the mountain streams moan through the cold arches of their foundations, green with weed, and rage over the heaps of their fallen towers. Far above in thunder-blue serration, stand the eternal edges of the angry Apennine, dark with rolling impendence of volcanic cloud.

Yet even among such scenes as these, Salvator might have been calmed and exalted, had he been, indeed, capable of exaltation. But he was not of high temper enough to perceive beauty. He had not the sacred sense—the sense of colour; all the loveliest hues of the Calabrian air were invisible to him; the sorrowful desolation of the Calabrian villages unfelt. He saw only what was gross and terrible,—the jagged peak, the splintered tree, the flowerless bank of grass, and wandering weed, prickly and pale. His temper confirmed itself in evil, and became more and more fierce and morose; though not, I believe, cruel, ungenerous, or lascivious. I should not suspect Salvator of wantonly inflicting pain. His constantly painting it does not prove he delighted in it; he felt the horror of it, and in that horror fascination. Also he desired fame, and saw that here was an untried field rich enough in morbid excitement to catch the humour of his indolent patrons. But the gloom gained upon him, and grasped him. He could jest, indeed, as men jest in prison-yards (he became afterwards a renowned mime in Florence); his satires are full of good mocking, but his own doom to sadness is never repealed.

Of all men whose work I have ever studied, he gives me most distinctly the idea of a lost spirit. Michelet calls him "Ce damné Salvator," perhaps in a sense merely harsh and violent; the epithet to me seems true in a more literal, more merciful sense,—"That condemned Salvator." I see in him, notwithstanding all his baseness, the last traces of spiritual life in the art of Europe. He was the last man to whom the thought of a spiritual existence presented itself as a conceivable reality. All succeeding men, however powerful—Rembrandt, Rubens, Vandyck, Reynolds—would have mocked at the idea of a spirit. They were men of the world; they are never in earnest, and they are never appalled. But Salvator was capable of pensiveness, of faith, and of fear. The misery of the earth is a marvel to him; he cannot leave off gazing at it. The religion of the earth is a horror to him. He gnashes his teeth at it, rages at it, mocks and gibes at it. He would have acknowledged religion, had he seen any that was true. Anything rather than that baseness which he did see. "If there is no other religion than this of pope and cardinals, let us to the robber's ambush and the dragon's den." He was capable of fear also. The grey spectre, horse-headed, striding across the sky—(in the Pitti palace)—its bat wings spread, green bars of the twilight seen between its bones; it was no play to him—the painting of it. Helpless Salvator! A little early sympathy, a word of true guidance, perhaps, had saved him. What says he of himself? Despiser of wealth and of death. Two grand scorns; but, oh, condemned Salvator! the question is not for man what he can scorn, but what he can love.

I do not care to trace the various hold which Hades takes on this fallen soul. It is no part of my work here to analyze his art, nor even that of Durer; all that we need to note is the opposite answer they gave to the question about death.

To Salvator it came in narrow terms. Desolation, without hope, throughout the fields of nature, he had to explore; hypocrisy and sensuality, triumphant, and shameless, in the cities from which he derived his support. His life, so far as any nobility remained in it, could only pass in horror, disdain, or despair. It is difficult to say which of the three prevails most in his common work; but his answer to the great question was of despair only. He represents "Umana Fragilita" by the type of a skeleton with plumy wings, leaning over a woman and child; the earth covered with ruin round them —a thistle, casting its seed, the only fruit of it. "Thorns, also, and thistles shall it bring forth to thee." The same tone of thought marks all Salvator's more earnest work.

On the contrary, in the sight of Durer, things were for the most part as they ought to be. Men did their work in his city and in the fields round it. The clergy were sincere. Great social questions unagitated; great social evils either non-existent, or seemingly a part of the nature of things, and inevitable. His answer was that of patient hope; and two-fold, consisting of one design in praise of Fortitude, and another in praise of Labour. The Fortitude, commonly known as the "Knight and Death," represents a knight riding through a dark valley overhung by leafless trees, and with a great castle on a hill beyond. Beside him, but a little in advance, rides Death on a pale horse Death is gray-haired and crowned;—serpents wreathed about his crown (the sting of death involved in the kingly power). He holds up the hour-glass, and looks earnestly into the knight's face. Behind him follows Sin; but Sin powerless; he has been conquered and passed by, but follows yet, watching if any way of assault remains. On his forehead are two horns—I think, of sea-shell—to indicate his insatiableness and instability. He has also the twisted horns of the ram, for stubbornness, the ears of an ass, the snout of a swine, the hoofs of a goat. Torn wings hang useless from his shoulders, and he carries a spear with two hooks, for catching as well as wounding. The knight does not heed him, nor even Death, though he is conscious of the presence of the last.

He rides quietly, his bridle firm in his hand, and his lips set close in a slight sorrowful smile, for he hears what Death is saying; and hears it as the word of a messenger who brings pleasant tidings, thinking to bring evil ones. A little branch of delicate heath is twisted round his helmet. His horse trots proudly and straight; its head high, and with a cluster of oak on the brow where on the fiend's brow is the sea-shell horn. But the horse of Death stoops its head; and its rein catches the little bell which hangs from the knight's horse-bridle, making it toll, as a passing bell.*

Durer's second answer is the plate of "Melencholia," which is the history of the sorrowful toil of the earth, as the "Knight and Death" is of its sorrowful patience under temptation.

Salvator's answer, remember, is in both respects that of despair. Death as he reads, lord of temptation, is victor over the spirit of man; and lord of ruin, is victor over the work of man. Durer declares the sad, but unsullied conquest over Death the tempter; and the sad, but enduring conquest over Death the destroyer.

Though the general intent of the Melencholia is clear, and to be felt at a glance, I am in some doubt respecting its special symbolism. I do not know how far Durer intended to show that labour, in many of its most earnest forms, is closely connected with the morbid sadness or "dark anger," of the northern nations. Truly some of the best work ever done for man, has been in that dark anger;† but I have not yet been

* This was first pointed out to me by a friend—Mr. Robert Allen. It is a beautiful thought; yet, possibly, an after-thought. I have some suspicion that there is an alteration in the plate at that place, and that the rope to which the bell hangs was originally the line of the chest of the nearest horse, as the grass-blades about the lifted hind leg conceal the lines which could not, in Durer's way of work, be effaced, indicating its first intended position. What a proof of his general decision of handling is involved in this "repentir!"

† "Yet withal, you see that the Monarch is a great, valiant, cautious, melancholy, commanding man."—Friends in Council, last volume, p. 269; Milverton giving an account of Titian's picture of Charles the Fifth. (Com-

able to determine for myself how far this is necessary, or how far great work may also be done with cheerfulness. If I knew what the truth was, I should be able to interpret Durer better; meantime the design seems to me his answer to the complaint, "Yet is his strength labour and sorrow."

"Yes," he replies, "but labour and sorrow are his strength."

The labour indicated is in the daily work of men. Not the inspired or gifted labour of the few (it is labour connected with the sciences, not with the arts), shown in its four chief functions: thoughtful, faithful, calculating and executing.

Thoughtful, first; all true power coming of that resolved, resistless calm of melancholy thought. This is the first and last message of the whole design. Faithful, the right arm of the spirit resting on the book. Calculating (chiefly in the sense of self-command), the compasses in her right hand. Executive—roughest instruments of labour at her feet: a crucible, and geometrical solids, indicating her work in the sciences. Over her head the hour-glass and the bell, for their continual words, "Whatsoever thy hand findeth to do." Beside her, childish labour (lesson-learning?) sitting on an old millstone, with a tablet on its knees. I do not know what instrument it has in its hand. At her knees, a wolf-hound asleep. In the distance, a comet (the disorder and threatening of the universe) setting, the rainbow dominant over it. Her strong body is close girded for work; at her waist hang the keys of wealth; but the coin is cast aside contemptuously under her feet. She has eagles' wings, and is crowned with fair leafage of spring.

Yes, Albert of Nuremberg, it was a noble answer, yet an

pare Ellesmere's description of Milverton himself, p. 140.) Read carefully also what is said further on respecting Titian's freedom, and fearless withholding of flattery; comparing it with the note on Giorgione and Titian.

imperfect one. This is indeed the labour which is crowned with laurel and has the wings of an eagle. It was reserved for another country to prove, for another hand to portray, the labour which is crowned with fire, and has the wings of the bat.

———o———

CARE FOR POSTERITY.

The benevolent regards and purposes of men in masses seldom can be supposed to extend beyond their own generation. They may look to posterity as an audience, may hope for its attention, and labour for its praise: they may trust to its recognition of unacknowledged merit, and demand its justice for contemporary wrong. But all this is mere selfishness, and does not involve the slightest regard to, or consideration of, the interests of those by whose numbers we would fain swell the circle of our flatterers, and by whose authority we would gladly support our presently disputed claims. The idea of self-denial for the sake of posterity, of practising present economy for the sake of debtors yet unborn, of planting forests that our descendants may live under their shade, or of raising cities for future nations to inhabit, never, I suppose, efficiently takes place among publicly recognised motives of exertion. Yet these are not the less our duties; nor is our part fitly sustained upon the earth, unless the range of our intended and deliberate usefulness include not only the companions, but the successors, of our pilgrimage. God has lent us the earth for our life; it is a great entail. It belongs as much to those who are to come after us, and whose names are already written in the book of creation, as to us; and we have no right, by anything that we do or neglect, to involve them in unnecessary penalties, or deprive them of benefits which it was in our power to bequeath. And this the more, because it is one of the appointed conditions of the labour of men that, in proportion to the time between the seed-sowing and the harvest, is the fulness of the fruit; and that generally, therefore, the farther off we place our aim, and the less we desire to be ourselves the witnesses of what we have laboured for, the more wide and rich will be the measure of our success. Men cannot benefit those that are with them as they can benefit those who come after them; and of all the pulpits from which human voice is ever sent forth, there is none from which it reaches so far as from the grave.

———o———

GLOOM.

It is not in the languor of a leisure hour that a man will set his whole soul to conceive the means of representing some important truth, nor to the projecting angle of a timber bracket that he would trust its representation, if conceived. And yet, in this languor, and in this trivial work, he must find some expression of the serious part of his soul, of what there is within him capable of awe, as well as of love. The more noble the man is, the more impossible it will be for him to confine his thoughts to mere loveliness, and that of a low order. Were his powers and his time unlimited, so that, like Frà Angelico, he could paint the Seraphim, in that order of beauty he could find contentment, bringing down heaven to earth. But by the conditions of his being, by his hard-worked life, by his feeble powers of execution, by the meanness of his employment and the languor of his heart, he is bound down to earth. It is the world's work that he is doing, and world's work is not to be done without fear. And whatever there is of deep and eternal consciousness within him, thrilling his mind with the sense of the presence of sin and death around him, must be expressed in that slight work, and feeble way, come of it what will. He cannot forget it, among all that he sees of beautiful in nature; he may not bury himself among the leaves of the violet on the rocks, and of the lily in the glen, and twine out of them garlands of perpetual gladness. He sees more in the earth than these,—misery and wrath, and discordance and danger, and all the work of the dragon and his angels; this he sees with too deep feeling ever to forget. And though when he returns to his idle work,—it may be to gild the letters upon the page, or to carve the timbers of the chamber, or the stones of the pinnacle,—he cannot give his strength of thought any more to the woe or to the danger, there is a shadow of them still present with him: and as the bright colours mingle beneath his touch, and the fair leaves and flowers grow at his bidding, strange horrors and phantasms rise by their side; grisly beasts and venomous serpents, and spectral fiends and nameless inconsistencies of ghastly life, rising out of things most beautiful, and fading back into them again, as the harm and the horror of life do out of its happiness. He has seen these things; he wars with them daily; he cannot but give them their part in his work, though in a state of comparative apathy to them at the time. He is but carving and gilding, and must not turn aside to weep; but he knows that hell is burning on, for all that, and the smoke of it withers his oak-leaves.

Now, the feelings which give rise to the false or ignoble grotesque, are exactly the reverse of these. In the true grotesque, a man of naturally strong feeling is accidentally or resolutely apathetic; in the false grotesque, a man naturally apathetic is forcing himself into temporary excitement. The horror which is expressed by the one, comes upon him whether he will or not; that which is expressed by the other, is sought out by him, and elaborated by his art. And therefore, also, because the fear of the one is true, and of true things, however fantastic its expression may be, there will be reality in it, and force. It is not a manufactured terribleness, whose author, when he had finished it, knew not if it would terrify any one else or not: but it is a terribleness taken from the life; a spectre which the workman indeed saw, and which, as it appalled him, will appal us also. But the other workman never felt any Divine fear; he never shuddered when he heard the cry from the burning towers of the earth,

"Venga Medusa; sì lo farem di smalto."

He is stone already, and needs no gentle hand laid upon his eyes to save him.

———o———

NOTHING BUT TRUTH.

Let me declare, without qualification—that partial conception is no conception. The whole picture must be imagined, or none of it is. And this grasp of the whole implies very strange and sublime qualities of mind. It is not possible, unless the feelings are completely under control; the least excitement or passion will disturb the measured equity of power; a painter needs to be as cool as a general; and as little moved or subdued by his sense of pleasure, as a soldier by the sense of pain. Nothing good can be done without intense feeling; but it must be feeling so crushed, that the work is set about with mechanical steadiness, absolutely untroubled, as a surgeon,—not without pity, but conquering it and putting it aside—begins an operation. Until the feelings can give strength enough to the will to enable it to conquer them, they are not strong enough. If you cannot leave your picture at any moment;—cannot turn from it and go on with another, while the colour is drying;—cannot work at any part of it you choose with equal contentment—you have not firm enough grasp of it.

It follows also, that no vain or selfish person can possibly paint, in the noble sense of the word. Vanity and selfishness are troublous, eager, anxious, petulant:—painting can only be done in calm of mind. Resolution is not enough to secure this; it must be secured by disposition as well. You may resolve to think of your picture only; but, if you have been fretted before beginning, no manly or clear grasp of it will be possible for you. No forced calm is calm enough. Only honest calm,—natural calm. You might as well try by external pressure to smoothe a lake till it could reflect the sky, as by violence of effort to secure the peace through which only you can reach imagination. That peace must come in its own time; as the waters settle themselves into clearness as well as quietness; you can no more filter your mind into purity than you can compress it into calmness; you must keep it pure, if you would have it pure; and throw no stones into it, if you would have it quiet. Great courage and self-command may, to a certain extent, give power of painting without the true calmness underneath; but never of doing first-rate work. There is sufficient evidence of this, in even what we know of great men, though of the greatest, we nearly always know the least (and that necessarily; they being very silent, and not much given to setting themselves forth to questioners; apt to be contemptuously reserved, no less than unselfishly). But in such writings and sayings as we possess of theirs, we may trace a quite curious gentleness and serene courtesy. Rubens' letters are almost ludicrous in their unhurried politeness. Reynolds, swiftest of painters, was gentlest of companions; so also Velasquez, Titian, and Veronese.

It is gratuitous to add that no shallow or petty person can paint. Mere cleverness or special gift never made an artist. It is only perfectness of mind, unity, depth, decision, the highest qualities, in fine, of the intellect, which will form the imagination.

And, lastly, no false person can paint. A person false at heart may, when it suits his purposes, seize a stray truth here or there; but the relations of truth,—its perfectness,—that which makes it wholesome truth, he can never perceive. As wholeness and wholesomeness go together, so also sight with sincerity; it is only the constant desire of, and submissiveness to truth, which can measure its strange angles and mark its infinite aspects; and fit them and knit them into the strength of sacred invention.

Sacred, I call it deliberately; for it is thus, in the most accurate senses, humble as well as helpful; meek in its receiving as magnificent in its disposing; the name it bears being rightly given to invention formal, not because it forms, but because it finds. For you cannot find a lie; you must make it for yourself. False things may be imagined, and false things composed; but only truth can be invented.

———o———

INFIDELITY.

It is written, "He that trusteth in his own heart is a fool," so also it is written, "The fool hath said in his heart, There is no God;" and the self-adulation which influenced not less the learning of the age than its luxury, led gradually to the forgetfulness of all things but self, and to an infidelity only the more fatal because it still retained the form and language of faith.

In noticing the more prominent forms in which this faithlessness manifested itself, it is necessary to distinguish justly between that which was the consequence of respect for Paganism, and that which followed from the corruption of Catholicism. For as the Roman architecture is not to be made answerable for the primal corruption of the Gothic, so neither is the Roman philosophy to be made answerable for the primal corruption of Christianity. Year after year, as the history of the life of Christ sank back into the depth of time, and became obscured by the misty atmosphere of the history of the world,—as intermediate actions and incidents multiplied in number, and countless changes in men's modes of life, and tones of thought, rendered it more difficult for them to imagine the facts of distant time,—it became daily, almost hourly, a greater effort for the faithful heart to apprehend the entire veracity and vitality of the story of its Redeemer; and more easy for the thoughtless and remiss to deceive themselves as to the true character of the belief they had been taught to profess. And this must have been the case, had the pastors of the Church never failed in their watchfulness, and the Church itself never erred in its practice or doctrine. But when every year that removed the truths of the Gospel into deeper distance, added to them also some false or foolish tradition; when wilful distortion was added to natural obscurity, and the dimness of memory was disguised by the fruitfulness of fiction; when, moreover, the enormous temporal power granted to the clergy attracted into their ranks multitudes of men who, but for such temptation, would not have pretended to the Christian name, so that grievous wolves entered in among them, not sparing the flock; and when, by the machinations of such men, and the remissness of others, the form and administration of Church doctrine and discipline had become little more than a means of aggrandizing the power of the priesthood, it was impossible any longer for men of thoughtfulness or piety to remain in an unquestioning serenity of faith. The Church had become so mingled with the world that its witness could no longer be received; and the professing members of it, who were placed in circumstances such as to enable them to become aware of its corruptions, and whom their interest or their simplicity did not bribe or beguile into silence, gradually separated themselves into two vast multitudes of adverse energy, one tending to Reformation, and the other to Infidelity.

Of these, the last stood, as it were, apart, to watch the course of the struggle between Romanism and Protestantism, a struggle which, however necessary, was attended with infinite calamity to the Church. For, in the first place, the Protestant movement was, in reality, not re*formation* but re*animation*. It poured new life into the Church, but it did not form or define her anew. In some sort it rather broke down her hedges, so that all they who passed by might pluck off her grapes. The reformers speedily found that the enemy was never far behind the sower of good seed; that an evil spirit might enter the ranks of reformation as well as those of resistance; and that though the deadly blight might be checked amidst the wheat, there was no hope of ever ridding the wheat itself from the tares. New temptations were invented by Satan wherewith to oppose the revived strength of Christianity: as the Romanist, confiding in his human teachers, had ceased to try whether they were teachers sent from God, so the Protestant, confiding in the teaching of the

Spirit, believed every spirit, and did not try the spirit whether they were of God. And a thousand enthusiasms and heresies speedily obscured the faith and divided the force of the Reformation.

But the main evils rose out of the antagonism of the two great parties; primarily, in the mere fact of the existence of an antagonism. To the eyes of the unbeliever the Church of Christ, for the first time since its foundation, bore the aspect of a house divided against itself. Not that many forms of schism had not before arisen in it; but either they had been obscure and silent, hidden among the shadows of the Alps and the marshes of the Rhine; or they had been outbreaks of visible and unmistakeable error, cast off by the Church, rootless, and speedily withering away, while, with much that was erring and criminal, she still retained within her the pillar and ground of the truth. But here was at last a schism in which truth and authority were at issue. The body that was cast off withered away no longer. It stretched out its boughs to the sea and its branches to the river, and it was the ancient trunk that gave signs of decrepitude. On one side stood the reanimated faith, in its right hand the book open, and its left hand lifted up to heaven, appealing for its proof to the Word of the Testimony and the power of the Holy Ghost. On the other stood, or seemed to stand, all beloved custom and believed tradition; all that for fifteen hundred years had been closest to the hearts of men, or most precious for their help. Long-trusted legend; long-reverenced power; long-practised discipline; faiths that had ruled the destiny, and sealed the departure, of souls that could not be told or numbered for multitude; prayers, that from the lips of the fathers to those of the children had distilled like sweet waterfalls, sounding through the silence of ages, breaking themselves into heavenly dew to return upon the pastures of the wilderness; hopes, that had set the face as a flint in the torture, and the sword as a flame in the battle, that had pointed the purposes and ministered the strength of life, brightened the last glances and shaped the last syllables of death; charities, that had bound together the brotherhoods of the mountain and the desert, and had woven chains of pitying or aspiring communion between this world and the unfathomable beneath and above; and, more than these, the spirits of all the innumerable, undoubting, dead, beckoning to the one way by which they had been content to follow the things that belonged unto their peace; —these all stood on the other side: and the choice must have been a bitter one, even at the best; but it was rendered tenfold more bitter by the natural, but most sinful animosity of the two divisions of the Church against each other.

On one side this animosity was, of course, inevitable. The Romanist party, though still including many Christian men, necessarily included, also, all the worst of those who called themselves Christians. In the fact of its refusing correction, it stood confessed as the Church of the unholy; and, while it still counted among its adherents many of the simple and believing,—men unacquainted with the corruption of the body to which they belonged, or incapable of accepting any form of doctrine but that which they had been taught from their youth,—it gathered together with them whatever was carnal and sensual in priesthood or in people, all the lovers of power in the one, and of ease in the other. And the rage of these men was, of course, unlimited against those who either disputed their authority, reprehended their manner of life, or cast suspicion upon the popular methods of lulling the conscience in the lifetime, or purchasing salvation on the death-bed.

Besides this, the reassertion and defence of various tenets

which before had been little more than floating errors in the popular mind, but which, definitely attacked by Protestantism, it became necessary to fasten down with a band of iron and brass, gave a form at once more rigid, and less rational, to the whole body of Romanist Divinity. Multitudes of minds which in other ages might have brought honour and strength to the Church, preaching the more vital truths which it still retained, were now occupied in pleading for arraigned falsehoods, or magnifying disused frivolities: and it can hardly be doubted by any candid observer, that the nascent or latent errors which God pardoned in times of ignorance, became unpardonable when they were formally defined and defended; that fallacies which were forgiven to the enthusiasm of a multitude, were avenged upon the stubbornness of a Council; that, above all, the great invention of the age, which rendered God's word accessible to every man, left all sins against its light incapable of excuse or expiation; and that from the moment when Rome set herself in direct opposition to the Bible, the judgment was pronounced upon her, which made her the scorn and the prey of her own children, and cast her down from the throne where she had magnified herself against heaven, so low, that at last the unimaginable scene of the Bethlehem humiliation was mocked in the temples of Christianity. Judea had seen her God laid in the manger of the beast of burden; it was for Christendom to stable the beast of burden by the altar of her God.

Nor, on the other hand, was the opposition of Protestant ism to the Papacy less injurious to itself. That opposition was, for the most part, intemperate, undistinguishing, and incautious. It could indeed hardly be otherwise. Fresh bleeding from the sword of Rome, and still trembling at her anathema, the reformed churches were little likely to remember any of her benefits, or to regard any of her teaching.

Forced by the Romanist contumely into habits of irreverence, by the Romanist fallacies into habits of disbelief, the self-trusting, rashly-reasoning spirit gained ground among them daily. Sect branched out of sect, presumption rose over presumption; the miracles of the early Church were denied and its martyrs forgotten, though their power and palm were claimed by the members of every persecuted sect; pride, malice, wrath, love of change, masked themselves under the thirst for truth, and mingled with the just resentment of deception, so that it became impossible even for the best and truest men to know the plague of their own hearts; while avarice and impiety openly transformed reformation into robbery, and reproof into sacrilege. Ignorance could as easily lead the foes of the Church, as lull her slumber; men who would once have been the unquestioning recipients, were now the shameless inventors of absurd or perilous superstitions; they who were of the temper that walketh in darkness, gained little by having discovered their guides to be blind; and the simplicity of the faith, ill understood and contumaciously alleged, became an excuse for the rejection of the highest arts and most tried wisdom of mankind: while the learned infidel, standing aloof, drew his own conclusions, both from the rancour of the antagonists, and from their errors; believed each in all that he alleged against the other; and smiled with superior humanity, as he watched the winds of the Alps drift the ashes of Jerome, and the dust of England drink the blood of King Charles.

Now all this evil was, of course, entirely independent of the renewal of the study of Pagan writers. But that renewal ound the faith of Christendom already weakened and divided; and therefore it was itself productive of an effect tenfold greater than could have been apprehended from it at another time. It acted first, as before noticed, in leading the attention of all men to words instead of things; for it was discovered that the language of the middle ages had been corrupt, and the primal object of every scholar became now to purify his style. To this study of words, that of forms being added, both as of matters of the first importance, half the intellect of the age was at once absorbed in the base sciences of grammar, logic, and rhetoric; studies utterly unworthy of the serious labour of men, and necessarily rendering those employed upon them incapable of high thoughts or noble emotions. Of the debasing tendency of philology, no proof is needed beyond once reading a grammarian's notes on a great poet: logic is unnecessary for men who can reason; and about as useful to those who cannot, as a machine for forcing one foot in due succession before the other would be to a man who could not walk: while the study of rhetoric is exclusively one for men who desire to deceive or be deceived; he who has the truth at his heart need never fear the want of persuasion on his tongue, or, if he fear it, it is because the base rhetoric of dishonesty keeps the truth from being heard.

The study of these sciences, therefore, naturally made men shallow and dishonest in general; but it had a peculiarly fatal effect with respect to religion, in the view which men took of the Bible. Christ's teaching was discovered not to be rhetorical, St. Paul's preaching not to be logical, and the Greek of the New Testament not to be grammatical. The stern truth, the profound pathos, the impatient period, leaping from point to point and leaving the intervals for the hearer to fill, the comparatively Hebraized and unelaborate idiom, had little in them of attraction for the students of phrase and syllogism: and the chief knowledge of the age became one of the chief stumbling-blocks to its religion.

But it was not the grammarian and logician alone who was thus retarded or perverted; in them there had been small loss. The men who could truly appreciate the higher excellencies of the classics were carried away by a current of enthusiasm which withdrew them from every other study. Christianity was still professed as a matter of form, but neither the Bible nor the writings of the Fathers had time left for their perusal, still less heart left for their acceptance. The human mind is not capable of more than a certain amount of admiration or reverence, and that which was given to Horace was withdrawn from David. Religion is, of all subjects, that which will least endure a second place in the heart or thoughts, and a languid and occasional study of it was sure to lead to error or infidelity. On the other hand, what was heartily admired and unceasingly contemplated was soon brought nigh to being believed; and the systems of Pagan mythology began gradually to assume the places in the human mind from which the unwatched Christianity was wasting. Men did not indeed openly sacrifice to Jupiter, or build silver shrines for Diana, but the ideas of Paganism nevertheless became thoroughly vital and present with them at all times; and it did not matter in the least, as far as respected the power of true religion, whether the Pagan image was believed in or not, so long as it entirely occupied the thoughts. The scholar of the sixteenth century, if he saw the lightning shining from the east unto the west, thought forthwith of Jupiter, not of the coming of the Son of Man; if he saw the moon walking in brightness, he thought of Diana, not of the throne which was to be established for ever as a faithful witness in heaven; and though his heart was but secretly enticed, yet thus he denied the God that is above.*

And, indeed, this double creed, of Christianity confessed and Paganism beloved, was worse than Paganism itself, inas-

* Job, xxxi. 26—28; Psalm lxxxix. 37.

much as it refused effective and practical belief altogether It would have been better to have worshipped Diana and Jupiter at once, than to have gone on through the whole of life naming one God, imagining another, and dreading none. Better, a thousandfold, to have been "a Pagan suckled in some creed outworn," than to have stood by the great sea of Eternity, and seen no God walking on its waves, no heavenly world on its horizon.

This fatal result of an enthusiasm for classical literature was hastened and heightened by the misdirection of the powers of art. The imagination of the age was actively set to realize these objects of Pagan belief; and all the most exalted faculties of man, which, up to that period, had been employed in the service of Faith, were now transferred to the service of Fiction. The invention which had formerly been both sanctified and strengthened by labouring under the command of settled intention, and on the ground of assured belief, had now the reins laid upon its neck by passion, and all grounds of fact cut from beneath its feet; and the imagination which formerly had helped men to apprehend the truth, now tempted them to believe a falsehood. The faculties themselves wasted away in their own treason; one by one they fell in the potters' field; and the Raphael who seemed sent and inspired from heaven that he might paint Apostles and Prophets, sank at once into powerlessness at the feet of Apollo and the Muses.

But this was not all. The habit of using the greatest gifts of imagination upon fictitious subjects, of course destroyed the honour and value of the same imagination used in the cause of truth. Exactly in the proportion in which Jupiters and Mercuries were embodied and believed, in that proportion Virgins and Angels were disembodied and disbelieved. The images summoned by art began gradually to assume one average value in the spectator's mind; and incidents from the Iliad and from the Exodus to come within the same degrees of credibility.

———o———

THE TWO BOYHOODS.

Born half-way between the mountains and the sea—that young George of Castelfranco—of the Brave Castle:—Stout George they called him, George of Georges, so goodly a boy he was—Giorgione.

Have you ever thought what a world his eyes opened on—fair, searching eyes of youth? What a world of mighty life, from those mountain roots to the shore;—of loveliest life, when he went down, yet so young, to the marble city—and became himself as a fiery heart to it?

A city of marble, did I say? nay, rather a golden city, paved with emerald. For truly, every pinnacle and turret glanced or glowed, overlaid with gold, or bossed with jasper. Beneath, the unsullied sea drew in deep breathing, to and fro, its eddies of green wave. Deep-hearted, majestic, terrible as the sea,—the men of Venice moved in sway of power and war; pure as her pillars of alabaster, stood her mothers and maidens; from foot to brow, all noble, walked her knights; the low bronzed gleaming of sea-rusted armour shot angrily under their blood-red mantle-folds. Fearless, faithful, patient, impenetrable, implacable,—every word a fate,—sate her senate. In hope and honour, lulled by flowing of wave around their isles of sacred sand, each with his name written and the cross graved at his side, lay her dead. A wonderful piece of world. Rather, itself a world. It lay along the face of the waters, no larger, as its captains saw it from their masts at evening, than a bar of sunset that could not pass away; but, for its power, it must have seemed to them as if they were sailing in the expanse of heaven, and this a great planet, whose orient edge widened through ether. A world from which all ignoble care and petty thoughts were banished, with all the common and poor elements of life. No foulness, nor tumult, in those tremulous streets, that filled, or fell, beneath the moon; but rippled music of majestic change, or thrilling silence. No weak walls could rise above them; no low-roofed cottage, nor straw-built shed. Only the strength as of rock, and the finished setting of stones most precious. And around them, far as the eye could reach, still the soft moving of stainless waters, proudly pure; as not the flower, so neither the thorn nor the thistle, could grow in the glancing fields. Ethereal strength of Alps, dream-like, vanishing in high procession beyond the Torcellan shore; blue islands of Paduan hills, poised in the golden west. Above, free winds and fiery clouds ranging at their will;—brightness out of the north, and balm from the south, and the stars of the evening and morning clear in the limitless light of arched heaven and circling sea.

Such was Giorgione's school—such Titian's home.

Near the south-west corner of Covent Garden, a square brick pit or well is formed by a close-set block of houses, to the back windows of which it admits a few rays of light. Access to the bottom of it is obtained out of Maiden Lane, through a low archway and an iron gate; and if you stand long enough under the archway to accustom your eyes to the darkness, you may see on the left hand a narrow door, which formerly gave quiet access to a respectable barber's shop, of which the front window, looking into Maiden Lane, is still extant, filled in this year (1860), with a row of bottles, connected, in some defunct manner, with a brewer's business. A more fashionable neighbourhood, it is said, eighty years ago than now—never certainly a cheerful one—wherein a boy being born on St. George's day, 1775, began soon after to take interest in the world of Covent Garden, and put to service such spectacles of life as it afforded.

No knights to be seen there, nor, I imagine, many beautiful ladies; their costume at least disadvantageous, depending much on incumbency of hat and feather, and short waists; the majesty of men founded similarly on shoebuckles and wigs;—impressive enough when Reynolds will do his best for it; but not suggestive of much ideal delight to a boy.

"Bello ovile dov' io dormii agnello:" of things beautiful, besides men and women, dusty sunbeams up or down the street on summer mornings; deep furrowed cabbage leaves at the greengrocer's; magnificence of oranges in wheelbarrows round the corner; and Thames' shore within three minutes' race.

None of these things very glorious; the best, however, that England, it seems, was then able to provide for a boy of gift: who, such as they are, loves them—never, indeed, forgets them. The short waists modify to the last his visions of Greek ideal. His foregrounds had always a succulent cluster or two of greengrocery at the corners. Enchanted oranges gleam in Covent Gardens of the Hesperides; and great ships go to pieces in order to scatter chests of them on the waves. That mist of early sunbeams in the London dawn crosses, many and many a time, the clearness of Italian air; and by Thames' shore, with its stranded barges and glidings of red sail, dearer to us than Lucerne lake or Venetian lagoon,—by Thames' shore we will die.

With such circumstance round him in youth, let us note what necessary effects followed upon the boy. I assume him to have had Giorgione's sensibility (and more than Giorgione's, if that be possible) to colour and form. I tell you farther, and this fact you may receive trustfully, that his sensibility to human affection and distress was no less keen than even his sense for natural beauty—heart-sight deep as eye-sight.

Consequently, he attaches himself with the faithfullest child-love to everything that bears an image of the place he was born in. No matter how ugly it is,—has it anything about it like Maiden Lane, or like Thames' shore? If so, it shall be painted for their sake. Hence, to the very close of life, Turner could endure ugliness which no one else of the same sensibility would have borne with for an instant. Dead brick walls, blank square windows, old clothes, market-womanly types of humanity—anything fishy and muddy, like Billingsgate or Hungerford Market, had great attraction for him; black barges, patched sails, and every possible condition of fog.

"That mysterious forest below London Bridge"—better for the boy than wood of pine, or grove of myrtle. How he must have tormented the watermen, beseeching them to let him crouch anywhere in the bows, quiet as a log, so only that he might get floated down there among the ships, and round and round the ships, and with the ships, and by the ships, and under the ships, staring and clambering;—these the only quite beautiful things he can see in all the world, except the sky; but these, when the sun is on their sails, filling or falling, endlessly disordered by sway of tide and stress of anchorage, beautiful unspeakably; which ships also are inhabited by glorious creatures—red-faced sailors, with pipes, appearing over the gunwales, true knights, over their castle parapets—the most angelic beings in the whole compass of London world. And Trafalgar happening long before we can draw ships, we, nevertheless, coax all current stories out of the wounded sailors, do our best at present to show Nelson's funeral streaming up the Thames; and vow that Trafalgar shall have its tribute of memory some day. Which, accordingly, is accomplished—once, with all our might, for its death; twice, with all our might, for its victory; thrice, in pensive farewel to the old Temeraire, and, with it, to that order of things.

Now this fond companying with sailors must have divided his time, it appears to me, pretty equally between Covent Garden and Wapping (allowing for incidental excursions to Chelsea on one side, and Greenwich on the other), which time he would spend pleasantly, but not magnificently, being limited in pocket-money, and leading a kind of "Poor Jack" life on the river.

In some respects, no life could be better for a lad. But it was not calculated to make his ear fine to the niceties of language, nor form his moralities on an entirely regular standard. Picking up his first scraps of vigorous English chiefly at Deptford and in the markets, and his first ideas of female tenderness and beauty among nymphs of the barge and the barrow—another boy might, perhaps, have become what people usually term "vulgar." But the original make and frame of Turner's mind being not vulgar, but as nearly as possible a combination of the minds of Keats and Dante, joining capricious waywardness and intense openness to every fine pleasure of sense, and hot defiance of formal precedent, with a quite infinite tenderness, generosity, and desire of justice and truth—this kind of mind did not become vulgar, but very tolerant of vulgarity, even fond of it in some forms; and, on the outside, visibly infected by it, deeply enough; the curious result, in its combination of elements, being to most people wholly incomprehensible. It was as if a cable had been woven of blood-crimson silk, and then tarred on the outside. People handled it, and the tar came off on their hands; red gleams were seen through the black, under neath, at the places where it had been strained. Was it ochre?—said the world, or red lead?

Schooled thus in manners, literature, and general moral principles at Chelsea and Wapping, we have finally to inquire concerning the most important point of all. We have seen the principal differences between this boy and Giorgione, as respects sight of the beautiful, understanding of poverty, of commerce, and of order of battle; then follows another cause of difference in our training—not slight,—the aspect of religion, namely, in the neighbourhood of Covent Garden. I say the aspect; for that was all the lad could judge by. Disposed, for the most part, to learn chiefly by his eyes, in this special matter he finds there is really no other way of learning. His father taught him "to lay one penny upon another." Of mother's teaching, we hear of none; of parish pastoral teaching, the reader may guess how much.

I choose Giorgione rather than Veronese to help me in carrying out this parallel; because I do not find in Giorgione's work any of the early Venetian monachist element. He seems to me to have belonged more to an abstract contemplative school. I may be wrong in this; it is no matter; —suppose it were so, and that he came down to Venice somewhat recusant, or insentient, concerning the usual priestly doctrines of his day,—how would the Venetian religion, from an outer intellectual standing-point, have *looked* to him?

He would have seen it to be a religion indisputably powerful in human affairs; often very harmfully so; sometimes devouring widows' houses, and consuming the strongest and fairest from among the young; freezing into merciless bigotry the policy of the old: also, on the other hand, animating national courage, and raising souls, otherwise sordid, into heroism: on the whole, always a real and great power;

served with daily sacrifice of gold, time, and thought; putting forth its claims, if hypocritically, at least in bold hypocrisy, not waiving any atom of them in doubt or fear; and, assuredly, in large measure, sincere, believing in itself, and believed: a goodly system, moreover, in aspect; gorgeous, harmonious, mysterious;—a thing which had either to be obeyed or combated, but could not be scorned. A religion towering over all the city—many buttressed—luminous in marble stateliness, as the dome of our Lady of Safety shines over the sea; many-voiced also, giving, over all the eastern seas, to the sentinel his watchword, to the soldier his war-cry; and, on the lips of all who died for Venice, shaping the whisper of death.

I suppose the boy Turner to have regarded the religion of his city also from an external intellectual standing-point.

What did he see in Maiden Lane?

Let not the reader be offended with me; I am willing to let him describe, at his own pleasure,what Turner saw there; but to me, it seems to have been this. A religion maintained occasionally, even the whole length of the lane, at point of constable's staff; but, at other times, placed under the custody of the beadle, within certain black and unstately iron railings of St. Paul's, Covent Garden. Among the wheelbarrows and over the vegetables, no perceptible dominance of religion; in the narrow, disquieted streets, none; in the tongues, deeds, daily ways of Maiden Lane, little. Some honesty, indeed, and English industry, and kindness of heart, and general idea of justice; but faith, of any national kind, shut up from one Sunday to the next, not artistically beautiful even in those Sabbatical exhibitions; its paraphernalia being chiefly of high pews, heavy elocution, and cold grimness of behaviour.

What chiaroscuro belongs to it—(dependent mostly on candle light),—we will, however, draw, considerately; no goodliness of escutcheon, nor other respectability being omitted, and the best of their results confessed, a meek old woman and a child being let into a pew, for whom the reading by candlelight will be beneficial.

For the rest, this religion seems to him discreditable—iscredited—not believing in itself, putting forth its authority in a cowardly way, watching how far it might be tolerated, continually shrinking, disclaiming, fencing, finessing; divided against itself, not by stormy rents, but by thin fissures, and splittings of plaster from the walls. Not to be either obeyed, or combated, by an ignorant, yet clear-sighted youth; only to be scorned. And scorned not one whit the less, though also the dome dedicated to *it* looms high over distant winding of the Thames; as St. Mark's campanile rose, for goodly landmark, over mirage of lagoon. For St. Mark ruled over life; the Saint of London over death; St. Mark over St. Mark's Place, but St. Paul over St. Paul's Churchyard.

Under these influences pass away the first reflective hours of life, with such conclusion as they can reach. In consequence of a fit of illness, he was taken—I cannot ascertain in what year—to live with an aunt, at Brentford; and here, I believe, received some schooling, which he seems to have snatched vigorously; getting knowledge, at least by translation, of the more picturesque classical authors, which he turned presently to use, as we shall see. Hence also, walks about Putney and Twickenham in the summer time acquainted him with the look of English meadow-ground in its restricted tates of paddock and park; and with some round-headed appearances of trees, and stately entrances to houses of mark. he avenue at Bushy, and the iron gates and carved pillars of Hampton, impressing him apparently with great awe and admiration; so that in after life his little country house is,—of all places in the world,—at Twickenham! Of swans and reedy shores he now learns the soft motion and the green mystery, in a way not to be forgotten.

And at last fortune wills that the lad's true life shall begin; and one summer's evening, after various wonderful stage-coach experiences on the north road, which gave him a love of stage-coaches ever after, he finds himself sitting alone among the Yorkshire hills.* For the first time, the silence of Nature round him, her freedom sealed to him, her glory opened to him. Peace at last; nor roll of cart-wheel, nor mutter of sullen voices in the back shop; but curlew-cry in space of heaven, and welling of bell-toned streamlet by its shadowy rock. Freedom at last. Dead-wall, dark railing, fenced field, gated garden, all passed away like the dream of a prisoner; and behold, far as foot or eye can race or range, the moor, and cloud. Loveliness at last. It is here then, among these deserted vales! Not among men. Those pale, poverty-struck, or cruel faces;—that multitudinous, marred humanity—are not the only things that God has made. Here is something He has made which no one has marred. Pride of purple rocks, and river pools of blue, and tender wilderness of glittering trees, and misty lights of evening on immeasurable hills.

Beauty, and freedom, and peace; and yet another teacher, graver than these. Sound preaching at last here, in Kirkstall crypt, concerning fate and life. Here, where the dark pool reflects the chancel pillars, and the cattle lie in unhindered rest, the soft sunshine on their dappled bodies, instead of priests' vestments; their white furry hair ruffled a little, fitfully, by the evening wind, deep-scented from the meadow thyme.

* I do not mean that this is his first acquaintance with the country, but the first impressive and touching one, after his mind was formed. The earliest sketches I found in the National collection are at Clifton and Bristol· the next, at Oxford.

Consider deeply the import to him of this, his first sight of ruin, and compare it with the effect of the architecture that was around Giorgione. There were indeed aged buildings, at Venice, in his time, but none in decay. All ruin was removed, and its place filled as quickly as in our London; but filled always by architecture loftier and more wonderful than that whose place it took, the boy himself happy to work upon the walls of it; so that the idea of the passing away of the strength of men and beauty of their works never could occur to him sternly. Brighter and brighter the cities of Italy had been rising and broadening on hill and plain, for three hundred years. He saw only strength and immortality, could not but paint both; conceived the form of man as deathless, calm with power, and fiery with life.

Turner saw the exact reverse of this. In the present work of men, meanness, aimlessness, unsightliness: thin-walled, lath-divided, narrow-garreted houses of clay; booths of a darksome Vanity Fair, busily base.

But on Whitby Hill, and by Bolton Brook, remained traces of other handiwork. Men who could build had been there; and who also had wrought, not merely for their own days. But to what purpose? Strong faith and steady hands, and patient souls—can this, then, be all you have left! this the sum of your doing on the earth!—a nest whence the night-owl may whimper to the brook, and a ribbed skeleton of consumed arches, looming above the bleak banks of mist, from its cliff to the sea.

As the strength of men to Giorgione, to Turner their weakness and vileness, were alone visible. They themselves unworthy or ephemeral; their work, despicable, or decayed. In the Venetian's eyes, all beauty depended on man's presence and pride; in Turner's, on the solitude he had left, and the humiliation he had suffered.

And thus the fate and issue of all his work were determined at once. He must be a painter of the strength of nature, there was no beauty elsewhere than in that; he must paint also the labour and sorrow and passing away of men; this was the great human truth visible to him.

Their labour, their sorrow, and their death. Mark the three. Labour; by sea and land, in field and city, at forge and furnace, helm and plough. No pastoral indolence nor classic pride shall stand between him and the troubling of the world: still less between him and the toil of his country,—blind, tormented, unwearied, marvellous England.

Also their Sorrow; Ruin of all their glorious work, passing away of their thoughts and their honour, mirage of pleasure, FALLACY OF HOPE; gathering of weed on temple step; gaining of wave on deserted strand; weeping of the mother for the children, desolate by her breathless first-born in the streets of the city, desolate by her last sons slain, among the beasts of the field.

And their Death. That old Greek question again;—yet unanswered. The unconquerable spectre still flitting among the forest trees at twilight; rising ribbed out of the sea-sand; —white, a strange Aphrodite,—out of the sea-foam; stretching its gray, cloven wings among the clouds; turning the light of their sunsets into blood. This has to be looked upon, and in a more terrible shape than ever Salvator or Durer saw it. The wreck of one guilty country does not infer the ruin of all countries, and need not cause general terror respecting the laws of the universe.

Turner was eighteen years old when Napoleon came down on Arcola. Look on the map of Europe, and count the blood-stains on it, between Arcola and Waterloo.

Not alone those blood-stains on the Alpine snow, and the blue of the Lombard plain. The English death was before his eyes also. No decent, calculable, consoled dying; no passing to rest like that of the aged burghers of Nuremberg town. No gentle processions to churchyards among the fields, the bronze crests bossed deep on the memorial tablets, and the skylark singing above them from among the corn. But the life trampled out in the slime of the street, crushed to dust amidst the roaring of the wheel, tossed countlessly away into howling winter wind along five hundred leagues of rock-fanged shore. Or, worst of all, rotted down to forgotten graves through years of ignorant patience, and vain seeking for help from man, for hope in God—infirm, imperfect yearning, as of motherless infants starving at the dawn; oppressed royalties of captive thought, vague ague-fits of bleak, amazed despair.

So taught, and prepared for his life's labour, sate the boy at last alone among his fair English hills; and began to paint, with cautious toil, the rocks, and fields, and trickling brooks, and soft, white clouds of heaven.

WORK AND PLAY.

What is the proper function of play, with respect not to youth merely, but to all mankind?

It is a much more serious question than may be at first supposed; for a healthy manner of play is necessary in order to a healthy manner of work: and because the choice of our recreation is, in most cases, left to ourselves, while the nature of our work is as generally fixed by necessity or authority, it may be well doubted whether more distressful consequences may not have resulted from mistaken choice in play than from mistaken direction in labour.

Observe, however, that we are only concerned, here, with that kind of play which causes laughter or implies recreation, not with that which consists in the excitement of the energies whether of body or mind. Muscular exertion is, indeed, in youth, one of the conditions of recreation; "but neither the violent bodily labour which children of all ages agree to call play," nor the grave excitement of the mental faculties in games of skill or chance, are in anywise connected with the state of feeling we have here to investigate, namely, that sportiveness which man possesses in common with many inferior creatures, but to which his higher faculties give nobler expression in the various manifestations of wit, humour, and fancy.

With respect to the manner in which this instinct of playfulness is indulged or repressed, mankind are broadly distinguishable into four classes: the men who play wisely; who play necessarily; who play inordinately; and who play not at all.

First: Those who play wisely. It is evident that the idea of any kind of play can only be associated with the idea of an imperfect, childish, and fatigable nature. As far as men can raise that nature, so that it shall no longer be interested by trifles or exhausted by toils, they raise it above play; he whose heart is at once fixed upon heaven, and open to the earth, so as to apprehend the importance of heavenly doctrines, and the compass of human sorrow, will have little disposition for jest; and exactly in proportion to the breadth and depth of his character and intellect, will be, in general, the incapability of surprise, or exuberant and sudden emotion, which must render play impossible. It is, however, evidently not intended that many men should even reach, far less pass their lives in, that solemn state of thoughtfulness, which brings them into the nearest brotherhood with their Divine

Master; and the highest and healthiest state which is competent to ordinary humanity appears to be that which, accepting the necessity of recreation, and yielding to the impulses of natural delight springing out of health and innocence, does, indeed, condescend often to playfulness, but never without such deep love of God, of truth, and of humanity, as shall make even its slightest words reverent, its idlest fancies profitable, and its keenest satire indulgent. Wordsworth and Plato furnish us with, perhaps, the finest and highest examples of this playfulness: in the one case, unmixed with satire, the perfectly simple effusion of that spirit

> "Which gives to all the self-same bent,
> Whose life is wise, and innocent;"

—in Plato, and, by the by, in a very wise book of our own times, not unworthy of being named in such companionship, "Friends in Council," mingled with an exquisitely tender and loving satire.

Secondly: The men who play necessarily. That highest species of playfulness, which we have just been considering, is evidently the condition of a mind, not only highly cultivated, but so habitually trained to intellectual labour that it can bring a considerable force of accurate thought into its moments even of recreation. This is not possible, unless so much repose of mind and heart are enjoyed, even at the periods of greatest exertion, that the rest required by the system is diffused over the whole life. To the majority of mankind, such a state is evidently unattainable. They must, perforce, pass a large part of their lives in employments both irksome and toilsome, demanding an expenditure of energy which exhausts the system, and yet consuming that energy upon subjects incapable of interesting the nobler faculties. When such employments are intermitted, those noble instincts, fancy, imagination, and curiosity, are all hungry for the food which the labour of the day has denied to them, while yet the weariness of the body, in a great degree, forbids their application to any serious subject. They therefore exert themselves without any determined purpose, and under no vigorous estraint, but gather, as best they may, such various nourishment, and put themselves to such fantastic exercise, as may soonest indemnify them for their past imprisonment, and prepare them to endure their recurrence. This sketching of the mental limbs as their fetters fall away,—this leaping and dancing of the heart and intellect, when they are restored to the fresh air of heaven, yet half paralyzed by their captivity, and unable to turn themselves to any earnest purpose,—I call necessary play. It is impossible to exaggerate its importance, whether in polity, or in art.

Thirdly: The men who play inordinately. The most perfect state of society which, consistently with due understanding of man's nature, it may be permitted us to conceive, would be one in which the whole human race were divided, more or less distinctly, into workers and thinkers; that is to say, into the two classes, who only play wisely, or play necessarily. But the number and the toil of the working class are enormously increased, probably more than doubled, by the vices of the men who neither play wisely nor necessarily, but are enabled by circumstances, and permitted by their want of principle, to make amusement the object of their existence. There is not any moment of the lives of such men which is not injurious to others; both because they leave the work undone which was appointed for them, and because they necessarily think wrongly, whenever it becomes compulsory upon them to think at all. The greater portion of the misery of this world arises from the false opinions of men whose idleness has physically incapacitated them from forming true ones. Every duty which we omit obscures some truth which we should have known; and the guilt of a life spent in the pursuit of pleasure is twofold, partly consisting in the perversion of action, and partly in the dissemination of falsehood.

There is, however, a less criminal, though hardly less dangerous condition of mind; which, though not failing in its more urgent duties, fails in the finer conscientiousness which regulates the degree, and directs the choice, of amusement, at those times when amusement is allowable. The most frequent error in this respect is the want of reverence in approaching subjects of importance or sacredness, and of caution in the expression of thoughts which may encourage like irreverence in others: and these faults are apt to gain upon the mind until it becomes habitually more sensible to what is ludicrous and accidental, than to what is grave and essential, in any subject that is brought before it; or even, at last, desires to perceive or to know nothing but what may end in jest. Very generally minds of this character are active and able; and many of them are so far conscientious, that they believe their jesting forwards their work. But it is difficult to calculate the harm they do, by destroying the reverence which is our best guide into all truth; for weakness and evil are easily visible, but greatness and goodness are often latent; and we do infinite mischief by exposing weakness to eyes which cannot comprehend greatness. This error, however, is more connected with abuses of the satirical than of the playful instinct; and I shall have more to say of it presently.

The men who do not play at all: those who are so dull or so morose as to be incapable of inventing or enjoying jest, and in whom care, guilt, or pride represses all healthy exhilaration of the fancy; or else men utterly oppressed with labour, and driven too hard by the necessities of the world to be capable of any species of happy relaxation. We have next to consider the expression throughout of the minds of men who indulge themselves in unnecessary play. It is evident that a large number of these men will be more refined and more highly educated than those who only play necessarily; their power of pleasure-seeking implies, in general, fortunate circumstances of life. It is evident also that their play will not be so hearty, so simple, or so joyful; and this deficiency of brightness will affect it in proportion to its unnecessary and unlawful continuance, until at last it becomes a restless and dissatisfied indulgence in excitement, or a painful delving after exhausted springs of pleasure.

THE STATES OF THE FOREST.

It was not from their lakes, nor their cliffs, nor their glaciers—though these were all peculiarly their possession, that the three venerable cantons or states received their name. They were not called the States of the Rock, nor the States of the Lake, but the States of the *Forest*. And the one of the three which contains the most touching record of the spiritual power of Swiss religion, in the name of the convent of the "Hill of Angels," has, for its own, none but the sweet childish name of "Under the Woods."

And indeed you may pass under them if, leaving the most sacred spot in Swiss history, the Meadow of the Three Fountains, you bid the boatman row southward a little way by the shore of the Bay of Uri. Steepest there on its western side, the walls of its rocks ascend to heaven. Far, in the blue of evening, like a great cathedral pavement, lies the lake in its darkness; and you may hear the whisper of innumerable falling waters return from the hollows of the cliff, like the voices of a multitude praying under their breath. From time to time the beat of a wave, slow lifted, where the rocks lean over the black depth, dies heavily as the last note of a requiem. Opposite, green with steep grass, and set with chalet villages, the Fron-Alp rises in one solemn glow of pastoral light and peace; and above, against the clouds of twilight, ghostly on the gray precipice, stand, myriad by myriad, the shadowy armies of the Unterwalden pine.

I have seen that it is possible for the stranger to pass through this great chapel, with its font of waters, and mountain pillars, and vaults of cloud, without being touched by one noble thought, or stirred by any sacred passion; but for those who received from its waves the baptism of their youth, and learned beneath its rocks the fidelity of their manhood, and watched amidst its clouds the likeness of the dream of life, with the eyes of age—for these I will not believe that the mountain shrine was built, or the calm of its forest-shadows guarded by their God, in vain.

———o———

THE PAGAN SYSTEM OF EDUCATION.

The Pagan system is completely triumphant; and the entire body of the so-called Christian world has established a system of instruction for its youth, wherein neither the history of Christ's Church, nor the language of God's law, is considered a study of the smallest importance; wherein, of all subjects of human inquiry, his own religion is the one in which a youth's ignorance is most easily forgiven*; and in which it is held a light matter that he should be daily guilty of lying, of debauchery, or of blasphemy, so only that he write Latin verses accurately, and with speed.

I believe that in a few years more we shall wake from all these errors in astonishment, as from evil dreams; having been preserved, in the midst of their madness, by those hidden roots of active and earnest Christianity which God's grace has bound in the English nation with iron and brass. But in the Venetian, those roots themselves had withered; and, from the palace of their ancient religion, their pride cast them forth hopelessly to the pasture of the brute. From pride to infidelity, from infidelity to the unscrupulous and insatiable pursuit of pleasure, and from this to irremediable degradation, the transitions were swift, like the falling of a star. The great palaces of the haughtiest nobles of Venice were stayed, before they had risen far above their foundations, by the blast of a penal poverty; and the wild grass, on the unfinished fragments of their mighty shafts, waves at the tide-mark where the power of the godless people first heard the "Hitherto shalt thou come." And the regeneration in which they had so vainly trusted,—the new birth and clear dawning, as they thought it, of all art, all knowledge, and all hope,—became to them as that dawn which Ezekiel saw on the hills of Israel: "Behold the day; behold, it is come. The rod hath blossomed, pride hath budded, violence is risen up into a rod of wickedness. None of them shall remain, nor of their multitude; let not the buyer rejoice, nor the seller mourn, for wrath is upon all the multitude thereof."

* I shall not forget the impression made upon me at Oxford, when, going up for my degree, and mentioning to one of the authorities that I had not had time enough to read the Epistles properly, I was told, that "the Epistles were separate sciences, and I need not trouble myself about them."

The fact is, we distrust each other and ourselves. We know that if, on any occasion of general intercourse, we turn to our next neighbour, and put to him some searching or testing question, we shall, in nine cases out of ten, discover him to be only a Christian in his own way, and as far as he thinks proper, and that he doubts of many things which we ourselves do not believe strongly enough to hear doubted without danger. What is in reality cowardice and faithlessness, we call charity; and consider it the part of benevolence sometimes to forgive men's evil practice for the sake of their accurate faith, and sometimes to forgive their confessed heresy for the sake of their admirable practice. And under this shelter of charity, humility, and faintheartedness, the world, unquestioned by others or by itself, mingles with and overwhelms the small body of Christians, legislates for them, moralizes for them, reasons for them; and, though itself of course greatly and beneficently influenced by the association, and held much in check by its pretence to Christianity, yet undermines, in nearly the same degree, the sincerity and practical power of Christianity itself.

———o———

THEOLOGY OF SPENSER.

The following analysis of the first books of the "Faërie Queen," may be interesting to readers who have been in the habit of reading the noble poem too hastily to connect its parts completely together; and may perhaps induce them to more careful study of the rest of the poem.

The Redcrosse Knight is Holiness,—the "Pietas" of St. Mark's, the "Devotio" of Orcagna,—meaning, I think, in general, Reverence and Godly Fear.

This virtue, in the opening of the book, has Truth (or Una) at its side, but presently enters the Wandering Wood, and encounters the serpent Error; that is to say, Error in her universal form, the first enemy of Reverence and Holiness; and more especially Error as founded on learning; for when Holiness strangles her,

> "Her vomit *full of bookes and papers was,*
> With loathly frogs and toades, which eyes did lacke."

Having vanquished this first open and palpable form of Error, as Reverence and Religion must always vanquish it, the Knight encounters Hypocrisy, or Archimagus: Holiness cannot detect Hypocrisy, but believes him, and goes home with him; whereupon Hypocrisy succeeds in separating Holiness from Truth; and the Knight (Holiness) and Lady (Truth) go forth separately from the house of Archimagus.

Now observe, the moment Godly Fear, or Holiness, is separated from Truth, he meets Infidelity, or the Knight Sans Foy; Infidelity having Falsehood, or Duessa, riding behind him. The instant the Redcrosse Knight is aware of the attack of Infidelity, he

> "Gan fairly couch his speare, and towards ride."

He vanquishes and slays Infidelity; but is deceived by his companion, Falsehood, and takes her for his lady: thus showing the condition of Religion, when, after being attacked by Doubt, and remaining victorious, it is nevertheless seduced, by any form of Falsehood, to pay reverence where it ought not. This, then, is the first fortune of Godly Fear separated from Truth. The poet then returns to Truth, separated from Godly Fear. She is immediately attended by a lion, or Violence, which makes her dreaded wherever she comes; and when she enters the mart of Superstition, this Lion tears

Kirkrapine in pieces: showing how Truth, separated from Godliness, does indeed put an end to the abuses of Superstition, but does so violently and desperately. She then meets again with Hypocrisy, whom she mistakes for her own lord, or Godly Fear, and travels a little way under his guardianship (Hypocrisy thus not unfrequently appearing to defend the Truth), until they are both met by Lawlessness, or the Knight Sans Loy, whom Hypocrisy cannot resist. Lawlessness overthrows Hypocrisy, and seizes upon Truth, first slaying her lion attendant: showing that the first aim of licence is to destroy the force and authority of Truth. Sans Loy then takes Truth captive, and bears her away. Now this Lawlessness is the "unrighteousness," or "adikia," of St. Paul; and his bearing Truth away captive, is a type of those "who hold the truth in unrighteousness,"—that is to say, generally, of men who, knowing what is true, make the truth give way to their own purposes, or use it only to forward them, as is the case with so many of the popular leaders of the present day. Una is then delivered from Sans Loy by the satyrs, to show that Nature, in the end, must work out the deliverance of the truth, although, where it has been captive to Lawlessness, that deliverance can only be obtained through Savageness, and a return to barbarism. Una is then taken from among the satyrs by Satyrane, the son of a satyr and a "lady myld, fair Thyamis," (typifying the early steps of renewed civilization, and its rough and hardy character "nousled up in life and maners wilde,") who, meeting again with Sans Loy, enters instantly into rough and prolonged combat with him: showing how the early organization of a hardy nation must be wrought out through much discouragement from Lawlessness. This contest the poet leaving for the time undecided, returns to trace the adventures of the Redcrosse Knight, or Godly Fear, who, having vanquished Infidelity, presently is led by

Falsehood to the house of Pride: thus showing how religion, separated from truth, is first tempted by doubts of God, and then by the pride of life. The description of this house of Pride is one of the most elaborate and noble pieces in the poem; and here we begin to get at the proposed system of Virtues and Vices. For Pride, as queen, has six other vices yoked in her chariot; namely, first, Idleness, then Gluttony, Lust, Avarice, Envy, and Anger, all driven on by "Sathan, with a smarting whip in hand." From these lower vices and their company, Godly Fear, though lodging in the house of Pride, holds aloof; but he is challenged, and has a hard battle to fight with Sans Joy, the brother of Sans Foy: showing, that though he has conquered Infidelity, and does not give himself up to the allurements of Pride, he is yet exposed, so long as he dwells in her house, to distress of mind and loss of his accustomed rejoicing before God. He, however, having partly conquered Despondency, or Sans Joy, Falsehood goes down to Hades, in order to obtain drugs to maintain the power or life of Despondency; but, meantime, the Knight leaves the house of Pride; Falsehood pursues and overtakes him, and finds him by a fountain side, of which the waters are

"Dull and slow,
And all that drinke thereof do faint and feeble grow."

Of which the meaning is, that Godly Fear, after passing through the house of Pride, is exposed to drowsiness and feebleness of watch; as, after Peter's boast, came Peter's sleeping, from weakness of the flesh, and then, last of all, Peter's fall. And so it follows: for the Redcrosse Knight, being overcome with faintness by drinking of the fountain, is thereupon attacked by the giant Orgoglio, overcome, and thrown by him into a dungeon. This Orgoglio is Orgueil, or Carnal

Pride; not the pride of life, spiritual and subtle, but the common and vulgar pride in the power of this world; and his throwing the Redcrosse Knight into a dungeon, is a type of the captivity of true religion under the corporal power of corrupt churches, more especially of the Church of Rome; and of its gradually wasting away in unknown places, while carnal pride has the preeminence over all things. That Spenser means, especially, the pride of the Papacy, is shown by the 16th stanza of the book; for there the giant Orgoglio is said to have taken Duessa, or Falsehood, for his "deare," and to have set upon her head a triple crown, and endowed her with royal majesty, and made her to ride upon a seven-headed beast.

In the meantime, the dwarf, the attendant of the Redcrosse Knight, takes his arms, and finding Una tells her of the captivity of her lord. Una, in the midst of her mourning, meets Prince Arthur, in whom, as Spenser himself tells us, is set forth generally Magnificence; but who, as is shown by the choice of the hero's name, is more especially the magnificence, or literally, "great doing" of the kingdom of England. This power of England, going forth with Truth, attacks Orgoglio, or the Pride of Papacy, slays him; strips Duessa, or Falsehood, naked: and liberates the Redcrosse Knight. The magnificent and well known description of Despair follows, by whom the Redcrosse Knight is hard bested, on account of his past errors and captivity, and is only saved by Truth, who, perceiving him to be still feeble, brings him to the house of Cœlia, called, in the argument of the canto, Holiness, but properly, Heavenly Grace, the mother of the Virtues. Her "three daughters, well upbrought," are Faith, Hope, and Charity. Her porter is Humility; because Humility opens the door of Heavenly Grace. Zeal and Reverence are her chamberlains, introducing the new comers to her presence; her groom, or servant, is Obedience; and her physician, Patience. Under the commands of Charity, the matron Mercy rules over her hospital, under whose care the knight is healed of his sickness; and it is to be especially noticed how much importance Spenser, though never ceasing to chastise all hypocrisies and mere observances of form, attaches to true and faithful *penance* in effecting this cure. Having his strength restored to him, the Knight is trusted to the guidance of Mercy, who, leading him forth by a narrow and thorny way, first instructs him in the seven works of Mercy, and then leads him to the hill of Heavenly Contemplation; whence, having a sight of the New Jerusalem, as Christian of the Delectable Mountains, he goes forth to the final victory over Satan, the old serpent, with which the book closes.

THE END.

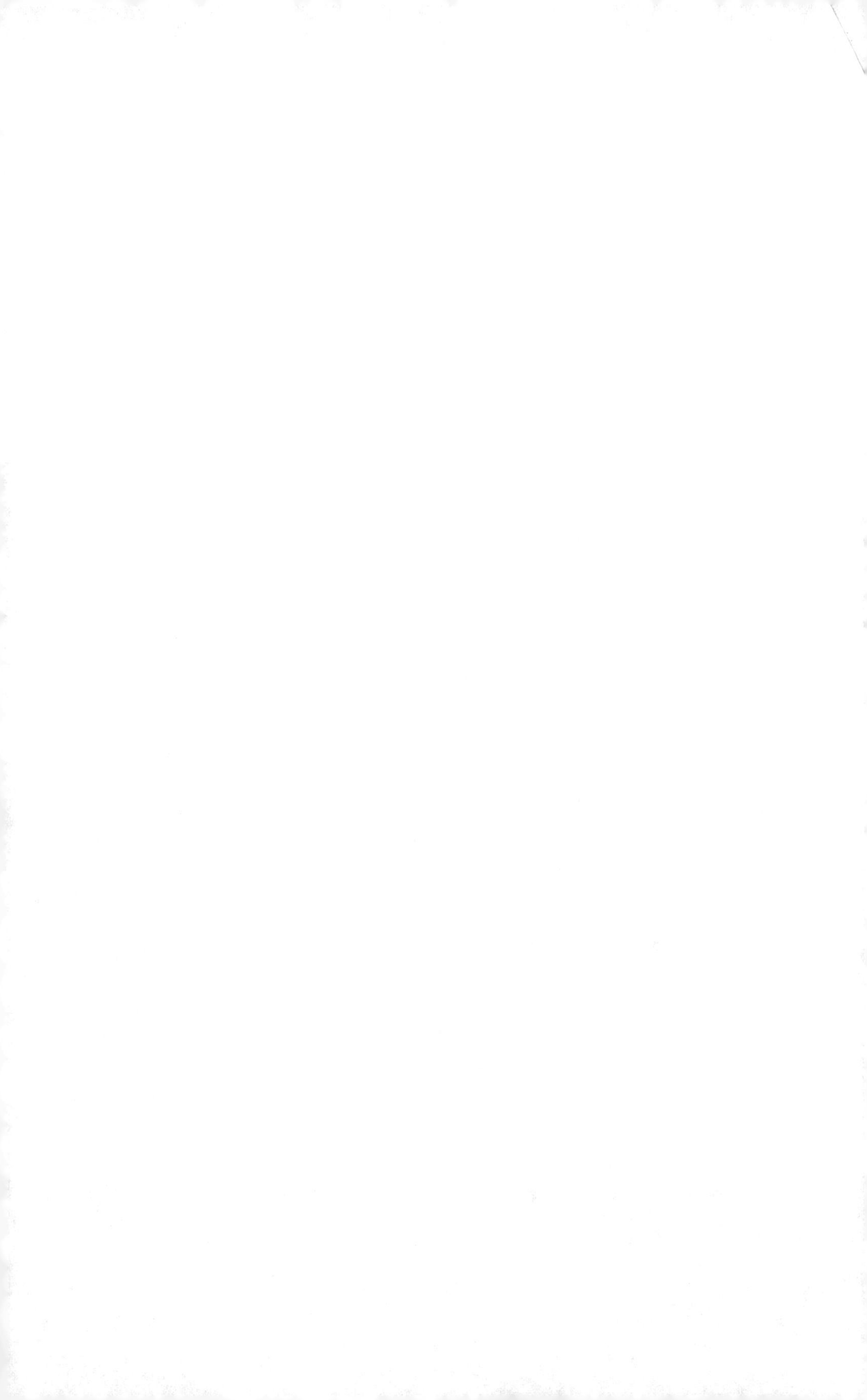

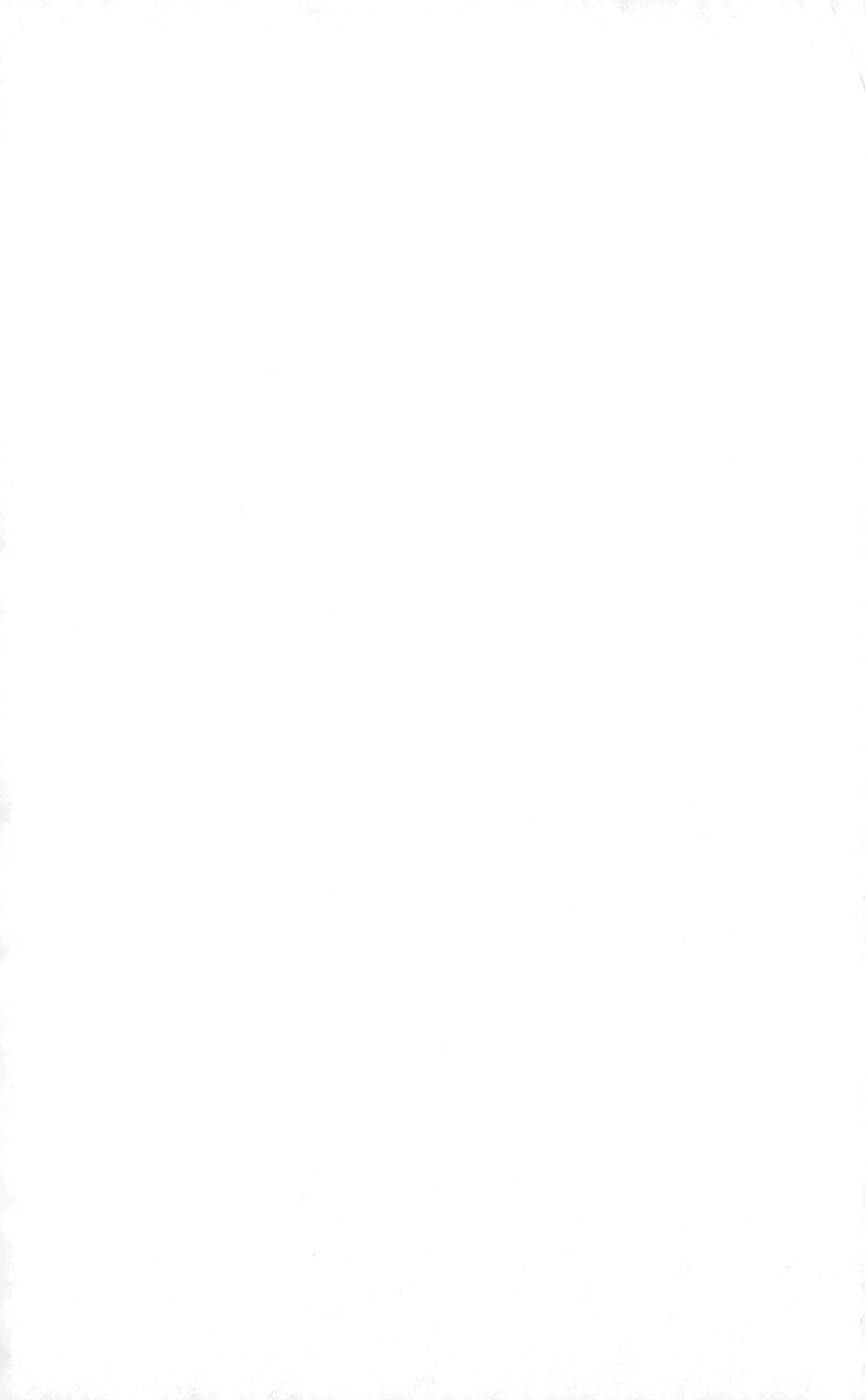

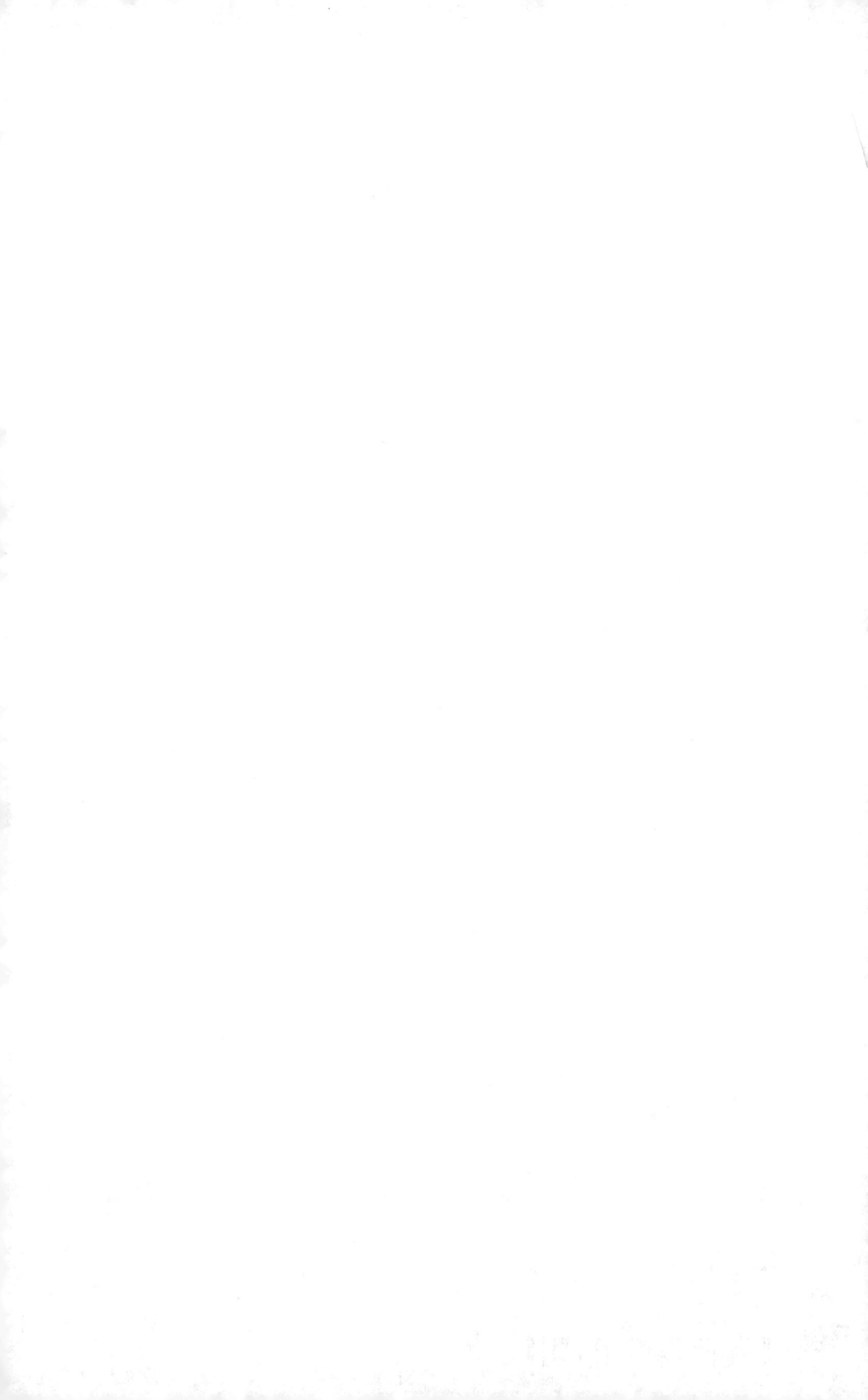

www.ingramcontent.com/pod-product-compliance
Lightning Source LLC
LaVergne TN
LVHW010148110826
845151LV00002B/455

* 9 7 8 1 4 2 5 5 3 8 0 0 2 *